The International Game of Power
Past, Present and Future

New Babylon

Studies in the Social Sciences
42

MOUTON PUBLISHERS · BERLIN · NEW YORK · AMSTERDAM

The International Game of Power

Past, Present and Future

Peter Bernholz

MOUTON PUBLISHERS · BERLIN · NEW YORK · AMSTERDAM

Peter Bernholz
Institut für Sozialwissenschaften
der Universität Basel
Basel
Switzerland

Library of Congress Cataloging in Publication Data

Bernholz, Peter. The international game of power. (New Babylon, studies in the social sciences ; 42) 1. International relations. I. Title. II. Series. JX1391.B43 1985   327   85-4820 ISBN 0-89925-033-5 (U.S.)

CIP-Kurztitelaufnahme der Deutschen Bibliothek

Bernholz, Peter: The international game of power : past, present, and future / Peter Bernholz. – 1. print. – Berlin ; New York ; Amsterdam : Mouton, 1985. (New Babylon ; 42) ISBN 3-11-009784-2 NE: GT

Printed on acid free paper

Typesetting: COPO Typesetting, Bangkok Thailand / Werksatz Marschall, Berlin. – Printing: Druckerei Hildebrand, Berlin. – Binding: Dieter Mikolai, Berlin. Printed in Germany.

Preface

There are a number of very good books on international relations on the market. Still, over the years the present author has become more and more dissatisfied with the available discussions of the problems of the international system. This does not mean that the respective books do not have their merits, given the objectives of their authors. But several ingredients seem to be missing. Thus, usually, the historical perspective is conspicuous by its absence; too much weight is given to recent approaches of minor importance which often turn out to be passing fashions of one or two decades; economic foundations of relative international power are neglected or even forgotten; sometimes states and other organizations are either seen as acting organicist entities or, on the contrary, as mere puppets in class wars; finally, often no clear distinctions are drawn between factual analysis and moral and legal issues of the international system.

Given this impression a different approach suggested itself for this book. First, the international system was sketched as a man-made, mainly anarchical, spontaneous and self-organizing system, which cannot be controlled by anybody and poses an increasing danger to mankind. Secondly, a long historical perspective has been taken, since different systems prevailed for decades and centuries, so that about the whole of written history is needed to get just a few examples of each system. Thirdly, because of this fact it seemed advisable to stress the deep insights of earlier observers of the international scene, namely of politicians, political philosophers, historians and social scientists. Quotations have been presented by such eminent men as Kalidasa, the early Indian politician, of Machiavel, of Louis XIV, George Washington, Frederick II of Prussia, de Tocqueville, Bismarck, the French historian Bainville, who predicted World War II, and George Kennan. Such quotations have especially then been given, when they contain interpretations and predictions which are well-reasoned and which have passed the test of history, like de Tocqueville's famous prediction of the 1830s that the USA and Russia would once dominate the world.

Fourthly, especially economic, but also geographic, demographic and scientific foundations of relative international power and its change over time have been widely discussed and analyzed in their importance for a possible future. Finally, terrorism, ideological and guerrilla warfare, whose importance rose strongly with the stalemate produced by the presence of nuclear arsenals, have been considered as important ingredients of the present international system.

The perspective taken can, perhaps, be best described as a public choice approach. This means to begin with the assumption that individuals try to choose rationally for themselves, their relatives and friends in a given institutional and organizational setting inherited from their forefathers, and with ideas, ideologies, and knowledge which have been shaped by their education and their life experiences in this very environment. Thus their knowledge is biased, it is necessarily limited and unexpected, and undesired consequences of their actions are usually inevitable. But this does not mean that men are mere pawns on the chessboard of history, of a totally unpredictable development. Nor does it mean that they are only manipulated or are only means of collective actors like classes, nations, religions or interest groups. An organicist interpretation of history is far from our understanding of the facts. Classes, nations etc. are potent man-made restrictions of human action, but they are no actors themselves.

The above presentation should indicate where the merits, if any, of this book can be found. It tries to present a fresh perspective, an unusual and perhaps illuminating integration of many facts, analytical and empirical results, which are widely scattered in the literature. It should thus, together with the historical examples and the easily accessible level of presentation, appeal especially to the educated layman, but also be useful to the undergraduate student as complementary reading.

It follows, on the other hand, that it has not been the ambition of the book to present and to discuss the wealth of the most recent literature in the field of foreign relations and of the international political system. Reasons of space would have prohibited such a discussion in any case, given the different aims set out above.

The following authors and publishers have kindly granted permission to quote from works mentioned in the book: Little, Brown & Co.; Westview Press; Biblio Verlag; Rowohlt Verlag; A. D. Peters & Co. Ltd.; Reimar Hobbing Verlag; Carl Ed. Schünemann KG.; American Political Association; American Journal of Medicine; Random House Inc.; Alfred A. Knopf; Inc.; Princeton University Press; Cornell University Press; University of Chicago Press; Hoffmann & Campe; Prof. Dr. Konrad Lorenz; Dr. Sebastian Haffner. I would like to express my gratitude to all of them. I am grateful to several people who have read and criticized the first drafts of the manuscript, especially to James M. Buchanan and to Gordon Tullock, both now at George Mason University. It is obvious that they do not share any responsibility for remaining weaknesses and mistakes. My family and especially my wife Elisabeth have again shown the forbearance and patience necessary to enable the completion of this book.

Moreover, I am grateful to my secretaries, Frau Baumgartner and Frau Ilg who have typed and corrected efficiently and patiently several versions of the manuscript. That they believed the book to be fascinating reading has been an encouragement.

Bottmingen, Switzerland
February 1985   Peter Bernholz

Table of Contents

Chapter 1

Human Artifacts, Social Dilemma and the International System

1. The International System as a Human Artifact

We live in an environment strongly shaped by ourselves. To a great degree, this is now true even with respect to our physical environment. In Europe scarcely a plot of earth exists which has not been turned over and cultivated again and again. Which plants are allowed to grow and which animals are permitted to live are determined largely by humans.

Our social environment, too, has been nearly totally created by us. Towns, church, state, democracy, money markets, agencies, goods, taxes and joint stock companies are all human artifacts. What is more, modern man himself is partly a manmade artifact. He is born into his social environment, which limits and determines his acquired behaviour. He is formally educated with the help of human inventions and institutions like the art of writing, schools, radio and television, to say nothing of the informal education provided by the surroundings in which he works and lives.

The fact that the social environment has been created by man does, however, not mean that it has been constructed by one or several individuals designing and executing one or more detailed plans. The Roman Empire, Russia, the English language or the Science of Physics have not been planned or constructed. No single human being or group would have been able to do so. All these human artifacts are the accumulated consequences of a great number of human actions which have led to many intended and perhaps to even more unintended outcomes. Thus most human institutions, rules and organizations have 'emerged' and have somehow successfully survived the struggle with other competing institutions, rules and organizations. The same is true for artifacts like markets, languages, tools, machines and consumer goods.[1]

The mainly unplanned nature of human artifacts does not mean that they are inadequate or inefficient for human purposes. They must have advantages for human beings to survive, they must have been better than competing artifacts because they have outlived them. Languages, cars, houses, joint stock companies, markets and mathematics must serve some human needs quite well, otherwise they would be on their way to extinction. And the workings of markets, organizations and languages are not chaotic, even though they have not been planned, but they have emerged as successful adapters in the ceaseless competition for survival.

The above remarks should not be misunderstood. Even if most human artifacts have emerged this does not mean that all of them have. New machines, companies, houses, streets, and even states (like Bismarck's Germany of 1871) have often been carefully planned and been constructed according to plan. But even in these cases the further developments of these artifacts may be quite different from those originally intended or even expected. For nobody can perfectly predict the impact of new, and especially of complex artifacts on social environment and the repercussions from the latter. To believe that any human being or human group could fully understand the present or even more, plan the future social environment, would be lunatic.

The consequences of these facts for man's image and his perception of the world can scarcely be exaggerated. His ideas and even his scientific theories are not only referring to a social environment created by his forefathers, but they are strongly influenced by this very environment. The individual often takes the institutions and organizations around him as if they were given by nature, since he himself can scarcely change them. He thus acts and reacts as if the system were immutable and as if it were ruled and determined by unchangeable laws. As a consequence, his expectations and actions are to a great extent dependent on the environment into which he has been born.

The behaviour just sketched is a rational one seen from an individual perspective. But this should not obscure the fact that our social environment can be changed by ourselves as collectivities since it has been, after all, created by men. This observation leads to important consequences. On the one hand, men may be so impressed with their views of an immutable social system that they form their ideas and act in such a way that society becomes in fact nearly static (like in old Egypt), or that no visions of alternative 'better' or 'worse' organizations of mankind than the existing one are developed. On the other hand, there may be people believing like the Marxists do that there are immutable laws governing social change which lead to a final stage of society, say communism and the withering away of the state, which cannot be prevented by anybody. Finally there may be people so influenced by the fact that social surroundings are artifacts that they believe human beings are able to plan and to bring about any kind of utopian environment they can dream of.

Even social science has often not been able to escape the dangers just mentioned. There are still social scientists who believe that their only job is to explore the social reality presently surrounding them and to find the laws determining its workings. It is obvious that such an attitude can be an obstacle to the use of creativity to invent new and 'better' social institutions and can serve interested groups as a weapon against changes of the status quo. Similar considerations apply to people like Marx who as an economist and philosopher was convinced he had found immutable laws of social change. If enough people believe in such a theory they may be able to bring about some of the changes thought to be inescapable. And, if the theory proves wrong, misery and oppression may result instead of the 'better' society hoped for.

The above considerations about the artifactual nature of social systems are of immediate relevance for foreign policy and for our understanding of it. We usually identify foreign policy as the 'behavior' of one state towards other states. But what if no such entities called 'states' exist? Then no foreign policy in the above sense can be present. But states are human inventions and even in their primitive forms not older than a few thousand years.[2]

Moreover, states have changed their characters during the course of history, and the number of states which were in contact with each other has not remained the same over time. There have been city states, national states and empires; feudal states, tyrannies, decentralized and centralized democracies. Systems have existed comprising many states (multipolar systems), some important states (balance of power systems), two important states (bipolar systems) or only one important state (world state systems). Do all these systems work in the same way? Is their functioning dependent on the nature and internal organisation of the states participating in the system?

The problems thus brought about by different social systems for the study of foreign policy could be easily handled if there existed a general theory able to explain or even to predict not only the behavior of different international systems, but also the changes from one system to another. Such a general theory is, however, not available. It is therefore necessary to use different approaches for different international systems, their developments and the changes between systems.

There are obvious dangers apt to mislead the social scientist following this road. If he is living in a world in which the balance of power system is prevailing, he may take the power relations and the Machiavellian outlook connected with this system as an immutable fact of life. Thus he may overlook the possibility that the system can be destabilized by important factors like revolutionary changes in weapons techniques or in social organization;

and that this change may lead, e.g. to a world state with an international law and ethics approaching those prevailing inside the nation state in which he presently lives. As a consequence of his time-determined outlook or his prejudices he may, moreover, also be unable to design and to propose better-functioning and more humane international systems.

The practising politician is liable to fall prey to similar dangers. Accustomed to, say, a balance of power system with a few important states he may overlook that there can arise participants like Napoleon or Hitler who make use of revolutionary developments to transform the system. Or, worse, not knowing the functioning of a balance of power system he may not realize (as a member of a victorious coalition like Wilson and Lloyd George after the First or Roosevelt and Truman during and after the Second World War) that the system can be destroyed and changed by the dissolution or division of important members (like Austria-Hungary and Germany, thus leaving the USA in a bipolar system with Soviet Russia).

In the following analysis we have strictly to keep in mind the manmade nature of the social environment and especially of international systems. These systems are not immutably given like the movement of the planets around the sun. It may be impossible under 'normal conditions' that they can be changed even by leading politicians. But conditions may change and thus open a chance even for individual actors to transform the existing system. And we should realize that our beliefs and our perceptions, which are formed by the social sciences, too, can be one of the most important factors responsible for such a transformation.

In Chapter 2 our study will begin by looking at different international systems, by studying their internal workings under the assumption that they are given. But we shall not stop there. Factors determining and transforming international systems will preoccupy us as much and we shall also turn to the question how a "better" international system should look, whether it can be established and whether factors working to bring it about exist.

2. States and the International System as a Response to the Social Dilemma and as a Means of Exploitation and Oppression

In a large group of human beings there are always some who find it easier to live from the fruits of the work of others than to work themselves. Thus they may cheat or use violence, theft and burglary to get hold of what other people have created, if the risk of being caught is not too high and the punishment to be expected not too severe.

The underlying situation can be described with the help of a simple example (Table 1.1). Let us assume that there are two people or groups *A* and *B* who can either devote all their time and resources to produce goods (*w*), e.g. wheat, or can use only half of them for productive work and the other half for stealing or defence against theft (*s*). The four cells of Table 1.1 give the amounts of goods (wheat) available to *A* and *B* in the four different possible outcomes.

If both *A* and *B* pursue activity *w*, (*w,w*), *A* gets 80 and *B*, who is perhaps less skilful or has smaller resources, 50 units. In case (*w,s*), in which only *B* steals, he gets 70 and *A* only 30 units. Note that the total product of both is now smaller than in case (*w,w*), namely 100 compared to 130 units, since *B* spends less of his time and resources on productive work. A similar outcome prevails, if *A* but not *B* steals, (*w,s*). Finally if both spend half of their time and resources on theft and on safeguarding against it, (*s,s*), *A* gets 40 and *B* 30, thus leaving a total of only 70 units.

Table 1.1

A	B	
	w	*s*
w	80, 50	30, 70
s	100, 20	40, 30

One realizes at once that activity *s* dominates activity *w*, so that the worst outcome (*s,s*) will result if both act independently. For consider *A*'s options. If he chooses the activity *s* he will be better off than with productive work (*w*) only, whatever *B* will do. For if *B* selects *w*, *A* can get 100 instead of 80, and if *B* prefers *s*, 40 instead of 30 units. *B* is in an analogous situation. But if *A* and *B* as a consequence both select strategy *s* then they are far worse off than if they had both followed strategy *w*, which would have resulted for *A* in 80 instead of 40 and for *B* in 50 instead of 30 units.

The example clarifies the nature of the social dilemma for the simplest possible case. The situation remains fundamentally the same if three or more people are involved. In fact, as we will see later, the dilemma gets more serious. Note again the essence of its nature: everybody follows his own self-interest rationally and independently, but all end up in a worse situation than could be achieved.

But given the situation just described, could not *A* and *B* easily escape the dilemma by cooperating, that is by agreeing to a contract in which they promise each other not to steal? Unfortunately the solution to the social dilemma cannot as easily be accomplished. For assume that A kept the contract but B did not. Then B would be better off again and get 70 instead of 50 units. It follows that both are motivated to break their agreement. Worse still, both have to expect that the other will renege on the contract. But if, say, A expects such a behaviour of B then it would be better for A, too, to break the agreement, since in this case he would get 40 instead of 30 units. Thus self-interest and (probably warranted) distrust would lead again to outcome (s,s).

What is needed, then, is a mechanism preventing the violation of the contract between A and B. Obviously, there exists such a solution to the social dilemma, namely the formation of a state guaranteeing with police and courts the punishment of violations of private contracts (Table 1.2). Let us assume, for our example, that it would take an amount of 10 units to keep up police and courts and that a violation of the contract between A and B would be punished with 25 units. Assume further that A and B had each to bear one half of the 10 units necessary for police and courts. Then the figures of Table 1.2 would result by deducting corresponding amounts from the figures of Table 1.1. E.g. if both choose w, then $80-5 = 75$ and $50-5 = 45$ units would be the resulting amounts. On the other hand, if only B would steal, he would have to pay the fine of 25 and 5 for police and courts thus leaving him $70-30 = 40$ units. A, however, would only have to pay 5, keeping $30-5 = 25$ units, etc. We realize at once that after these changes strategy w dominates s for both A and B, whatever the other does. As a consequence (w,w) will be the outcome, giving 75 units to A and 45 to B, which is much better than the 40 and 30 units they receive in outcome (s,s) in Table 1.1 without the existence of a state enforcing contracts. It follows that they both can accept the state and the chance of being punished in case of violation of contract, since this institution benefits them.

We should like to stress several points concerning our example. First, and least important, the penalty has to be big enough or the punishment would not work. Thus one observes at once that a penalty of 5 or even 10 units would not be sufficient to bring about (w,w) as an outcome. Secondly, we have assumed that a violation of contract will be detected and punished with certainty. If there are many people present this will not be true. But then the threatened punishment has to be more severe the smaller the probability that the violator of the contract or legal rule forbidding theft will be apprehended. Thirdly, the existence of the state and thus of the solution to the social dilemma is not costless. Outcome (w,w) leaves A and B with a total of 130 units without (Table 1.1), but only with 120 units with the state (Table 1.2).[3]

A fourth point remains to be made. In a small group (especially, of course, in one with only two people) the sanctions required to reach an outcome like (*w,w*) in Table 1.2 can obviously be brought about in an informal way and do not need the existence of a state. Social disapproval by relatives and friends, an education teaching children to respect adequate norms may be quite sufficient to prevent the violation of agreements.

Table 1.2

A	*B*		
		w	*s*
w		75, 45	25, 40
s		70,15	10, 0

Moreover, the situation described in Table 1.1 will usually repeat itself, or at least be followed by similar situations. In game theoretic language, there will be an indefinite number of plays of the same or of similar games. To return to our example, *A* and *B* do not only live, work and possibly steal in the next week, but also during an indefinite number of later weeks. If this is the case, however, then they may be motivated to keep their agreements even if no outside sanctions exist. For assume that B would break the contract concluded for next week. In this case he could gain 20 units (see Table 1.1), but had to expect that *A* would as a consequence either not conclude or break an agreement in one or more of the following weeks. This would, taking into account his own response, lead to outcome (*s,s*), bringing about a reduction of 20 units per week. It follows that *B* will be better off if he keeps the agreement in the first week, whenever he has to expect that *A* will be around during the weeks to come. But *A* is in a similar situation. Consequently both will be strongly motivated to keep their agreements, even if they only follow their narrow self-interest and if no outside sanctions exist.

Having discussed these additional factors we note that they are mainly valid for small groups. This is certainly true for the iterative game just mentioned. Even within a group of, say, 100 people it would be extremely difficult to detect the violator of a contract or a rule against theft without the help of a specialized agency, like the police. It follows that it would not be possible to punish a thief just by not concluding or by breaking an agreement with him the next week. But if this is true, then two problems arise. The motivation to steal would be present again. And since everybody could be the violator people would be more reluctant to make and to keep agreements with others. Thus the outcome (w,w) would either not result or become more and more improbable in time.

In a large group, social disapproval and an education inculcating moral values would probably not be sufficient to secure an outcome like (w,w). First, again, there is the difficulty of detecting the violators. Secondly, it is much less likely that the action is disapproved by all members of a large group, most of whom have not been hurt by the violation or have scarcely or not at all heard about it. Finally, people usually feel themselves the less bound by inculcated norms the greater the distance and the less they know the people with whom they have to deal. We conclude that informal internal sanctions of the kind mentioned become less reliable as the size of the group in question increases. Thus results the importance of the state, of laws, police and courts to secure personal and property rights against violations and to bring about outcomes like (w,w), which can be preferred by all members of society.

The existence of states, however, unfortunately entails new problems. True, police and army should only be used to protect citizens against violence and against the violation of property rights. But it is also true that both can be misused by minorities or majorities to exploit and to oppress people within and without the state. Indeed, Marxism envisions the state mainly in this function, namely as an instrument of the ruling class to exploit the rest of the population and to maintain their own dominance.[4] It is because of this possibility that constitutional theories have tried to design adequate democratic constitutions safeguarding the rule of law, and providing adequate human and minority rights.[5]

Turning to the international system we are at once impressed by the fact that no international government, no international police or army exist to sanction the violation of international agreements. If national governments like those of the Soviet Union or the USA ponder to invade Afghanistan or to fight a war in Vietnam, they are certainly not influenced in their calculations by the possible sanctions on the part of a "World Government", its police or armed forces. The factors they take into account are the possible reactions of other national governments and perhaps their own populations. Thus, at least to a certain degree, the international system is still ruled by anarchy preventing outcomes like (w,w) in Table 1.2, and furthering outcomes like (s,s) in Table 1.1. Indeed, we can reinterpret A and B as states, and w and s as peaceful relations and war efforts, respectively, to describe the situation of a simplified international system with two actors. Then the example would at least show that the social dilemma has not been solved in this system.

To say that an international system composed of independent states is at least partly anarchic does not imply, however, that no international law, no rules of conduct and no cooperation exist. First with even only two states we have to take into account that for many issues about which both are concerned cooperation may be rewarding. This may be true, indeed, in situations like those described in Table 1.1, if they are repetitive games played an indefinite number of times. But note that conquering another state once and for all is not a repetitive game.

Secondly, with more than two states it is often useful to form coalitions with one or more states against others either to attack them or to defend against them (see Chapter 2).

Finally, governments will usually be interested that their citizens keep contracts with foreigners and observe foreign law in other states if they are on friendly terms with them. It follows, then, that states may well agree to set up international organizations, to adhere to a certain body of international law and to set up international courts to adjudicate certain conflicts arising between them or between their citizens.[6]

But in spite of all this, each state remains free to decide for itself, when and to which degree to agree to and to keep international treaties, to follow international law, to keep peace or to go to war. The international system keeps its basically anarchical traits as long as no international government exists which can apply adequate sanctions against states. This fact has been sadly confirmed by the great number of wars and invasions which took place even since World War II, by the armaments race, the breach of international agreements, by threats and reprisals among states in spite of the existence of the United Nations and many other international organizations and courts.

We recall that modern states and the international system have emerged as human institutions, as artifacts. Nobody has planned or even predicted them and their consequences. These institutions and the system they compose have been successfully developed and survived in fierce competition with other organizations of society like the feudal or tribal system and with other states. But their survival does not mean that they are 'better' in the moral sense of the word. It is true that the nation state has brought a high measure of order and suppression of internal violence. But, as we have already pointed out, it can be used for purposes of internal and external exploitation and oppression. The international system composed of states is still largely anarchical, encourages overspending on armaments, leads to wars and other actions inimical to world developments. It has not solved the social dilemma on an international scale.

Furthermore, if we look around, we realize that oligarchies, dictatorships and military regimes abound, and that only a minority of states can be judged to be free democratic societies with constitutional safeguards for human and minority rights and the rule of law. As we will see later

(Chapter 3.4) it is quite possible that these societies may be outmanoeuvred and suppressed in time by non-democratic states because of the nature of the existing international system. If such a development should in fact happen, these states would have proved themselves as institutions better capable to survive, but we would certainly not believe them to be "better" from a moral point of view.

3. Nature of International Actors, of International Aims and Issues

We are interested in the workings of the international system in the past, the presence and future. In approaching this problem several questions come to mind, namely:

(1) Who are the international actors?

(2) What are the issues with which they are confronted and which they try to solve?

(3) What are the aims of the international actors?

We do not intend to discuss questions (2) and (3) in this section in a substantive way. This will be done in Chapter 5. Similarly, the actors in the international system will be at the center of our interest throughout the book. At the moment, their nature, like that of issues and aims, will only concern us from a more general, formal and introductory point of view closely related to the discussion of the previous sections.

In a strict methodological sense, only human beings can be actors of the international system. Institutions and organizations like states, churches, multinational and international organizations are human artifacts, not organisms. They can have no aims, no issues can exist for them and they cannot act. On the other hand, human beings are confined and restricted in their behaviour by the institutional setting surrounding them. People would not have problems with the Internal Revenue Service, be drafted into the army and be forced to fight a war, or be obliged to send their children to school, if no state or no international system, no school and no Internal Revenue Service existed. The freedom of action of human beings is thus strongly limited or even determined by the kind of social system in which they live. In some cases people have scarcely any choice, since the institutional setting fully determines their actions. In such cases one might even argue that the relevant institutions and not the individuals concerned are acting.

In modern, well-ordered states it is especially the use of force which is strongly regulated by law. Individuals are not allowed to use force, or in many states even to possess weapons, save under highly restrictive conditions. In this sense the modern state or the people dominating it, have often successfully secured a monopoly of power. It is because of this that the state as an artifact plays a dominant role in the international system. Individuals can only play an important role in this system if they are influential in the state machinery so that they are able to use its agencies and, if necessary, its armed forces. For only then can they meet the threats or actual use of military power by other states, threaten themselves with military intervention, engage in war and enforce obedience domestically. It is in this sense that we may speak of states as the main international actors: individuals have to act through a state and have to take into account the reality of the existence of other states wielding a monopoly of power in their territories, if they want to be influential or important participants of the international system.

There is still another meaning in which organizations and especially states can be said metaphorically to have ends and to act. We all know that many people identify with 'their' church, 'their' nation, 'their' company and are prepared to sacrifice a lot, sometimes even their lives for these entities. The ideas with which they identify are handed down possibly from generation to generation and can usually only be slowly changed by the present membership. A single individual has only negligable influence on the heritage of ideas and rules of Islam, of Communism, of General Motors or of France. But if this is true, then the emerged tradition, the special cultural traits of an organization, an institution can in a sense 'dictate' aims to individuals who identify with it. Thus these human artifacts gain because of their deadweight as it were, their own lives; they have aims and act with their traditions and rules through the acts of individuals educated in and restricted by their cultural heritage.

Given the complicated relationship between human beings and the artifacts which have emerged in history, it cannot be surprising that long and heated controversies have raged over the question of who are the relevant international actors, what are their aims and what issues do they confront. The so-called 'realist' school of the discipline concerned with international relations has always emphasized nation states as international actors. We are able to appreciate this view because states more or less monopolize the use of power and have been able, at least during the last two hundred years, to a surprising degree to attract the allegiance of their citizens. We shall see, moreover, that often the restrictions caused by a given international system are such that the leading politicians of a state do not have much of a choice if they want to secure the survival of their nation.

Since the late 1960s, another school of thought, the so-called 'globalists' have debated the 'realists' view of the international system and of its operation.[7] The position of the globalists has been expressed by Puchala and Fagan as follows:[8]

> ... national governments are but some actors among many on the international scene. Other prominent actors include international organizations and directorates, multinational corporations, functionally linked transnational groups such as regional political parties and international guerilla organizations, and subnational groups such as departments of agriculture, ministries of finance or major labor unions, business firms or philanthropic foundations – all formulating and executing their own foreign policies in quasi-autonomous fashion. (p. 40)

Concerning the issues the two authors point out that

> ... it would seem that many of today's most pressing international issues have little to do with the relative military security of states, with their relative coercive power, with their territoriality, or even with the ideology of their regimes. Governments today appear increasingly absorbed in enhancing the economic, social, and intellectual well-being of their citizens via their foreign policies and international interactions. (p. 39)

Marxists have always taken an even stronger position against the relevance of states as national or international actors. For them, states are only instruments of the dominating class in society. To quote Friedrich Engels:

> Since the state has developed out of the need to restrain contradictions between classes, and since it has arisen at the same time amidst the conflict of these classes, it is regularly the state of the most powerful, economically dominating class. This class becomes with its help also the politically dominating class and gets thus with its help new means to keep down and to exploit the suppressed class . . . .[9]

It follows that classes are the real national and international actors in the Marxist's image of the world. Now, from our perspective classes as well as churches, international and multinational organizations, departments of agriculture and ministeries of finance are only human organizations and cannot have aims or act in the strictest methodological interpretation. In this they are quite similar to the state. Moreover, there can be no doubt that the actions of human beings are restricted by the existence of these social artifacts and that the aims of individuals are influenced by the traditions and rules embodied in these organizations and their membership. As a consequence, if non-state organizations are able to gain the allegiance of people more than the state, then the aims of the state, the issues perceived by its members can also be changed in the direction of the traditions of these organizations. For aims and issues in collectivities like states are formed as an aggregation of the ends followed by different individuals with changing influence in the political process.

We are thus not surprised about the controversy concerning the relevant international actors, the nature of issues and aims. To get a complete theory one would have to start from all the individuals in the world, their aims or preferences and from the restrictions given by the existence of all kinds of organizations, institutions and rules, and then have to deduce their decisions, reactions and the ensuing consequences for the international system. But it is obvious that this is far too ambitious to ever be accomplished. It follows that the science of international politics has to simplify drastically, has to reduce the number of actors if it wants to gain some understanding of reality. This means, unfortunately, that it has to take collective actors into account and to work with them as if they had aims, were confronted by issues and could act.

Given these problems, one has to decide which collective actors to select. It is our conviction that judged from the problems specific to the international system − anarchy, no worldwide organization with the power to sanction the violation of international law, of treaties and contracts, and on the whole successful monopolization of power by the states − that judged from these problems, states have to be the main actors to be considered when one tries to find the most important characteristics of the international system.

Some people may contradict these views by pointing out the influence of multinational corporations on the formation of the policies of states, the importance of international organizations like the International Monetary Fund on the domestic policies of countries in need of credit, etc. Now, we are the last to deny the existence of such influences. It is true that the United States Fruit Company has been able in the past to influence Central American countries or even to topple their governments, that the International Monetary Fund has set in 1982/1983 strict credit conditions influencing domestic economic policies of, say, Mexico and Brazil and that interest groups like unions, churches, agricultural organizations and business firms can have influence on the formation of the national and international politics of industrialized nations. We grant these facts and take them into account up to a certain point.

But we assert that all these facts are not the most important ingredients of the international system, and that their influences are usually rather weak. For first, international organizations or their members are strongly dependent in their policies on their member governments. Their importance is vastly smaller than that of a council of ministers. For instance, the Commission of the European Market is no match to the European Council of Ministers. Secondly, even rather weak countries have been able to nationalize their oil or copper industries belonging to 'powerful' international firms. Customs duties and tariffs have been raised, prices of pharmaceuticals been controlled by government agencies in spite of the fierce opposition of multinational corporations. Finally, the activities of firms, unions, churches, etc. are strongly regulated by the laws of nation states, and communist governments do not even allow the existence of independent private organizations. Even in western democracies these organizations are usually far removed from the possibility of dominating legislation. But if they were able to dominate it, then they would determine the aims of the state, and would also have to take into account the international environment of independent states wielding monopolies of power. If a multinational corporation, a union or church would, in fact, be able to control a state, then it would no longer act as a mere corporation, union or church.

On the whole, we prefer, because of these considerations, to take thus the position of the realists and to put the states at the center of the international system. But it follows from our general perspective that we shall not forget that there are other collective 'actors' and that in a strict sense only individuals can act, have aims and confront issues.

One major conclusion following from this perspective has yet to be mentioned. Collective actions can only be the outcome of individual decisions, usually an aggregation of the decisions of *many* persons. Now, since no individual has full information about all relevant facts and since nobody has full control of governmental actions, it follows that there may be actions which are inconsistent with each other or actions which nobody in the country wanted. A simple example helps to make this point clear. Take a group of three people I, II and III, who decide by simple majority voting about what their organization should do. Assume that three possible outcomes exist A, B and C and that the preferences of the group members are given by Table 1.3. The outcomes are valued the higher by the respective individual the closer they are to the top of the column.

Table 1.3

I	II	III
A	B	C
B	C	A
C	A	B

It follows that in this example a majority, namely I and III, prefer A to B, and another one, I and II, B to C. Now, consistency would require that A would be preferred to C by a majority. But this is not the case. For II and III prefer C to A.

This result means, first, that nobody can be sure about the collective outcome in spite of all group members having consistent preferences. For it depends on the sequence of the pairs of alternatives put to the decision, which outcome will be selected. If the group votes first on pair AB and then on the winner chosen, A, put against C, C will be selected. But the outcome would be different, namely A or B respectively if BC or AC would be first voted on.

Secondly, assume that the group would first take action B after having voted on B and C only, then similarly A after a vote on AB and finally C after voting on AC. Obviously this would lead to inconsistent behavior, since B is preferred by a majority to C.

We have stressed some of the problems of collective decision making. Nobody has full information or is in full control of the collective 'actor'. Even if all would act fully informed and rationally, inconsistent group behaviour might result. Consequently the outcome may not be wanted by anybody. Add the fact that several collective actors are members of the international system. Then it is difficult to doubt that, to put it mildly, the development of the international system cannot be planned or fully foreseen by anybody. Its events and characteristics are at least partly unintended consequences of human actions, they emerge.

It is thus not surprising that different interpretations of the international system have been presented. To Tolstoi in *War and Peace*, war and international politics are uncontrollable and unpredictable events or catastrophies like earthquakes or thunderstorms. For Clausewitz foreign policy and war as its "continuation with other means" are calculable by rational statesmen wisely leading monolithic states competing for power.

For Marxists war and international politics are another battlefield of class struggle, with the states as instruments wielded by the economically dominating class, that is presently the capitalist class in non-socialist countries. But since classes will vanish after the inevitable victory of the proletariat — inevitable because of the development of the means of production — and the introduction of communism, states will wither away, and with it the wars and anarchy of the present international system.[10]

If follows from the above considerations that all of these images of the international system may contain some partial truth. But the workings and the development of the system are neither totally unpredictable nor perfectly predictable. The course of its development is not predetermined and not fully controllable. But it can be partly influenced in a direction wanted by individual actors and it can to a greater degree be partially predicted by science. In the following chapters we shall try to substantiate this view.

Notes

[1]   Compare Friedrich A. Hayek: *The Constitution of Liberty*, University of Chicago Press, Chicago 1960.

[2]   For a discussion of many of the problems for human conflict and war stemming from the artifactual nature of man's social environment compare: Anatol Rapoport: *Conflict in Man-made Environment*, Penguin Books, Harmondsworth (Middlesex), 1974; and, Anatol Rapoport (ed.): *Carl von Clausewitz on War*. Penguin Books, Harmondsworth (Middlesex), 1968, Introduction by Anatol Rapoport, pp. 11–80.

[3]   The social dilemma has been treated in Gordon Tullock: *The Social Dilemma. The Economics of War and Revolution*. Center for the Study of Public Choice, Blacksburg (Va.) 1974.

[4]   See Friedrich Engels: *Der Ursprung der Familie, des Privateigentums und des Staates.* 17th edition, Stuttgart 1919.

[5]   The idea of a constitutional contract and thus of the state as a solution to the social dilemma has been discussed in depth by James M. Buchanan in *The Limits of Liberty. Between Anarchy and Leviathan.* University of Chicago Press, Chicago 1975.

[6]   Compare with Hedley Bull: *The Anarchical Society. A Study of Order in World Politics,* Macmillan, London 1981.

[7]   Concerning the discussion between 'realists' and 'globalists' see the articles in Ray Marghroori and Bennett Ramberg (eds.): *Globalism versus Realism. International Relations' Third Debate.* Westview Press, Boulder (Colorado) 1982, Copyright (c) 1978 by James Petras.

[8]   Donald G. Puchala and Stuart I. Fagan: "International Politics in the 1970s: The Search for a Perspective." *International Organization*, vol. 28, 1974. Reprinted in Maghroori and Ramberg, op. cit., pp. 37–56.

[9]   Friedrich Engels, op. cit., p. 180. A modern Marxist analysis concerning especially the present relationships between developed capitalist and developing countries is offered by James Petras in *Critical Perspectives on Imperialism and Social Class in the Third World*. Monthly Review Press, New York and London, 1978.

[10]   Friedrich Engels, op. cit.

Chapter 2

International Political Systems

> *"War is a mere continuation of Policy by other means."*
> Carl v. Clausewitz, Prussian General, 1832[1]

1. Basic Laws of the International Political System

Between the years 321–296 *B.C.* Kautilya, minister of the first Maurya emperor in India, Chandragupta, wrote an important treatise on politics and diplomacy. It is fascinating to read several passages of this work:

The king who, being possessed of good character and bestfitted elements of sovereignty . . . is termed the conqueror.
The king who is situated anywhere immediately on the circumference of the conqueror's territory is termed the enemy.
The king who is likewise situated close to the enemy, but separated from the conqueror only by the enemy, is termed the friend of the conqueror.
A neighbouring foe of considerable power is styled an enemy; and when he is involved in calamities or has taken himself to evil ways, he becomes assailable; and when he has little or no help, he becomes destructible; otherwise (i.e. when he is provided with some help), he deserves to be harassed or reduced. . . .
The possession of power and happiness in a greater degree makes a king superior to another; in a less degree, inferior; and in an equal degree, equal. Hence a king shall always endeavour to augment his own power and elevate his happiness. . . ."[2]

In these sentences we find already all essential traits of international power politics, traits which are so contradictory to the teachings of Christ, his gospel of love, and those of the Buddha asking his followers not to kill any living being. What are then these main characteristics which have dominated hundreds and thousands of years of human history leading to bloodshed, incredible misery and devastation? And what are the reasons that these forces have not been checked by the prescriptions of brotherly love preached by the major world religions for centuries?

Kautilya obviously suggests the following propositions and postulates:
(1) Strengthen your own country so that it gains power relative to other states.
(2) All your immediate neighbor states are potential enemies. Defeat and conquer them whenever possible, that is if they are weak and have no reliable allies.
(3) Do everything to weaken your potential enemies.
(4) The states neighboring your enemies but not your own territory are potential allies. Try to gain their help either to withstand your (potentional) enemies or to defeat them.

(5) As soon as your former allies become neighbours they are turned into potential enemies.

Most of Kautilya's treatise tries to work out the specific means and measures which are adequate to strengthen the state internally and externally, to defeat and conquer the enemies and to expand the territory of one's own country. It is perhaps interesting to know that Kautilya's king Chandragupta succeeded in defeating the dynasty of Magadha, taking their capital Pataliputra (Patna) and conquering from there the whole of northern India. He destroyed the Greek-Macedonian troops left by Alexander the Great in the northwest of India and established the Maurya empire. His Prime Minister, Kautilya, probably played a leading role in designing and executing this policy.

It is not always clear whether Kautilya'a statements are meant as a description of reality or recommendations given to princes who want to be successful conquerors. Certainly both kinds of sentences can be found in his work. We should, therefore, ask ourselves whether there exist compelling reasons for statesmen to build up the relative strength of their nations and to embark on adventurous expansionary policies. This seems to be very doubtful at least at first glance. Increasing the military strength of a country implies the diversion of resources from increasing wealth and the well-being of the population. If a number of states rearm by about the same magnitude, their relative strengths remain unchanged, so that their efforts amount to a sheer waste of resources. The same is, of course, even more true for wars, if their outcomes are not rather clear from the very beginning. Following this line of reasoning one has to ask to what extent it would not only be morally better but domestically more rewarding for statesmen to pursue peaceful policies and to concentrate on the task of creating the best conditions for domestic economic and cultural development?

Unfortunately this kind of reasoning overlooks several facts which account for the instability of the international political system so well-known for the whole of human history. First there are always at least *a few people and politicians* who want to extend their power and the territory of their states, because they love power itself, want to spread their beliefs (ideas, doctrines or religions) to other people or to rob others of their wealth. We may call this fact the *Law of the Existence of an Expansionary Minority*. But why should the 'law' just stated lead to the sad state of international affairs reflected in the passages written by Kautilya? Would it not be possible to contain a presumably small minority of power-hungry human beings? Here we can state two more laws which easily explain the *Law of the Jungle of International Politics*, namely the *Law of the Rule of Minimal International Morality* and the *Law of the Attraction of Power-Hungry Minorities towards Political Offices*.

The second of these laws can be easily explained. People who love power and prestige and like to dominate others will usually strive harder than their fellow-men to move into state positions connected with power and prestige. People interested in ethics and religion are not as probable to become politicians as are people interested in power and prestige. Moreover, the more or less ruthless who are not hindered by moral or ethical norms have a bigger chance to move up in the political and bureaucratic hierarchy than do those with a more scrupulous conscience. As a consequence there is a high probability to find a preponderance of more or less unscrupulous men interested in power and prestige in leading positions of the government.

The *Law of the Rule of Minimal International Morality* can be best explained with the help of a numerical example. Let us assume that only two important states called the Soviet Union and USA are present. The Soviet Union is bent on expansion to deliver the world from the scourge of capitalism and to advance the final salvation of humanity by communism bringing about the withering away of the state and of all future wars. The Soviet Union and the USA have both the possibility to rearm or not (see Table 2.1). If both do not rearm we have the situation described by the figures in the upper left cell. If both rearm the situation given in the lower right cell prevails. In the former case all resources can be spent on economic development, whereas part of them has to be spent on military expenditures in the latter. Thus the situation of both countries is worse than in the former case. This is described by the smaller figures (representing a kind of utility measure) for both countries. Citizens of the USA enjoy only a well-being of 7 as compared to 10 (in which case no rearmament of both powers takes place) and those of the Soviet Union of 5 compared to 8. This implies, of course, that both states would rearm by about the same magnitude so that none would be able to wield military superiority.

Table 2.1: The Rearmament Problem with one Agressor

USSR USA	Does not rearm	Rearms
Does not rearm	10, 8	0, 12
Rearms	8, 4	7, 5

Now consider the upper right cell where only Russia but not the USA rearms. If this happened the Soviet Union or the 'Communist World Movement' could apply its military strength either by using it or by threatening to use it to subjugate the USA to communism, a situation felt to be very bad by the American population. This is symbolized by a utility of 0. The Soviet leadership would, however, consider this the best possible situation since it implies the final defeat of capitalism connected with world domination by the USSR. Its utility is therefore given to be 12.

The final case would be a rearmament of the USA but not of the Soviet Union. Assuming that the former does not want to dominate the latter, it has no advantage from rearming one-sidedly. In fact, its utility drops to 8 because of the military expenditures. On the other hand, the utility of the Soviet Union drops to 4 but not to 0. It drops because the hope for communist world domination deteriorates sizably. But it remains above 0 since there is no danger of US aggression.

Table 2.2: The Rearmament Dilemma with two Perceived Aggressors

USA \ USSR	Does not rearm	Rearms
Does not rearm	10, 8	0, 12
Rearms	12, 0	7, 5

Assume now that the state of affairs just sketched is well-known to the respective leadership. Which of the two options, to arm or not to arm, would be selected? It is obvious that rearmament will be the selected strategy for both countries. For consider the Soviet Union. It is better off if it rearms, whatever the USA decides to do. For 12 is greater than 8 and 5 greater than 4. Given this situation, which is known to the USA, the latter will also decide in favour of rearmament, because Russia decides for rearmament and because 7 is better than 0 for the USA.

It is important to visualize the full importance of these conclusions. First, only the Soviet Union strives for expansion. But because of this, the USA has also to rearm. Second, as a consequence both nations are worse off than they could be without rearming. Now, in our example the Soviet Union could unilaterally disarm, because it knows that the USA would follow this policy (since 10 is greater than 8). This would be a rational policy for the Soviet Union in spite of its plans for world domination, since with US rearmament there would be no hope to realize its aim.

Our example has, however, assumed that there is full information about the situation on the part of the politicians of both countries and that, for example, no uncertainty about their future domestic developments exists. Things look somewhat different if we remove these unrealistic assumptions. What is the change in the situation, if the leadership of the Soviet Union (perhaps wrongly) assumes that the capitalistic USA strives, too, for world domination and for eradication of the communist threat? This scenario as perceived by the Soviet leadership is described in Table 2.2, where the figures in the left lower cell have been changed to 12 for the USA and to 0 for the Soviet Union. Obviously, now neither the USA nor Russia could risk to move to disarmament because in the changed situation not only the USSR but also the USA would have the possibility and the perceived wish (12 is greater than 10 for USA) to gain world domination. But even now disarmament would still be beneficial to both countries.

This time, however, one-sided disarmament would not do even from the point of view of the Soviet leadership. Thus only a treaty concluded between both powers to disarm could help. But how would it be possible to control and to enforce such an agreement? This shows that it is not easy to remove the dilemma in which both powers find themselves, because there exists no super-organization able to force them not to violate the treaty (since the states are still the only organizations wielding final military power). Moreover, we get as a further result that both leaderships may wrongly suspect expansionary aims of the other power, therefore they start to rearm themselves and by doing so reinforce the initial suspicion of the other country.

Finally, let us consider the possibility of future internal changes in one of the countries. If in the case of Table 2.1 the leadership of the Soviet Union believes for instance that the American public and the politicians may change their perceptions of Soviet aims over time (perhaps even because of communist propaganda for 'peaceful coexistance'), then they could expect that the USA would disarm one-sidedly. But in this case it would pay for the Soviet Union not to disarm but to wait for the future disarmament of the USA to use the chance to gain world domination.

The discussion of our examples should clarify the following relationships:
(1) If there is (are) some aggressive nation(s) then the other powers are forced to rearm and to enter the arena of international power politics.
(2) With uncertainty present as to the aims of different nations, there is strong motivation to rearm as a precautionary measure. But each rearmament 'confirms' and strengthens the initial suspicions and reinforces the rearmament race.
(3) All participating nations are usually in a worse position with than without the arms race. But the dilemma cannot be easily solved because of the difficulty to control and to enforce disarmament treaties.

(4) Nations with an aggressively-minded leadership may even prefer to keep up their armaments in spite of the high costs, since they hope for domestic or other changes unfavourable to their potential enemy leading to disarmament or to a lack of will-power to use military force.

All the above factors obviously favor tendencies to elevate the relative power of states into an end itself and to build up international tensions and suspicions. Together with the domestic tendencies for power-hungry minorities to move into leading governmental positions, this leads to the rule of the law of the jungle in the relations between independent organizational unities, called states, wielding the monopoly of power in their respective territories.

Let us, after this analysis, return to Kautilya's time for a moment. Before the Maurya empire was created by Chandragupta, India was composed of quite a number of independent kingdoms and principalities. Such a setting seems to be fertile soil for the development of a theory of how to gain, maintain and expand power. A theory of this kind nearly necessarily develops out of the observed relationships in an environment of states competing for predominance and which may be even 'forced' to do so as it were by the Laws described above. It is therefore not surprising that theories like that which developed in Old India and culminated in the writings of Kautilya 300 years *B.C.*, grew up in similar settings, namely in the 'China of the Warring States' at about the same time and in Renaissance Italy about 1500 *A.D.* In the latter case the corresponding ideas were put forward by Niccolo Machiavelli after more than two hundred years of fierce competition among quite a number of Italian city and territorial states.[3] Even today we still speak of 'Machiavellian politics' when we want to describe shrewd, amoralistic, ruthless power politics using all available means. In Europe, Machiavellian ideas were developed further by the Prussian general von Clausewitz in his book *On War*[1] as a consequence of the observation of the competition of European states for hegemony, to which we will return later.

In the 'China of the Warring States' there had been, too, several hundred years of fierce competition among a number of independent states. Here the so-called legalistic school developed and put forward ideas similar to those presented in the works of Kautilya and Machiavelli. The Chinese doctrine obviously culminated in the thinking of Su Ch'in and Chang I[10] who were leading ministers on different sides of the fence during the final period of the 'Warring States'. After Su Ch'in had been murdered by political enemies the kingdom of Ch'in with its minister Chang I won the upper hand over the competing states. Finally Cheng, the king of Ch'in (who called himself later Shih Huang Ti as emperor), and his able Machiavellian minister Li Ssu, conquered them and formed a unified Chinese Empire (221 *B.C.*). It may be a credit to the realism of the theory of international relations, the essentials of which have been sketched above, that Kautilya as well as Chang I were advising or even partly leading the victorious states and that powerful empires resulted, thus ending the period of independent states vying for power in an atmosphere of intrigue, bloodshed and destruction. We will turn to the importance of these developments later on when we deal with the 'World State'. Machiavelli, however, did not succeed with his ideas to unify Italy and to liberate it from its sufferings under the hands of foreign 'barbarians'. Machiavelli dedicated his book *The Prince* (Il Principe) to Lorenzo de Medici of Florence and wrote in the concluding chapter:

If I consider everything which I have said until now and ponder whether times are presently favourable for a new ruler and whether a shrewd and capable man would have a chance to shape the present situation to promote his own fame and the welfare of the whole Italian people, then so many factors seem to work in favour of a new ruler that I would know of no time which could be more adequate.[3]

Machiavelli's judgement was probably wrong, even if there had been a more capable man present than Lorenzo de Medici, (who earned the hatred of the Florentines because of his pride and his licentiousness, and who died at the early age of twenty-seven). For already foreign powers, especially France and Spain had intervened several times in Italian affairs and the domestic states were not able to match their powers. As a matter of fact the Spanish under King Ferdinand were already on the brink of dominating Italy, a domination which became final when in 1519 Habsburgian Charles V, the grandson of Ferdinand, combined the Spanish crown with that of the German Holy Empire and the Habsburgian dominions in the Netherlands, Belgium and Burgundy.

2. The Multipolar International System

Until now we have only shown why in a system of a number of independent states there are tendencies for each state to increase its relative power: to rearm, to form and to change alliances and to use wars and the threat of wars to conquer enemies and to expand its own territory. The question of whether differences in the number or size of states leads to differences in the character of this game of international power politics has not been asked until now.

Postponing the question concerning the importance of the size of states until later, we will take up now the question of numbers. The most preliminary considerations already suggest that a difference should exist between

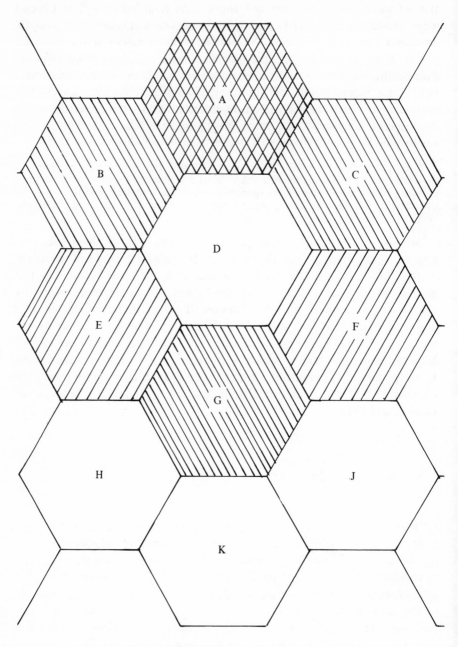

Figure 2.1: An Idealized Multipolar System of States

systems containing two, five and, let's say thirty essential states, that is, states of roughly comparable power. In a situation in which only two important states exist it does not make much sense for an alliance to be formed between them, and there is no possibility to shift it. It is true that both "big powers" can add states of minor importance to form alliances, but each of them will always find itself at the helm of one of the two opposing alliances.

With thirty states of about equal strength present things are different. In this case it is certainly possible for the relevant states to enter many different alliances and to switch easily from one alliance to another. But it makes usually no sense to form, let's say, alliances containing far removed allies who are not themselves neighbours of neighbouring countries. Alliances comprising a large number or even a majority of all relevant states are usually not very rewarding. The costs to build such alliances become too expensive and the expected spoils have to be divided among too many participants. Because of this there is a tendency, confined of course by considerations of uncertainty, towards minimal winning coalitions.[4] The situation is again different if there are, for instance, only five or seven states of about equal strength. Here two alliances can be meaningful which contain all powers and here, too, an easy shift among alliances is often promising.

In this section we will be concerned with a multipolar system, that is, with a system comprising a great number of states of about equal power. Ideally this system would look like that sketched in Figure 2.1, if no differences of geography, of the densities of the populations, the fertility of the land and of the kinds and degrees of development of industries and of agriculture were present. We can see that even in such a simple and unrealistic system ambiguities of the positions of countries in respect to each other are present. According to Kautilya, countries B, C and D would be potential enemies of state A. E, G and F would be potential friends and allies against D. But G has E and F as potential enemies and B, C as potential allies against E, D and F. This fact should not be without importance for the relationship between A and G. One may even argue that B and C, too, could be useful to A as allies against D, even if it were mainly for the purpose of preventing them to join a coalition against A. After a possible defeat of D and its division among the victorious alliance, let's say A, E, G and F, A and G will presumably be new neighbors. This fact has, however, already to be taken into account during the formation of the victorious alliance, during the war and especially during the time of the division of D. If we consider all these different factors, we get a rather complicated situation. It is therefore not surprising that a lot of maneuvering, intrigue, formation, shifting and breaking of alliances takes place in a multipolar system. Many mistakes and miscalculations will be made from the point of view of the individual states and the outcome of the struggle for power and the history of the development of the total system may look like a chance process to outside observers. In many cases the results will be quite surprising and unexpected to the leading politicians and nobody will feel himself to be in full control of the situation.

Things are even more complicated und unpredictable in reality. Geographical features may lead to certain advantages or disadvantages for several states. One or the other country may be protected by the sea or by inaccessible mountains in one or several directions. Others may be centrally located among and border many countries without having any natural protection. The help provided by natural frontiers depends, however, on the kind of weapons available. The development of fleets, planes and missiles has severely lowered the protective value of an insular position. Still, Britain would certainly have been conquered by German forces during World War II had it not been an island.

A different growth of the respective populations and economies as well as the influence of new ideas and ideologies may also change the relative power of states in different ways. These factors are not fully controllable. We will return to them later. Let it suffice for the moment to mention that an increased population, a better educational system and the development of technology and industry can all be used to build up stronger military forces, thus leading to the ascendancy or relatively more rapid development of some countries, which can be exploited for the expansion of these favored states.

Another factor of importance to be considered is the size of countries. A small territory will usually reduce the possibilities of waging a successful war and history shows that countries which have been reduced in their size have usually become more peaceful organizations. Sweden had been a very belligerent power after King Gustav Adolf had successfully intervened in the Thirty Years War (1618–1648) against the Catholic imperial forces on behalf of the Protestant princes and free cities in the German Holy Roman Empire. But after Sweden had suffered a decisive defeat under King Charles XII by Russian Tsar Peter the Great in the battle of Poltawa (1709), she became more and more peaceful. The same happened to Denmark, which had been a very aggressive country comprising big parts of Scandinavia and the Baltic and parts of England in early medieval times.

It is interesting to note that Kautilya was aware of the importance of many of the factors just mentioned. He writes:

Possessed of capital cities both in the centre and the extremities of the kingdom, productive of subsistence not only to its own people, but also to outsiders on occasions of calamities . . . containing fertile lands, mines, timber and elephant forests, and pasture grounds, . . . full of cattle, not depending upon rain for water, possessed of land and waterways, rich in various kinds of commercial articles, capable of bearing the burden of a vast army and heavy taxation, inhabited by agriculturalists of good and active character, full of intelligent masters and servants, and with a population noted for its loyality and good character – these are the qualities of a good country.[5]

Whoever thinks himself to be growing in power more rapidly both in quality and quantity than his enemy, and the reverse of his enemy, may neglect his enemy's progress for the time.

Whoever is inferior to another shall make peace with him; whoever is superior in power shall wage war; whoever thinks, 'No enemy can hurt me, nor am I strong enough to destroy my enemy,' shall observe neutrality; . . ."[6]

Let us turn to a final, but important observation concerning multipolar systems. Such systems have existed several times in history in different places. The first such system known is the many city states of Sumer and Akkad in old Mesopotamia (now Iraq) in the third and early second millennium B.C. The Greek city states down from the eighth or seventh century B.C. are another example. The same situation prevailed in Old India before Kautilya, in China from the eighth century B.C. and in Italy after the power of the Holy Roman Empire had vanished in the thirteenth century with the defeat of the Hohenstaufen Emperors in their epic fight with the popes.

In Japan there happened to be a Feudal Period with similar characteristics at least from about 1300–1600 A.D. Finally the whole feudal system of Europe in the Middle Ages may be considered to have been a situation in which a very great number of independent states existed, governed either by feudal lords, princes of the church like bishops and abbots, or as rather independent, fortified cities. It is nowadays customary to speak about these periods as being dominated by civil wars and plagued by rubber barons. But this is a completely wrong perspective taken from a period in which the nation states of Western Europe had been firmly established. The ideology of the nation state preferred to interpret the forced formation of its later territory as a 'reunification'. Consequently the international intrigues, alliances and wars of the rather independent entities (states) of the earlier period were looked at as internal strife, dissensions and civil wars. Only in cases where 'rebellious' entities like the original Swiss Cantons or the Dutch Netherlands were successful to form independent countries (they seceded from the German Holy Roman Empire) are these wars now called wars of liberation. But this is an inadequate analysis of the real situation, even if there existed a French or English king or a Holy Roman emperor being at the same time King of Germany, Lombardy, Burgundy and the Arelat (the region around Arles in what is now the Provence in Southern France), and who considered himself the ultimate sovereign of the whole of Europe as the legal successor of the Roman Emperors. For the power of emperor and kings was shaky, more often than not only nominal and not real. In the feudal system these sovereigns had to rely for military help on the Barons, so that they were not able to monopolize military power. As a matter of fact the dukes, counts, bishops and later the free cities were the real holders of power in their territories most of the time. They often even had nominal obligations to different kings, to the emperor and the pope and played them out against each other. It is thus not surprising that these princes and cities behaved more often than not like independent powers and vied for domination in a multipolar system. The many castles, fortresses, city walls and towers preserved in many places in Western Europe and Japan are evidence of this state of affairs.

Map 1: The Italian Balance of Power System of the Renaissance

We have convinced ourselves that human history had quite a number of multipolar systems. But it seems that all these systems proved to be rather unstable over time. They usually were reduced to balance of power systems within a couple of centuries, i.e. to systems containing only three to seven actors of about equal strength. The remaining essential states were considered to be the 'big powers' of the new system. It is true that a number of smaller states survived, too. But they were reduced to international impotence, which usually meant a peaceful and prosperous existence, as long as it was tolerated by the big powers or required for the balance of power between them.

Map 2: The European Balance of Power System in the nineteenth Century

Historical evidence for the reduction of the number of states in a multipolar system and its transformation into a balance of power system with only a limited number of actors abounds. In Renaissance Italy only Venice, Milan, Florence, the states of the Holy See and the Kingdom of Naples (with Sicily) remained as 'big powers' in the second half of the fifteenth century (see Map 1). Similarly about 1770 only France, England, Austria (or better: the Habsburgian dominions), Russia and Prussia remained or had formed as members of the European balance of power, whereas Spain, Turkey and Sweden had already lost their former positions as important members. This system survived the Napoleonic wars and lasted until the end of World War I (see Map 2).

In old China a balance of power system formed out of the former multipolar feudal system, which existed since about 800 B.C. In the end phase of the 'Warring State Period' around 300 B.C. there existed only six 'great powers', namely Han, Chao, Wei, Ch'u, Yen, Ch'i and Ch'in (see Map 3). As for Greece it is well-known that the power of Sparta and Athens increased all the time at least from the Persian Wars around 480 B.C. and that their rivalries culminated in the Pelopennesian War which lasted nearly thirty years and saw the final victory of Sparta. But other, more or less important powers like Thebes, Syracuse on the island of Sicily (Southern Italy had been colonized by the Greeks and enjoyed the presence of quite a number

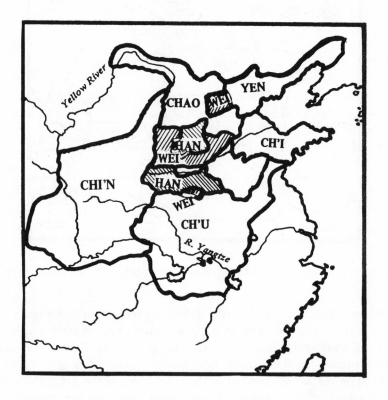

Map 3: The Chinese Balance of Power System, The Warring States, before 220 B.C.

of Greek city states), Macedonia and perhaps Corinth remained. It is, however, dubious whether a real balance of power system developed in this Greek setting of the fifth century B.C. The same is true for old Mesopotamia. Here, too, the number of independent states decreased and increased again over time.

Intermittently several states dominated the system or even created 'universal' empires (similar to that consolidated in China by Ch'in in 221 B.C. or by the the Maurya Empire in India). In this connection Ur, Lagash, Umma, Akkad, Isin and the old Babylonian Empire of King Hammurabi have to be mentioned (see Map 4). Because of lack of historical knowledge, it is not clear whether all these empires were following a period in which a balance of power system ruled. But we know that for instance at the beginning of the rule of Hammurabi of Babylon six powers fought for hegemony: Larsa, Eshnunna, Babylon, Qatna, Iamkhad (Aleppo) and Assur. Hammurabi became member of a tripartite alliance with Larsa and Mari which was able to defeat Eshnunna, Elam, the Mountain Peoples and Assur after fifteen years of fighting. After this Babylon turned against her former allies and subjugated them, too.

The historial facts show that the multipolar system is not a stable one and that the fierce competition for power and domination reduces more and more the number of participating vital actors. Usually, but probably not necessarily, a balance of power system is the next stage in the historical development, often followed (this will be discussed more fully in the next sections) by a bipolar system (see the example of Athens and Sparta) or a 'Universal Empire' like in the case of Babylon, the Maurya Empire, China and Rome.

What are the reasons of the instability of the multipolar system? Why is it mostly followed by a balance of power system? Is this system more stable? What are the reasons for its transformation into a bipolar system or a 'universal empire'? Can there be a direct development from a multipolar into a bipolar system or a universal empire? Why and under what conditions? These are obvious questions following from the historical evidence and which have to be answered in the concluding paragraphs of this and in the following sections.

We have seen how complicated the possible manoeuvring among alliances and counteralliances is even in an idealized multipolar system. On top of this we have the often unforeseen shifts of power brought about by technical and economic change, by different growth of populations, not to speak of the differing capabilities, the degrees of education and relevant information on the part of the leading politicians, who are also replaced over time. Given these factors it is not at all surprising that from time to time one or the other

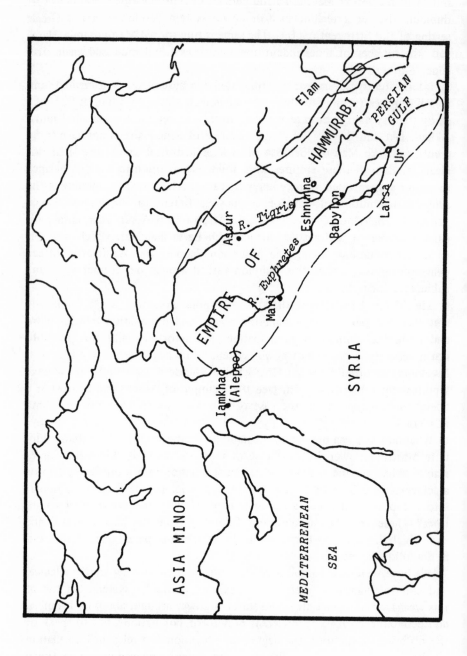

Map 4: Babylonia (Mesopotamia) before 1700 B.C.

state will become weak enough relative to its enemies to be conquered or threatened into subjugation and finally to be annexed if no countervailing tendencies are at work. Countervailing tendencies could, however, only be sufficient to prevent a decrease of the number of essential states over time, if enough other states would support each weakened state in case of crisis. Such persistant support of weak countries can, however, not be expected in a multipolar system, since it is often not in the self-interest of potential allies.

The self-interest of these states would usually only be motivated to help endangered states if either some spoils could be expected for the efforts or if the increasing power of the victorious country (countries) had to be feared because of lack of potential allies in cases of later crises. But now it is less probable that an alliance to help a weakened state promises the same gains as an alliance with a stronger country. Thus there is not much motivation to assist an endangered state because of the hope of direct benefits. Moreover, in a multipolar system the great number of participants assures that there will be no want of future potential allies. The territorial growth of a victorious state will be considered as threatening only if it is quite out of proportion with the growth of the other more successful countries. It follows, therefore, that except for the latter development no reason exists for member states to always support the weaker and threatened countries. On the contrary, since each state has only to try to keep up as much as possible with the power and territorial growth of other successful countries there lures a temptation to participate in the division of the weaker states whenever possible. We conclude that the multipolar system provides ample opportunity for a reduction of the number of member states over time and that no sufficient forces to counterbalance this tendency are at work. The system is by its own characteristics unstable in the long run and transforms itself into a balance of power system or possibly even into a bipolar system or a universal empire.

3. Balance of Power Systems

I developed for the King [Wilhelm I of Prussia] the political and military reasons speaking against a continuation of the war [against Austria-Hungary in 1866].
To mutilate Austria, to leave bitterness and a need for revenge had to be avoided. On the contrary, we had to keep open the option to make friendship again with our present opponent and at least to look at the Austrian state as a good figure on the European chessboard. . . . If Austria would be damaged heavily, it would become an ally of France

and of each enemy; it would even sacrifice its anti-Russian interests for its revenge against Prussia.
. . . not to speak of the fact that a prolongation of the war would open the path for French intervention. We had to conclude [the peace treaty] quickly before France would gain time to develop further diplomatic action towards Austria.

Otto von Bismarck
(Prussian Prime Minister and later Chancellor
of the German Reich of 1870/71)[7]

The quotation from Bismarck's memoirs brings out clearly the essential differences of a balance of power system with a limited number of essential participants as compared to multipolar systems. Whereas we have seen that there are no factors at work to preserve stability in the latter, this is not true for the former. According to Bismarck, the greater stability of such a system follows since the limited number of participants makes it important to preserve present enemies as potential allies for possible future conflicts with other strong countries. Secondly, the duration of a war with another state should, if at all possible, be limited so that no alliance with other relevant actors will be formed. Both ideas speak against a long and decisive war to destroy, to divide and to annex an enemy.

What are the reasons behind this kind of reasoning of one of the leading politicians of the European balance of power system of the second half of the nineteenth century? We know already (see Map 2) that there were five big powers present in Europe at that time, namely France, Great Britain, Russia, Austria-Hungary and Prussia. The War of 1866 between the German states Austria and Prussia was led for the domination of Germany. After its success in this war Prussia excluded Austria from the smaller Germany to be formed after the French-Prussian war of 1870/71. It is important to recall here that Austria (directed most of the time by its minister Metternich, who came from the Rhineland) had been the leading member of the loose German Confederation formed after the Napoleonic War at the Vienna Congress in 1815. Before that time the Habsburgians had been for centuries the emperors of the German Holy Roman Empire until they were deposed by Napoleon in 1806. Vienna had been the capital of this empire. In a sense Prussia's victory and its domination of the greater parts of Germany meant a secession from the formerly leading centers of Germany.

This process, of course, was a bitter event for many Germans, especially in Austria and the non-Prussian states, which had mostly fought on the Austrian side. Let me just show this with a quotation by the German historian Constantin Frantz, who expresses these feelings as follows: *For this is certainly without example in the history of other nations that a mutilation of the national body, which at that time happened with the separation of*

Austria, has been presented as a restauration of the national body and been praised as such by many.[8]

For the Austrian-Hungarian leadership the defeat of 1866 meant a sizable loss of power, and for Prussia a more than corresponding gain. It was the first time that Prussia was able to connect its territories within Germany by annexing states like Hannover, Hesse-Cassel and Hesse-Nassau. The new German empire to be formed a few years later was much more easy to defend than Prussia before 1866 and constituted a more meaningful, but at the same time more nationalistic political and economic unit.

The shift of power taking place in 1866 could not be unimportant for the other European powers, especially for France and Russia. Had Prussia tried in 1866 to march into Vienna and to annex Austrian territory (as intended by the Prussian generals and the King), the two powers would have felt endangered even more by the threat of a Prussian-German hegemony on the continent. There is scarcely any doubt that Bismarck was right in his fear that a prolongation of the war would have led France and possibly Russia into an alliance with Austria-Hungary taking away from Prussia the limited gains he was striving for. Moreover, he already foresaw the possibility of future conflicts with other countries and the possible value of Austria-Hungary as a future ally or at least as a neutral country in later emergencies.

The important conclusion we have to draw is that no participant in a balance of power system can be uninterested in the fate of its weaker and endangered members. There is always the danger that the strongest country may strive for hegemony, for the domination of the system or even for a universal empire. Thus, it is dangerous to allow its power to grow too much. And it is dangerous to allow the disappearance of one or even more of the members of the system because the remaining states may need them badly as potential allies against the strongest participant(s). One would, therefore, expect the following additional relationships to hold in a balance of power system:

Law of Behavior of States in a Balance of Power System: Join alliances against the strongest member or against an alliance of the two strongest members to prevent domination. If this country has (these countries have) been defeated weaken them, but not too much so that they can be used as allies against remaining future strongest power(s).

European history between the end of the Thirty Years War in 1648 and the end of the nineteenth century provides ample proof for the working of these tendencies. Britain joined forces with Habsburg and the Netherlands against Louis XIV's wars of aggression in the seventeenth and the beginning of the eighteenth centuries, for instance in the War of Spanish Succession. Britain allied with Prussia to prevent the Austrian-French-Russian coalition to prevail on the continent during the Seven Years War. This in spite of the fact that about fifteen to twenty years earlier during the War of Austrian Succession France joined Prussia against a British-Austrian coalition. Again during the French revolution and the Napoleonic wars several coalitions fought against the danger of French hegemony on the European continent. Napoleon I was finally defeated in 1814/15 by a coalition of Russia, Prussia, Austria-Hungary and Great Britain. Several decades later, when Russian power had strengthened more and more, Britain and France found themselves in a coalition with ailing Turkey to fight the Crimean War.

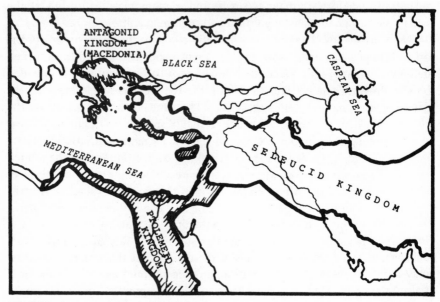

The Hellenistic kingdoms in ca. 240 B.C.

The Hellenistic kingdoms in ca. 185 B.C., the time of
the breakdown of the balance of power system

Map 5: The Hellenistic Balance of Power System

It is important to realize, moreover, that in all these cases the defeated powers were not weakened so much that they lost their usefulness as potential future allies, that is they always stayed as essential members of the system. For instance in the Vienna Peace Treaty of 1815 France could keep all its European territory from before the revolution, even German speaking Alsace (Elsass in German), which had partly been conquered by Louis XIV in 1681 and partly been annexed like the city of Mulhouse (Mühlhausen) during the revolutionary period.

The European Balance of Power was not the only period in history dominated by such an international system. We have already observed that China had a balance of power system during the period of 'Warring States' and that the same was probably true for several periods of early Mesopotamian history around 2000 B.C. Other balance of power systems were present in late Renaissance Italy and also at the time of the hellenistic successor states of the empire of Alexander the Great, which was split up among several of his generals soon after his death in 323 B.C. (see Map 5). It seems that as far as one can judge from the remaining historical evidence, help was usually given to endangered essential member states of the system, that is coalitions were formed against the aggressive strongest state or stronger states, and that defeated countries were mostly not divided or not so much reduced in their power that they could not serve any longer as future potential allies.

Concerning the Italian Balance of Power we find an interesting description of its workings in a book written by the learned statesman Rucellai, a brother-in-law of Lorenzo de Medici. The book deals with the intervention by French King Charles VIII in Italy. In the introduction, Rucellai turns to the period before this first outside intervention into the system and points out that four powerful Italian states existed during the second half of the fifteenth century. One of them, Venice, had expanded her power steadily 'for one hundred years' and by doing so threatened the other countries, namely Florence, Milan and Naples (the states of the Holy See are not mentioned). These three states had, therefore, waged together several wars against Venice "to maintain their common liberty". At last, a final peace had been reached because of the skilful efforts of two princes, King Ferdinand of Naples and Lorenzo de Medici. These two princes, who were the shrewdest in Italy, had again allied to defend "the common freedom" against Venice. And they had pursued "according to their own words" with all their strength the aim *to keep the political conditions of Italy in a state of calm and balance. Each weakening of another Italian state they had considered as a decrease of their own power.*[9]

It is obvious these statements by Rucellai provide an early and clear description of the essential prerequisites of a balance of power system. It seems clear that not only the author, but at least King Ferdinand of Naples and Lorenzo de Medici as principal political actors understood well the nature of its workings.

How far have the characteristics of the balance of power system been comprehended by even earlier writers and politicians? We find no references of a similar kind in the works of Machiavelli and of Kautilya. Perhaps both were too much preoccupied with the multipolar system. In the case of Kautilya it may even be true that no balance of power system developed between the end of the multipolar system and the advent of the Maurya Empire. It seems, on the other hand, that the importance to form alliances against the strongest country to preserve the balance of power was understood by Su Ch'in, the great opponent of Chang I in China during the period of the 'Warring States'. For he succeeded to forge the great alliance against Ch'in which prevented its ultimate domination of China at least during his lifetime.[10]

For the later period of the Greek city states and the development of Macedonian predominance under King Philip, the father of Alexander the Great, in the fourth century B.C., we have evidence that the Athenian orator and politician Demosthenes clearly saw the need to form a counteralliance to contain the power of Macedon. He said in his First Olynthiac:

I wonder if any one of you in this audience watches and notes the steps by which Philip, weak at first, has grown so powerful. First he seized Amphipolis, next Pydna, then Potidaea, after that Methone, lastly he invaded Thessaly. Then having settled Pherae, Pagasae, Magnesia, and the rest of that country to suit his purposes, off he went to Thrace, and there, after evicting some of the chiefs and installing others, he fell sick. On his recovery, he did not relapse into inactivity, but instantly assailed Olynthos. . . . If he takes Olynthos, who is to prevent his marching hither? . . . 'But, my friend,' cries someone, 'he will not wish to attack us.' Nay, it would be a crowning absurdity if, having the power, he should lack the will to carry out the threat which today he utters at the risk of his reputation for sanity. It is the duty of all of you to grasp the significance of these facts, and to send out an expedition that shall thrust him back into Macedon.[11]

It is well-known that Demosthenes succeeded to form a Greek coalition, even including such old adversaries as Athens and Boiotia (with Thebes), with Sparta remaining neutral, however. But it was too late. The better trained army of Macedon with its highly qualified cavalry remained victorious in the battle of Chaeronea in Central Greece in 338 B.C. A council of Greek states (with the exception of Sparta) had to accept the leadership of Macedon. Philip was murdered in 336 B.C. but his young son Alexander left Europe two years later to conquer the whole Persian Empire and to march to the end of the known world, to far-away India.

A similar awareness of certain features of the balance of power system was shown by the Greek Polybius in his description of the ascendancy of the power of Rome and of the reasons thereof. During the first and second wars between Rome and Carthage for the domination of the western Mediterranean there existed only one more state of some power and resources in this region, namely the Greek state of Syracuse on the island of Sicily. Concerning this state Polybius wrote in his histories:

Now Hiero, of Syracuse, had during this war been all along exceedingly anxious to do everything which the Carthaginians asked him; and at this point of it was more forward to do so than ever, from a conviction that it was for his interest, with a view alike to his own sovereignty and to his friendship with Rome; that Carthage should not perish, and so leave the superior power to work its own will without resistance. And his reasoning was entirely sound and prudent.[11]

It is never right to permit such a state of things, nor to help anyone to build up so preponderating a power as to make resistance to it impossible, however just the cause.[11/12]

Again, Syracuse did not succeed to prevent the defeat and final annexation of Carthage and of itself at the hands of Rome, but this does not distract from the validity of the above statement.

Turning to the European Balance of Power System of the last centuries, which ended definitely with the end of World War II, we can observe that there exists a huge literature, all discussing the different aspects of this system. Moreover, as we have already seen from the quotation taken from Bismarck's memoirs, many important statesmen were well aware of the workings of the system and sought to reach their aims by using or taking into account its characteristics. Former US Secretary of State Henry Kissinger has well-described how Prince Metternich, the Austrian-Hungarian, and Lord Castlereagh, the British Foreign Minister, joined to restore and to preserve the balance of power against Russian predominance after the near breakdown of this balance under the forces of French revolutionary ideas and the military and political genius of Napoleon.[13]

It is instructive to study a few more quotations from statesmen involved in the decision-making process which determined the development of the European Balance of Power System. Let us begin with Prince Metternich:

Modern history, however, has shown the use of the principal of solidarity and of the equilibrium between states and reveals to us the spectacle of the united efforts of several states against the momentary superiority of a single one to check the expansion of its influence and to force it to return into the common (international) law.[14]

A few decades earlier Frederick II, (the Great), King of Prussia, then still a Crown Prince is even more outspoken in describing his ideas:

The tranquillity of Europe is mainly caused by the preservation of a wise equilibrium which consists in the fact that the united forces of the other powers keep in balance the greater power of a single ruler. Each disturbance of this equilibrium brings about the danger of a general transformation.

Thus it seems to be a question of life or death for the princes of Europe, never to lose sight of the bargaining, the treaties and alliances through which it is possible to maintain a certain equilibrium among the most powerful rulers, and to timidly evade everything, which could sow the weeds of disunity among them; for sooner or later they would grow into their own ruin. Outspoken predilections and dislikes against this or that nation, prejudices in the ways of women, quarrels and disputes of individual persons, petty special and irrelevant interests should never obscure the sight of a man, who is a leader of whole peoples.[15]

The above sentences reveal a remarkable insight into the workings of the system. Let us conclude these quotations by turning to a statement made by Lord Halifax, British Foreign Minister, towards the very end of the European Balance of Power System. Halifax said on January 21, 1940:

The instinct of our people has always throughout their history driven them to resist attempts by any one nation to make itself master of Europe; they have always seen in any such attempt a threat both to their own existence and to the general cause of liberty in Europe ... If the British people have been right, as they have before, in resisting domination by any one Power in Europe, they are doubtly so right today.[16]

One may seriously doubt whether Britain was always opposed to making herself master of Europe. In a sense Britain attemped to become master of Europe during and after the Seven Years War, when she gained Canada and Louisiana from France and established her predominance over India by defeating the French. It was only through the anti-British coalition which was formed between France, Spain and the USA during the American War of Independence, that her search for hegemony was defeated.

In 1940, however, the situation was quite different. Great Britain was not any longer capable of gaining European preponderance, or even of defeating Germany and to contain Russia. But the European or world balance of power system could still have been saved if the United States had made it its policy to preserve Germany and Russia as big powers, say, within their borders of 1938. This was, however, impossible because of the domestic policies of the United States, a problem to which we have to return later.

4. Factors Causing the Breakdown of Balance of Power Systems

In the preceding section the reasons for the greater stability of balance of power compared to multipolar systems have been discussed. In spite of the presence of such stabilizing factors all historical balance of power systems have broken down at least after some centuries. Given this fact one might be inclined to assert that these breakdowns are just the consequence of the final frailty of all human institutions and organizations. For we know that most states of the distant future have vanished like Ur and Babylon, like the glory of Athens and the power of Rome.

It seems, however, that the above statement is not a sufficient explanation for the destruction of balance of power systems. First of all, one would like to know why certain states or even certain cultures have come to an end. For it is well-known that the Chinese empire and even Egypt and Persia could be said to have survived several millennia. However, concerning Persia and Egypt one wonders already whether they can be considered to be in any sense the same entities, or if there is enough historical continuity to consider them offsprings of the ancient nations. Fortunately, we don't have to analyse the general reasons for the destruction or vanishing of nations. Especially since one may well doubt, whether any general factors causing their final demise existed.

Second, it is beyond doubt that there are cases in which the very breakdown of a balance of power system was itself responsible for the end of several of its member states. This has been certainly true for the end of Austria-Hungary and of Germany as a consequence of World Wars I and II. Somebody might object here that Germany still exists and has only been divided into the Federal Republic of Germany (West Germany) and the German Democratic Republic (East Germany). He might point out that if the Soviet Union and its East German puppet regime only allowed free elections in the German Democratic Republic the reunification of Germany would happen very soon, as witnessed by the more than two out of eighteen million people who left East for West Germany before the communist regime put a halt to the exodus of its population by building the Berlin Wall. Thus, it might be concluded, even given the presence of the Soviet Union and the character of the present regime, it will only be a question of time until the reunification of Germany takes place at some more or less distant future date. The same has happened before with other nations. Poland had been divided by Russia, Austria-Hungary and Prussia during the eighteenth century, but was reestablished after 130 years of foreign domination in 1918. The military defeat of all of these big powers was necessary to allow the formation of a new Polish state.

One cannot quarrel with these arguments and it may well be that we or our children may witness one day in the future the reunification of Germany. But first, this is not a certainty, at present. Second, would the new state called Germany really be the old Germany again? In fact, we pointed out already that the formation of the 'German Reich' by Bismarck may be considered to have been a secession from the part of Germany which had ruled the German Holy Roman Empire from Vienna for centuries, namely Habsburgian Austria. Moreover, the Netherlands, Belgium, Switzerland and parts of Czechoslovakia (namely Bohemia and Moravia) belonged for centuries to the German Holy Roman Empire, which was ruled from Prague for several decades. Finally, even Bismarck's Germany has lost about one-fourth of its territory to present Poland as a consequence of the two World Wars, though only a minority of Poles lived in its eastern provinces.

So it seems that it was only by historical accident that out of the many successor states of the Holy Roman Empire just two but not the others are called 'Germany'. These two states called now Germany might as well have been baptized 'Rhenish Federal Republic' and 'Great Brandenburg' or 'Greater Saxony'. Certainly there is not much continuity between the organizations of the present states and that of the Bismarck Reich, not to speak of the German Holy Roman Empire.

This rather lengthy excursion should have established the fact that not only Austria-Hungary but also the German Reich founded by Bismarck vanished because of the breakdown of the European Balance of Power System. The same happened with the Chinese states when Ch'in succeeded to gain the hegemony in this region of the world in 221 B.C. and founded the Chinese Empire. Rome brought down the Hellenistic Balance of Power System (see Map 5), which had dominated the eastern Mediterranean region after the death of Alexander the Great in 223 B.C. Its end implied the demise of the main actors of this system, namely Egypt, Macedonia and Syria together with several medium-sized and minor states, which had lived and survived in the lee of this system.

We conclude that the survival of states has been in many respects dependent on the existence of a balance of power system, just as should be expected, given the fact that several states usually strive for universal domination. If this is true, however, we have to look for independent reasons for the breakdown of balance of power systems, not relying on the general hypothesis that all states have to vanish one day because of the frailty of human organizations.

It may be helpful in solving the just stated problem to look a bit more closely into the necessary conditions for the stability of balance of power systems. Morton A. Kaplan has formulated a number of such "essential rules of conduct":

(1) Act to increase capabilities but negotiate rather than fight.
(2) Fight rather than pass up an opportunity to increase capabilities.
(3) Stop fighting rather than eliminate an essential national actor.
(4) Act to oppose any coalition or single actor that tends to assume a position of predominance with respect to the rest of the system. . . .

(5) Permit defeated or constrained essential actors to reenter the system as acceptable role partners or act to bring some previously inessential actor within the essential actor classification. Treat all essential actors as acceptable role partners.[17]

The reader realizes at once that these are exactly the traits of working balance of power systems which we have derived before from the very nature of this system and the interests of the essential actors. Conditions (3)–(5) describe the factors preserving the stability of the system, (1)–(2) the forces caused by the quest of individual states for security, greater relative power and expansion. We have thus to examine why the factors mentioned in (3)–(5) may not work at all or may be too weak to counter the forces described in (1)–(2).

It has already been pointed out that important domestic political and ideological developments, different growth rates of populations, of the economies and of technologies, especially of military technologies may lead to a change of the relative powers of the essential states in the system. The same is true if one or the other of the actors is able to increase its territory disproportionately or if some states lack capable statesmen, who are well-informed about the workings of the system. Let us assume that one or more of these developments become pronounced before they have been corrected, say, by a victorious coalition of a number of countries against the most powerful states or state. Given such a development it may well happen that the relative power (powers) of one or more actors becomes (become) so strong that it (they) cannot be contained any longer by the united forces of other states.

Looking back we cannot escape the impression that similar developments have happened several times in history. Thus the implications of the growth of Ch'in seem not to have been realized in the beginning by the other members of the Chinese Balance of Power System. This happened, since Ch'in first started to occupy and to annex territories which were outside of the original region comprised by the system. The half-barbarian states Chu and Pa found, therefore, no help on the part of the other big powers. But it was just because of the additional territory and population won by their annexation together with the internal reorganization of Ch'in that its relative power grew disproportionately. Afterwards it had become more difficult and took an alliance of probably all remaining states to contain Ch'in. We know already that Su Chin succeeded to forge such an alliance. But after his death Chang I and his King Cheng succeeded to split up this alliance presumably because not all remaining statesmen had a sufficient knowledge of the characteristics of the system. One or two of the remaining actors alone were not a sufficient counterbalance for the increased power of Ch'in.

A similar development led to the destruction of the Hellenistic Balance of Power System by Rome. Rome was first a power outside of the region of this system. So it succeeded in increasing its power quietly by annexing more and more territory in Italy. Even when Rome entered its epic wars with Carthage for the domination of the western Mediterranean in the third century B.C. and finally annexed Northern Africa in the second century B.C., the hellenistic big powers, preoccupied with their own problems and the balance of power between them paid not enough attention to the development of these wars and to their outcomes. Only Philipp V of Macedon seems to have been aware of the danger of possible further growth of Roman power and concluded an alliance with the Carthaginian leader Hannibal who had invaded Italy during the Second Punic War (219–202 B.C.). But the Romans were able to form a counter-alliance with the Aitolian Federation and the Kingdom of Pergamum in Asia Minor against Philipp, so that finally a separate peace treaty was agreed on with the King of Macedon. One may, therefore, even suspect that the very balance of power among the states in the Eastern Mediterranean hindered Macedon in preventing the downfall of Carthage. Of course, this was only possible, if at least some of the statesmen of the other essential states did not see the imminent danger threatening because of the success of Rome.

We have already mentioned the reason for the doom of the Renaissance Balance of Power System in Italy, namely the interventions of France and Spain beginning in the end of the fifteenth century A.D. with the Italian expedition of French King Charles VIII. This breakdown was certainly not a surprising development for the regional Italian System, since it depended from its very beginning on the non-intervention on the part of the bigger European powers.

In spite of this we have to realize that usually quite a number of different factors have to combine to bring about the downfall of a balance of power system. It has just been shown that inadequate knowledge and information on the part of some of the participating statesmen as well as developments taking place outside or from the outside of the system may all be important factors in destroying the balance of power. It is therefore, perhaps a good idea, to examine more closely the destruction of the last of these systems, the European Balance of Power System, which since the end of the last century, with the advent of the USA and Japan as big powers, had already extended into a 'world system'. We have, because of historical proximity, much more information about the possible reasons for the downfall of this than of earlier balance of power systems, so that we may be able to form a better judgment about the relative importance of these reasons.

5. Factors Causing the End of the European Balance of Power System

Let us discuss the possible causes for the end of the European Balance of Power System one after the other. The first important reason has been the spectacular growth (dwarfing those of other formerly big powers) of the USA and Russia in terms of territory, human resources and, especially in the case of the USA, in economic capabilities (see Chapter 3, Sections 2 and 3). It is important to realize that this growth took place mainly outside of the traditional region where the balance of power prevailed. Observe that this is similar to the examples of Ch'in and Rome given above. That the growth occurred outside of the balance of power region is quite obvious for the USA which kept away from any entanglement with the system following the precious advice given by George Washington and Thomas Jefferson. Let me quote both. Washington said in his famous Farewell Address:

Europe has a set of primary interests, which to us have none, or a very remote relation. Hence she must be engaged in frequent controversies, the causes of which are essentially foreign to our concerns. Hence, therefore, it must be unwise in us to implicate ourselves, by artificial ties, in the ordinary vicissitudes of her politics, or the ordinary combinations and collisions of her friendships or enmities.
Our detached and distant situation invites and enables us to pursue a different course. If we remain one people, under an efficient government, the period is not far off when we may defy material injury from external annoyance; when we may take such an attitude as will cause the neutrality we may at any time resolve upon to be scrupulously respected; when belligerent nations, under the impossibility of making acquisitions upon us, will not lightly hazard giving us provocation; when we may choose peace or war, as our interest, guided by justice, shall counsel.
Why forego the advantages of so peculiar a situation? Why quit our own to stand upon foreign ground? Why, by interweaving our destiny with that of any part of Europe entangle our peace and prosperity in the toils of European ambition, rivalship, interest, humor, or caprice?
It is our true policy to steer clear of permanent alliances with any portion of the foreign world . . . [18]

Jefferson expressed himself similarly[19]

Peace, commerce and honest friendship with all nations, entangling alliances with none.

Following this advice the USA were free to expand on the North American continent, where no other power was present which could have checked the annexation of the vast territories in the middle west and west stretching from the Alleghanies to the Pacific Ocean (see Maps 6 and 7).

Turning to Russia we have to concede that it became a member of the European Balance of Power System already in the beginning of the eighteenth century, when Tsar Peter the Great defeated Charles XII of Sweden in the

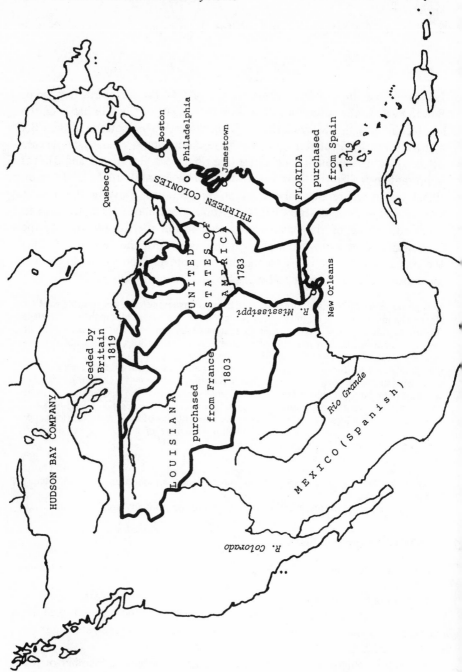

Map 6: Expansion of the United States until 1820

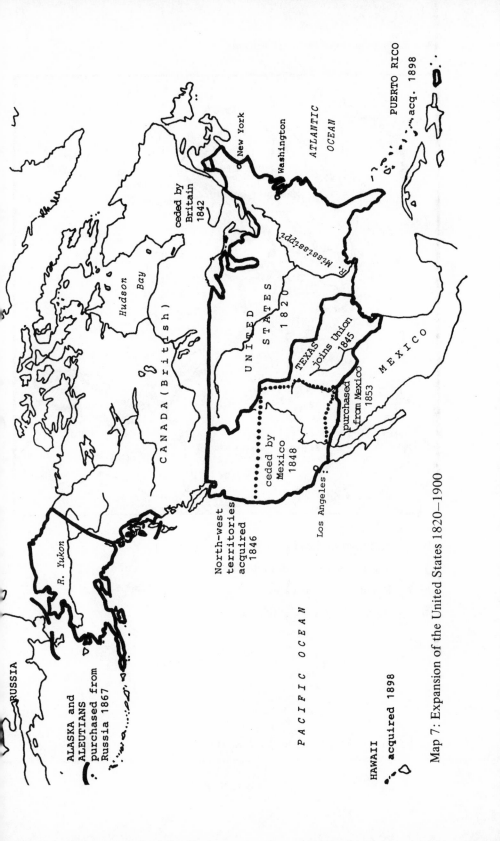

Map 7: Expansion of the United States 1820—1900

RUSSIA

ALASKA and
ALEUTIANS
purchased from
Russia 1867

R. Yukon

PACIFIC OCEAN

HAWAII

acquired 1898

North-west
territories
acquired
1846

ceded by
Mexico
1848

Los Angeles

purchased
from Mexico
1853

CANADA (British)

Hudson
Bay

ceded by
Britain
1842

UNITED
STATES
1820

R. Mississippi

TEXAS
joins union
1845

MEXICO

New York

Washington

ATLANTIC
OCEAN

PUERTO RICO

acq. 1898

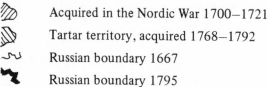 Acquired in the Nordic War 1700–1721

Tartar territory, acquired 1768–1792

Russian boundary 1667

Russian boundary 1795

Map 8: Russian Expansion in the West 1667–1792

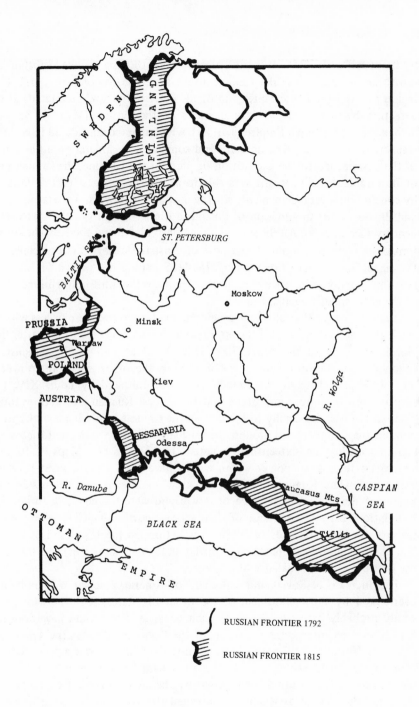

RUSSIAN FRONTIER 1792

RUSSIAN FRONTIER 1815

Map 9: Russian Expansion in the West 1792–1815

battle of Poltava (1709). It is true, moreover, that Russia annexed substantial territories in the west, like Finland (only after the Napoleonic wars), the region of the later Baltic States and of St. Petersburg (now Leningrad) after defeating Sweden, until then a member of the system (Map 8). Several defeats of the Ottoman Empire (Turkey), which may be considered in certain respects to have been, too, an early and somewhat peripheral essential actor of the system, led to the acquisition of parts of the Ukraine, the Crimea and of Bessarabia. Finally, Russia was able to acquire the biggest part of Poland by concluding several agreements with two other big powers, Austria-Hungary and Prussia about the division of Poland in the second part of the eighteenth century (see Map 9). All these gains were consolidated and the Russian Polish territories expanded again at the cost of Austria-Hungary and especially of Prussia at the Vienna Congress of 1814/15 ending the period of the Napoleonic wars, in which Russia had been perhaps the most powerful member of the great alliance against France.

Again it is true that all these developments took place more or less within the European system, even if the appearance of Russia as a main actor after the Nordic War against Sweden (1700–1721 A.D.) as well as the expansion following the Swedish defeat probably took the other important powers, who were just checking the French expansion initiated by Louis XIV, by surprise. But it is more important that the biggest Russian annexations took place in the east, especially in Siberia, on the Chinese borderlands, in Central Asia, in the Caucasus and around the Caspian Sea. Here vast territories were acquired during the sixteenth to nineteenth centuries (see Maps 9, 10 and 11), again finding no power which would have been able to resist Russian expansion. Thus Russia and the USA grew mainly or totally outside the region of the European Balance of Power and were thereby able to lay the foundations for a vast increase of their relative powers, which were probably decisive for the outcomes of World War I (through the USA) and of World War II (through the combination of Soviet and American power) and thus for the destruction of the balance of power.

The increase of Soviet and especially of American power was probably overlooked by most statesmen of the other big states, for otherwise they would probably have tried to check their advance. They could have done so for instance by intervening on behalf of the Confederates into the American Civil War (Britain and France) or by joining the Crimean War against Russia (Prussia and Austria-Hungary). On the other hand some statesmen may have been aware of the future dangers posed by the increasing relative strength of these powers. As far as Russia is concerned this certainly has been true for the Austrian minister Metternich. Together with the British statesmen Castlereagh, he was at least able to contain Russia during the last phase of the Napo-

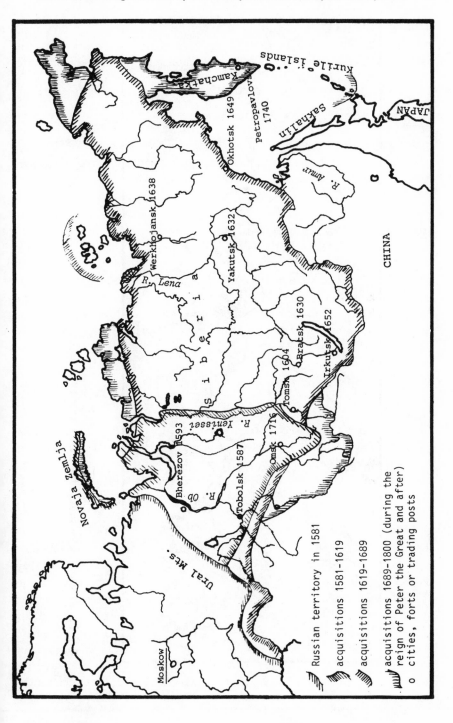

Map 10: Russian Expansion in the East until 1800

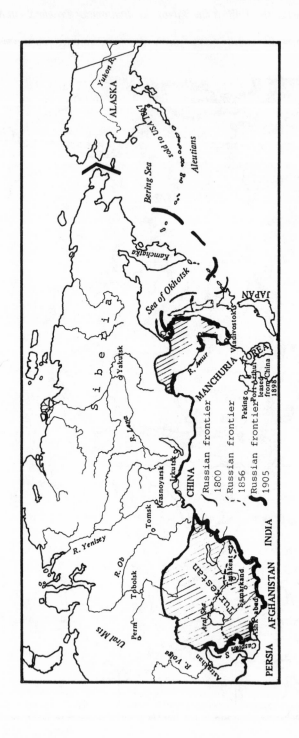

Map 11: Russion Expansion in the East 1800–1905

leonic wars and at the Vienna Congress (1814/15) and to prevent it from taking over even more Polish territories.[13] But given the relative power situation he had obviously no chance to roll back the western frontiers of Russia nor to stop its Asian expansion.

Some decades earlier Frederic the Great had already realized the future dangers stemming from Russian expansion. He wrote:

Civil wars in Russia and even more the division of this empire would be the most favourable events which could happen to Prussia and all the nordic Powers.[20]

But Prussia and even more the other nordic states lacked the power to help such a development in any way, especially given the Prussian-Austrian tensions resulting from Frederic's annexation of Silesia a few years before in the Austrian War of Succession. Frederic II was fully aware of Prussia's relative weakness and advised Prussian statesmen to move very cautiously against Russia.

The danger of Russian expansion was very clearly understood by the German political writer Constantin Frantz, who turned against German nationalism and advocated a kind of permanent alliance between Prussia (later Bismarck's Germany) and Austria-Hungary together with a close cooperation with other Central European nations including Poland. He became very outspoken in describing the development of Russian expansion and of its consequences for Central Europe and concluded:

Thus it has become fatal, indeed, that Russia has been allowed to intervene into the problems of civilized Europe [des abendländischen Europas] since Peter the Great, for out of this has developed through the chain of events the whole present plight of European affairs. There is, therefore, no hope to escape from this situation until Russia has first been forced out of Poland and Lithuania and thrown back behind the Dvina river. This is my ceterum censeo [my last word] and with it I will live and die.[21]

It may be mentioned in passing that Frantz saw quite clearly the dangers brought about for Germany by the creation of the Bismarck Reich and of the antagonisms caused in France through the annexation of Alsace-Lorraine, to which we will return later.

The only one who not only realized the potential growth of the USA and of Russia as early as 1835, but who also predicted accurately its consequences for the international political situation, was the French nobleman Alexis de Tocqueville, who later became for a short time French foreign minister. He wrote in his *Democracy in America*:

There are at present two great nations in the world, which started from different points, but seem to tend towards the same end. I allude to the Russians and the Americans. Both of them have grown up unnoticed; and while the attention of mankind was directed elsewhere, they have suddenly placed themselves in the front rank among the nations, and the world learned their existence and their greatness at almost the same time.
All other nations seem to have nearly reached their natural limits, and they have only to

maintain their power; but these are still in the act of growth. All the others have stopped, or continue to advance with extreme difficulty; these alone are proceeding with ease and celerity along a path to which no limit [1835] can be perceived. The American struggles against the obstacles that nature opposes to him; the adversaries of the Russian are men. The former combats the wilderness and savage life; the latter, civilization with all its arms. The conquests of the American are therefore gained by the plowshare; those of the Russian by the sword. The Anglo-American relies upon personal interest to accomplish his ends and gives free scope to the unguided strength and common sense of the people; the Russian centers all the authority of society in a single arm. The principal instrument of the former is freedom; of the latter, servitude. Their starting-point is different and their courses are not the same; yet each of them seems marked out by the will of Heaven to sway the destinies of half the globe.[22]

Truly a remarkable statement, the statement of one of the greatest social scientists of all time. It not only predicts the development of a bipolar world power system with Russia and the USA as the essential actors but also points out long-lasting differences in their internal political organizations and developments, namely despotism versus democracy and freedom against coercion. Moreover, the reasons given in other paragraphs of the same book by de Tocqueville for the unbreakable expansion of the USA, the growth of its population to be expected and the causes of its economic development are still convincing today and have well passed the test of history.

We have thus an example of the possibility to predict decades in advance the changes of relative international power, the eventual downfall of a balance of power system and its substitution by a bipolar system. Still, the impressive accuracy of the prediction should not blind us to the fact that international developments *could* have taken another course and that the predicted one was at best a highly probable one in 1835, and became more and more probable later on, say, especially around 1890, when more and more possible measures or steps were not taken, which could have bent the strong tendencies of historical development underlying the prediction. Otherwise, if the predicted events would have been a certainty, then the above mentioned factors promoting the growth of the relative strengths of the USA and Russia would have been necessary as well as sufficient causes for the breakdown of the European Balance of Power System. But this is certainly not true, as we will see in a moment when we discuss the other factors which also seem to have been responsible for these developments.

Before doing so it seems to be advisable, however, to show that the approach of a terrible World War has been predicted by one of the founding fathers of Marxism, Friedrich Engels, as early as 1887:

No other war is possible for Prussia-Germany than a World War. And this would be a World War of an extension and intensity which has never been seen before. Eight to ten million soldiers will strangle each other. . . . The devastations of the Thirty Years' War condensed into three to four years and extended over the whole continent, famine, epidemics, general disorder of the armies as well as of the masses of the population caused by bitter misery, hopeless disorder of our artificial bustle in trade, industry and the credit system; all this ending in general bankruptcy, breakdown of the old states and of their traditional wisdom to govern, such that dozens of crowns will roll along the pavement of the streets with nobody caring to pick them up; absolute impossibility to predict how all of this will end and who will come out of this battle victorious; only one result happening without any doubt: the general exhaustion and the creation of conditions for the final victory of the working class.

This is the prospect, if the extreme system of the competitive arms race will finally bear its inevitable fruits. To that end, my dear Kings and Statesmen, has your wisdom brought Old Europe.[23]

In these impressive sentences we find already mentioned one of the factors leading to the outbreak of World War I: the mutual arms race. Lewis F. Richardson has reformulated this idea in a mathematical model and checked the available figures about the spending on armaments on the part of the big powers in the years before the war.[24] The result seems to show that the mutual arms race was an inherently unstable dynamic system, so that, given certain parameter values, the development had to end in catastrophe. The evidence must, however, remain inconclusive since we cannot reenact history to get a different development. This would be necessary, if we wanted to check whether Richardson has selected the right model to describe reality.

Let us now discuss a number of other factors which may have been necessary to bring about the two World Wars and the demise of the balance of power system. One of the conditions for the survival of balance of power systems given by Kaplan, namely condition (4), contains the statement: "Treat all essential actors as acceptable role partners." Now several people have observed that this condition, which requires a high flexibility of states among different coalitions, has been violated years before the outbreak of World War I. Patrick J. McGowan and Robert H. Hood have tested the hypothesis that the frequency of new alliances has decreased before the war with the help of a quantitative empirical study. They conclude that the evidence supports the hypothesis, for during the period 1910–1914 there happened to be the

lowest measured alliance formation rate of the century except for 1820–1824, the quiet period after the burst of diplomatic activity that concluded the Napoleonic Wars. . . . Whichever way we look at it, a clearcut decline in system flexibility occurred after 1909, and this period immediately preceded an event that destroyed the European balance of power, perhaps forever.

While we would not want to push it too far, this appears to be a serendipitous finding of some theoretical interest . . . . Note that in four out of five instances of change [during the century from 1814–1914] from one diplomatic period to another a decline in the alliance formation rate occurred. . . . These five points represent the times at which war was most intense . . . and when diplomatic historians point to changes in the structure of the system. This finding would appear to lend further credence to our third hypothesis [that "in a balance of power international system, a decline in the systemic rate of alliance formation precedes system changing events, such as general war"] and it certainly merits further research.[25]

It should be clear from these results how important the readiness to form and to join new alliances has been for the stability of the European Balance of Power System during the nineteenth century and that is first breakdown after World War I followed a dramatic decrease of the rate of alliance formation from 1909–1914.

A next step is to look into possible reasons for the decrease of the rate of alliance formation and of the destabilizing arms race before 1914. Morton A. Kaplan points to the following explanation:

> If we recognize, as there is reason to believe that Bismarck foresaw, that the seizure of Alsace-Lorraine by Prussia led to a public opinion in France that was ineluctably revanchist, this . . . permits engineering the theory [of the balance of power] in a way consistent with the developments that followed. As long as Germany was unwilling to return Alsace-Lorraine to France, France would be Germany's enemy. Thus France and Germany became the poles of rigid opposed alliances, as neither would enter − or at least remain in − the same coalition regardless of specific common interests.[26]

This is certainly a plausible explanation, even if it does not account for the fact, that the rate of alliance formation decreased dramatically only from 1909–1914 and not immediately after 1870/71. Another explanation, which need not contradict Kaplan's has been given by a contemporary observer, Lewis Einstein, an American diplomat who wrote anonymously in January 1913. Mr. Einstein rightly felt the grave danger of an imminent war and discussed the different elements responsible for this situation as well as the signs confirming its existence. He argues:

> The sources of European unrest could, however, be more lightly discussed without the antagonism between Great Britain and Germany. . . . [it should not] be regarded as a mere contest for commercial supremacy on the part of two countries, one seeking to preserve, the other to gain new markets. Intelligent Germans are the first to recognize that neither their merchants nor their trade suffer in British Colonies. Beneath it lies the deeply conscious rival ambition of two great nations, the one to maintain undimished the heritage conquered by its forbears, the other to obtain the place "under the sun" which it regards as its right. And the magnitude of this issue is enhanced by the hardly lesser constellations gravitating around the rivals [see Map 12 for the two alliances of World War I], each with its own historic traditions and interests. . . .

> Paradoxical as it may seem, the grave danger of the present relations between Great Britain and Germany lies in the fact that there is no real difficulty between the two Powers. . . . Their antagonism presents nothing concrete save rival ambition. Both powers are logical and right in their attitude. From England's point of view she is carrying out her traditional policy of wellnigh four centuries. . . . The same causes have made her the enemy of Russia and France, and the friend of Prussia, which make her to-day the friend of Russia and France and the adversary of a united Germany seeking oversea expansion.

> The position of Germany is no less logical. Having achieved her unity and imperial

position by blood and iron, there is no reason why she should abandon the element of armed force which has been the mainspring of her triumph. . . . the nation is practically united with regard to the importance of maintaining her military supremacy, both by reason of an exposed central continental position and because of the unhealed wound inflicted on her Western neighbour, ... Nor is she to blame if in the quest for new outlets all efforts at expansion under her own flag are thwarted by the Colonial Empires of her rivals.[27]

Mr. Einstein thus considers British-German rivalry as the main reason for the rigidity of alliances and the accompanying tensions which led to the outbreak of World War I. Franco-German antagonism because of Alsace-Lorraine is for him only a secondary factor. One might suspect, however, that both factors had to come together to bring about the rigidity of alliances observed for 1909–1914. Otherwise either Britain or France might have changed alliances and thus prevented the beginning of the Great War.

There is another factor to be considered. Great Britain had over time become the balancer of the European System. Why did it not act in the same way to prevent the war before 1914? It may be true that British statesmen thought Germany to be the strongest power striving for supremacy at that time and that they therefore joined the alliance against it with the purpose of containment. But this does not explain the fact that Britain did not leave the alliance when Germany's power had been broken during the last phases or immediately after the war. It even allowed the very harsh peace treaties which severely weakened one of the essential members of the system, Germany, and dismembered another one, Austria-Hungary. One possible explanation for this behavior would be to assume that British statesmen had no longer the knowledge of the workings of the balance of power system which their predecessors so amply possessed and which is so necessary for its further duration. For if statesmen no longer know of the necessity to keep former enemies as essential actors for future alliances then there is no way to prevent the breakdown of the system.

If one looks into the historical literature covering that time, one easily gets the impression that such a deterioration of knowledge may have occurred, not only as far as British politicians are concerned, but probably even more so on the part of the statesmen of the nations on the continent.[27] Still there may be an additional aspect of the problem. The terrible losses of life, the wounds and damages inflicted by World War I (the number of deaths alone has been estimated to have amounted to about 15.8 million[28]) created so much hate and resentment in the populations, that it may simply have been impossible for politicians (especially in democracies) to leave alliances or to engage in favor of mild peace treaties.

In this respect, however, another power, the USA, found itself in a quite different position. It was not involved in any way in European quarrels and animosities before World War I. Its losses during the war were relatively minor and it had no direct aims in Europe. One has, therefore, to ask the question: Why did the USA not use its influence to prevent as a balancer first, the outbreak of the war and secondly, the harsh peace treaties of 1919/20 severely weakening Germany and dividing Austria-Hungary? This question is especially important, since World War II may be — as we will see — considered as a direct consequence of World War I and the peace treaties following it. The consequences of this second war certainly put the United States into a situation very much removed from its own traditional aspirations and its self-understanding, leaving it as one of the only surviving super-powers involved in the dirty and bloody game of international power politics.

One can formulate several objections against this understanding of the American position and against the question asked above. For nobody seemed to be able to foresee in 1913 the consequences of the deterioration of the state of the European Balance of Power System and even less the consequences of the approaching war. Could World War II be predicted as a consequence of the peace treaties of 1919/20 already in that year? Surprisingly enough, it could, as we will see later.

More important still, Mr. Lewis Einstein argued already in 1913 that the USA should give up its traditional hands-off policies concerning European affairs and should take over the role of a balancer neglected by Britain. This with the expressed purpose of preserving the international balance of power on which depended the security and comfortable freedom from heavy military expenditures enjoyed by the United States.

The belief prevailed [in the USA] that since in Europe, America had no territorial interests nor ambitions, it had likewise no solicitude and could with impunity remain indifferent to whatever occurred on its political plane. A brief retrospect suggests, however, ample proof to the contrary. The European balance of power has been such a permanent factor since the birth of the republic that Americans have never realized how its absence would have affected their political status. The national existence was first brought about by European dissension. When Pitt resisted Napoleon, the justifiable irritation felt against British high-handedness at sea caused Americans to forget that England's fight was in reality their own, and that the undisputed master of Europe would not have been long in finding pretexts to reacquire the Louisiana territory which, except for England, he would never have relinquished. . . .

Fifty years later, had England joined France in recognizing the Confederacy or in her abortive Mexican adventure, the history of the United States might have run a different course. . . . The undisputed paramountcy of any nation, both by land and sea, most inevitably make that Power a menace and a peril to every other country. . . .

. . . If Germany and England choose to indulge in the luxury of war such is their right. However much one may lament the loss of life, it is no affair of the United States even though England were defeated, so long as the general balance is preserved. But if ever decisive results are about to be registered of a nature calculated to upset what has for

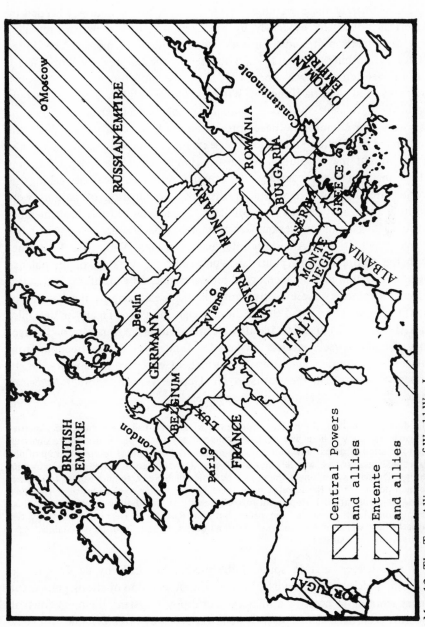

Map 12: The Two Alliances of World War I

centuries been the recognized political fabric of Europe, America can remain indifferent thereto only at her own eventual cost. If it then neglects to observe that the interests of the nations crushed are likewise its own, America will be guilty of political blindness which it will later rue.[29]

Unfortunately these warnings of Mr. Lewis Einstein were not heeded by American politicians, especially by President Wilson. It is perhaps revealing that the American diplomat Einstein had to write anonymously. The United States did nothing to use its power to prevent the outbreak of World War I. Its intervention into war since 1917 had the unfortunate result to crush Germany and Austria-Hungary. Without this a military stalemate would probably have developed as a consequence of mutual exhaustion, opening the way to a compromise peace preserving the balance of power. When the war ended the United States did not use its most favorable position adequately to prevent the dissolution of Austria-Hungary and the severe weakening of Germany. On the contrary, the popular American ideas of making the world safe for democracy and of the self-determination of nations were skilfully used by French Prime Minister Clemenceau as tools to dismember Austria-Hungary and to weaken Germany and Soviet Russia.

We conclude that American intervention during World War I together with the ignorance of its politicians concerning the workings of the balance of power system and the ideological pressures guided by wishful thinking in a popular democracy were instrumental in the weakening of the balance of power system. The United States did not sign the Peace Treaty of Versailles in 1919 and went back to its attitude of isolationism, unaware of the fact that she had herself severely shaken the fundament of her freedom from international conflict and from the burden of excessive armaments. Or, to present this result in the words of Mr. George Kennan, another American diplomat, who wrote about forty years later:

The damage had been done. The equilibrium of Europe had been shattered. Austria-Hungary was gone. There was nothing effective to take its place. Germany, smarting from the sting of defeat and plunged into profound social unrest by the breakup of her traditional institutions, was left nevertheless as the only great united state in Central Europe. Russia was no longer there, as a possible reliable ally, to help France to contain German power. From the Russian plain there lured a hostile eye, skeptical of Europe's values, rejoicing at all Europe's misfortunes, ready to collaborate solely for the final destruction of her spirit and her pride. Between Russia and Germany were only the pathetic new states of Eastern and Central Europe, lacking in domestic stability and the traditions of statesmanship. . . .[30]

We have seen that in spite of the predictions made by de Tocqueville in 1835, which were certainly based on the observation of strong permanent forces working in favor of a bilateral world power system, the breakdown of the European Balance of Power System was probably not inevitable. Bismarck could have foregone to rejoin Alsace-Lorraine with Germany, especially since the mainly German-speaking population did mostly dislike Prussia. His successors in the German government could have refrained from colonial and naval expansion to keep Great Britain on more friendly terms. They could have tried, too, to keep closer contacts to Russia as Bismarck always did, to keep it out of an alliance with France. Finally Britain could have remained the balancer of the system or the United States have taken up this role as proposed by Mr. Lewis Einstein. Then World War I as well as the breakdown of the European Balance of Power could have been prevented.

Still, one may ask, would it have been possible for Bismarck not to annex Alsace-Lorraine given the popular German nationalism of that time and the attitude of the Prussian general staff? Would it have been possible to prevent the decline of knowledge on the part of German and British politicians about the workings of the system, not to speak of their colleagues in Austria-Hungary and Russia? Could Woodrow Wilson, Colonel House or Robert Lansing, the main American actors, have learned this indispensable knowledge? Would American democracy have been able to enter the war without the enthusiastic feelings that the Allies were fighting to make the world safe for democracy, for the destruction of Prussian militarism, the self-determination of peoples and the final advent of long-lasting peace founded on common understanding, open diplomacy and the absence of old-fashioned power politics?

But if the answers to these questions cannot be distinctively positive, as it seems to be the case, was then the history of Europe and the world not predetermined to move into the direction outlined by de Tocqueville's prophesy? We would not like to agree to this proposition, but the probability of the predicted outcome was certainly high. Even George Kennan has only a rather helpless remark in referring to the American policies of that time:

If you say that mistakes of the past were unavoidable because of our domestic pre-dilections and habits of thought, you are saying that what stopped us from being more effective than we were was democracy as practiced in this country. And, if that is true, let us recognize it and measure the full seriousness of it – and find something to do about it. A nation which excuses its own failures by the sacred untouchableness of its own habits can excuse itself into complete disaster. I said . . . that the margin in which it is given to us to commit blunders has been drastically narrowed in the last fifty years. If it was the workings of our democracy that were inadequate in the past, let us say so. Whoever thinks the future is going to be easier than the past is certainly mad. And the system under which we are going to have to continue to conduct foreign policy is, I hope and pray, the system of democracy.[31]

We shall return to the relationship of democracy to the efficiency of foreign policy later on. At the moment let us turn to the final period of the European Balance of Power System which had been severely weakened, but not perfectly destroyed, by the peace treaties following World War I. For Germany as well as Russia regained their strengths during the thirties and Italy entered the system instead of Austria-Hungary, even if it remained a rather weak actor.

In studying the developments of the system until its final demise in 1945 one is struck by another astonishing prediction, this time made by the reputed French historian Jacques Bainville. Bainville accurately foresaw as early as 1920 the general events before and including the outbreak of World War II. He convincingly deducts these events from the very logic of the situation created by the peace treaties ending World War I. The fact that he was able to make these correct predictions again leads to the embarassing question, whether World War II was an unavoidable consequence of these earlier events and whether there existed any chance at all after 1919 to prevent its outbreak and the resulting destruction of the European Balance of Power System. But before trying to answer this question, let us quote from Bainville's work to provide a bit of the flavor of his predictions:

For more than a generation, the Germans have to pay tributes to the Allies. They have to pay the main part to the French who are one third less in number than they: forty million Frenchmen have as debtors sixty million Germans, the debt of whom will not be payed before thirty years, perhaps half a century has passed . . . .

To the young and weak Polish state it [Germany] had to give Posen. It is in danger to have to give back to it Upper Silesia . . . and the Treaty of Versailles has recreated the island of Eastern Prussia . . . .

One therefore cannot say that the treaty does not dismember Germany. It dismembers her strongly in the east . . . for the profit of Poland which has only one third of the density of its population. . . . Look only at this revealing map. Cowering in the Center of Europe like a malevolent animal Germany has only to extend one paw to reunite again the island of Koenigsberg. In this sign are inscribed the next misfortunes of Poland and Europe. . . .

For Poland there is no choice, it has only to fight and to die. But the state of Czechoslovakia? . . . It is surrounded by the Germans which hinder it, as it were, to breathe. . . . And, moreover, . . . there are three million Germans in Bohemia. A war with Germany would mean the suicide of Czechoslovakia. The government in Prague has to move with extreme prudence. And prudence means neutrality. And an unconditional and absolute neutrality is called very soon subjugation.

It is worse further south. There is Austria, an authentic piece of Germany. . . . Too great is the temptation for the state of Vienna to rejoin a big and powerful community. . . . There again, for 60 million Germans, the temptation is too big. The signal for the future is too evident. . . .

Between Germany and Russia there is no need for treaties: Poland brings them together. . . . There is no more natural alliance. . . .

Italy will certainly recover from the great moral, social and political troubles from which it suffers at this moment. Then it will realize that it counts forty million inhabitants and that the Allies have unjustly done wrong to it when they did not give it what it demanded, to prefer its direct competitors (Greece, Jugoslavia). . . to guard the Brenner and Triest against the eternally descending Germans it will think of the method by which it guarded Venetia. Not to get war with Austria it allied itself with Austria. A similar and only more complex situation will not fail to suggest the idea to enter into good relations with the German people. . . .

. . . if one day Poland would be attacked by the Germans, Russia would be prepared to profit from its disaster and to stab it from the back.

The march of Germany is totally indicated. It is through the east that she will begin her liberation and her revenge . . . .

The future difficulties, the designs of which are already showing, will have a double character. First they will be of a growing gravity. In the beginning the danger will only appear to trained eyes and to perspicacious men. The masses will remain insensitive to them and the governments will be tempted to deny them.[32]

This was certainly a breathtaking prediction and an impressive analysis, especially if one considers its early date (1920). Still, it is interesting to note that Bainville did not realize the unfavorable consequences of the alternative policies he preferred. According to him France should have kept Austria-Hungary as a big power but have divided Germany using the particularistic tendencies of its constituent states, without separating from it some of its provinces. He thus followed age-old French traditions which had been pursued by French statesmen at least since the time of Cardinal Richelieu. Now, Germany has been divided after World War II and been deprived of even more of its territory. But what has been the consequence of this for France and Europe? The predominance of Russia and the end of the French position as a big power! Bainville never hints at these possible consequences, which were quite clear to Metternich, Konstantin Frantz and others already mentioned. One is, therefore, inclined to ask, whether his penetrating sight has been clouded by nationalism in this respect.

Bainville's analysis poses the question whether World War II and the dissolution of the European Balance of Power could have been prevented after the peace treaties of 1919/20 had severely violated the rules of the game of this system. We still believe that some probably meagre chances to bring about a different development could have been used in the interwar period.

First, a better treatment of the Weimar Republic by the Allies could have helped the democratic forces in Germany who were striving, like foreign minister Stresemann (together with French minister Briand), for reconciliation of the former enemies. A more skilful economic policy would probably have prevented the most terrible slumps of the Great Depression beginning in 1929. For empirical research starting from political-economic hypotheses has confirmed that the Nazi as well as the Communist parties would never have gained so many votes without the excesses of the depression, especially the resulting high rate of unemployment.[33]

Finally, the Western Allies could have supported the internal opposition in Nazi Germany (perhaps even by military measures to assist a coup d'état). To support this the Allies should not have asked for unconditional German surrender. An alliance with a Germany weakened by the war, but undiminished in its territory and governed by the former resistance members would have been at least thinkable to contain the Soviet Union. This would have meant a readiness to shift alliances if a successful coup d'état would have happened inside Germany, certainly a difficult but not impossible maneuver.

All these alternative policies or decisions certainly look not very promising, but at least they were possible. Saying this does amount to the fact, again, that the developments predicted by Bainville were not necessary, but still highly probable, given the situation of 1919/20.

In concluding this chapter we should not forget the importance of uncontrollable and therefore unpredictable variables on the course of events. The fulfillment of de Tocqueville's prediction of the predominance of two superpowers, Russia and the USA, the implied defeat, subjugation or unimportance of the other earlier big powers and the implied end of the European Balance of Power may have been highly probable. But as Herman Kahn reminds us, they still might have been thwarted by accidental factors:

For example, the Germans *might* have won World War I in a few weeks just as Schlieffen had hoped, and the whole history of our times would have been different. In particular, the disillusionment experienced by – and with – Europe's society in the interwar years might not have occurred, and such commonplace beliefs as that 'war is unthinkable', 'war never pays' and 'war does not decide anything' would quite possibly never have become commonplace. Indeed, war, in the 1920's and 1930's, might have been seen as advantageous and useful. Similarly, Hitler came very close to winning World War II. One can argue that if Mussolini had never attacked Greece, or if the Yugoslavs had not resisted Hitler's attack, or if the 1941 winter in the Soviet Union had not been so severe, Hitler might have won at least the war against Russia. . . .[34]

6. The Bilateral Power System (Bipolar System)

The treaties of Yalta and Potsdam during and immediately after World War II gave the final blow to the Balance of Power. The German Reich was amputated and divided. In fact, it had ceased to exist. Italy and Japan (the latter surrendered a few months later on September 2, 1945, after the USA had erased two of its cities with the first attack using atomic bombs) were severely weakened and demilitarized. Even Great Britain and France, though finding themselves among the victorious powers, were relatively weak as compared to the two super-powers. In a few years it became obvious

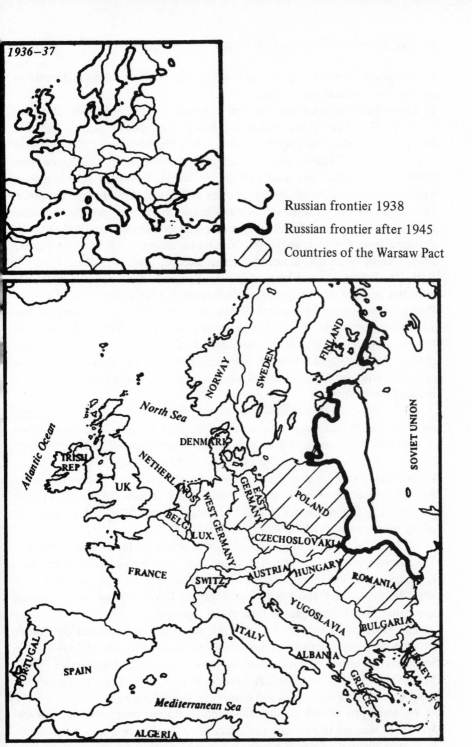

Maps 13 and 14: Russian Expansion after World War II (Europe before and after the War)

to everybody that they could and would play only a subordinate role on the stage of international politics.

Given these facts a power vacuum had been created in Europe. But there exists another *Law of international politics*: Each power vacuum will soon be filled by the remaining big powers. Thus the division of Germany and the weakening of Britain and France had as their necessary consequence the division of Europe, and even that of the world. From the very beginning Stalin had no illusions about this state of affairs and skilfully used the power vacuum in Europe first to get as many concessions from the Western Allies as possible (see Maps 13 and 14). In this way he gained Eastern Carelia and Petsamo from Finland, subjugated the Baltic States, took parts of Eastern Prussia from Germany, annexed Eastern Poland, took Carpathian Ruthenia from Czechoslovakia and Bessarabia from Rumania. Poland was compensated with the purely German provinces Pommerania, Silesia, and parts of Eastern Prussia and Brandenburg. Next Stalin engineered with his communist collaborators a number of clever maneuvres and coups d'état supported by the Soviet army to secure the domination of the German Democratic Republic, Poland, Czechoslovakia, Hungary, Rumania and Bulgaria. Only the guerilla warfare in Greece did not succeed and Yugoslavia moved away from Russian domination.

The USA was rather late to realize the nature of the new international order which it had helped to create. The illusions of a 'final crusade for democracy' and 'peace in Europe and the world' needed time to be shattered by the brutal facts of Soviet intrusion into the regions where a power vacuum had been created. But finally a tough stand was taken, the North Atlantic Alliance created and a containment policy instituted. This all amounted to the consequence that the United States filled in the other half of the power vacuum left in Europe.

In Asia, too, the vacuum created by the defeat of Japan was soon filled. The communists led by Mao Tse Tung took over the government of China in a rapid military success against Chiang Kai-shek. Korea was divided like later Vietnam, and the USA waged war in Korea against North Korean aggression, thus filling again its part of the vacuum.

The situation which finally emerged saw both superpowers confronted in an antagonistic stalemate, suspicious of each other, deeply involved in an armament race and surrounded by their medium-sized and smaller allies, which were directly or indirectly dependent on their military and economic support, and were sometimes not more than puppet regimes.

We have just sketched how the bipolar system developed after World War II. It remains to examine the characteristics of such a system and to see how it is different from a balance of power system. In doing so we state first that there exists no motivation for the big powers in a bipolar system to shift alliances and not to severely weaken or even to obliterate the other big power if it has been defeated. For since there is only one powerful potential enemy left, an essential actor has only to heed against a possible attack of this enemy or only to wrestle its power down, if it strives for world domination. As a consequence each of the two big powers has to be prepared not to be overwhelmed by the other some future day. It will, therefore, try to build up enough military power to be armed for possible future emergencies and to assemble as many minor allies as possible around it. For once defeated there may be no chance for recovery.

The above antagonistic tendencies have to be expected between the two superpowers because of the following reasons. Both states feel themselves to be in a precarious position since a victorious enemy has no incentives to spare the defeated as a future essential ally. One or both powers may actually strive for universal domination. Thus each of the superpowers looks suspiciously at any move of the other and tends to evaluate or even to perceive all developments in each part of the world in terms of its situation compared to its main opponent. The dilemma of the armament race is nearly inescapable (see Section 1), especially since disarmament agreements are difficult to achieve and to control given the mutual distrust, the strong motivation for cheating and the prize of world domination waiting for the more ruthless actor.

It can thus be concluded that a bipolar system is usually less stable than a balance of power system. The possibility of alliances with other essential actors does not exist. It is difficult not to mistrust the opponent, since world power waits as a reward. The incentives for an armament race are big. All world conflicts are more or less seen from the vantage point of the relative situation compared with the other super-power. If we take these factors together and recall that economic and population growth as well as domestic political and technological developments may be different in the two nations, then we have to expect that after some time one or the other state will feel itself to be stronger and may use its power to try to gain world domination. It follows that there is a good chance that a bipolar system will not last for very long but will be replaced by a universal empire with only one essential actor.

Let us now look at the historical evidence. It is interesting to note that we know only of a smaller number of bipolar than of balance of power or of multipolar systems. Moreover, bipolar systems usually did not last very long, a fact which seems to support the hypothesis of a smaller stability of this system. We have already seen that a kind of bipolar system existed in the Western Mediterranean in the third century B.C. between Rome and

Carthage and that this situation ended after only a few decades with the victory of Rome. Again, Athens and Sparta were members of a mitigated bipolar system from about 470 to 400 B.C. This system broke down, too, before the end of the century when Athens was defeated by Sparta and her allies in the Peloponnesian War.

It seems that in some cases a bipolar system has even not really existed between the end of balance of power or multipolar systems and the beginning of universal empires. This has probably been true when the Mauryan Empire was created in India by Chandragupta and the Chinese Empire by King Chen of Ch'in. In these cases the only remaining opponent was perhaps too weak, when all the other states had been defeated, to withstand the victorious state for any extended period. In these cases one of the two potential members of a bipolar system was not even able to build up its relative strength in a manner that could maintain the equilibrium between the two powers at least for a limited time.

What conclusions can be drawn from these historical facts for the present bipolar system? We have to be careful not to conclude at once that the existing bipolar system will also be overthrown at least within a few decades. For this time the situation has been drastically changed by technical progress, namely by the introduction of atomic weapons. Both superpowers are today able to destroy each other with the terrible arsenals of nuclear weapons they have accumulated, an unprecedented situation. It should be obvious that this factor is working in favor of the stability of the present bipolar system. The prize of world domination can at the moment only be won militarily at the risk of self-destruction.

Does this mean that the present 'bipolar world system' will stay with us into an indefinite future? We cannot be sure about this, because other means of expansion like ideological, economic and guerilla warfare are available in addition to traditional wars. Moreover, domestic developments within one of the superpowers may destroy the credibility of a counter-attack with atomic weapons in case it is attacked or threatened into subjugation. For instance, the leading politicians or the majority of the population in a democracy may not believe that the opposing government has aggressive intentions and thus neglect the balance of military power. Or taking into account the horrors of a possible war, strong groups in a democracy may be prepared to give up freedom and independence to prevent war. Finally, the two superpowers may be split-up by civil wars or revolutions or new big powers may develop in other regions of the world. We will discuss these possible developments in the last chapter, but we should not be blinded by them to the fact of the great stability of the present bipolar world system.

7. The Universal Empire

It is self-evident that between any two princes, neither of whom owes allegiance to the other, controversy may arise either by their own fault or by the fault of their subjects. For such, judgement is necessary. And inasmuch as one owing no allegiance to the other can recognize no authority in him (for an equal cannot control an equal), there must be a third prince with ample jurisdiction, who may govern both within the circle of his right . . . And this judge will be Monarch, or Emperor. [Universal] Monarchy is therefore indispensable to the world, . . .

Dante Alighieri,
Italian poet, 1265–1321 [35]

In discussing the 'universal empire' or 'world state' we move into a different world. In such a system no outside state of relevant power remains which is competing with the empire for world domination. Competition for power is limited to internal struggles, which may take the form of competition regulated by law like parliamentary or presidential elections, or the form of coups d'état, revolutions or civil wars. Even if the latter three prevail, so that violent means are used by two or more armed factions, two facts have to be kept in mind which make these kinds of armed fights quite different from clashes between independent states. First, it has been proved by Lewis F. Richardson by taking into account more than 100 years of deadly quarrels including all wars and civil strifes all over the world, that the unification of a number of independent organisational entities (states) into one nation reduces the amount of violence in that region.[36] It is well-known that there is certainly less violence now within France, Britain and Japan than during the feudal times of the Middle Ages. Second, no participants in the internal fight for power perceive the regions dominated by them as separate states. Quite the contrary. They all want to return to legality for the whole system and to ban all violence *after* their success. Of course, they and their opponents may not be able to do so and the universal empire may remain divided for some time or for an indefinite period. But even then the population still consider themselves to be citizens of the empire and the pretenders strive for power over the whole system even after several generations have passed. No question that such a perception of reality is itself a powerful force working towards the restoration of unity.

But can we speak about a universal empire from historical experience? Can it not be argued that a world state has never existed? This is certainly true if we take the concept of 'world state' or 'world empire' in its literal meaning. Never in human history has there been an empire comprising the whole earth. There are, however, good reasons to speak at least of the Roman and the Chinese Empires as universal empires. For both united the whole or nearly the whole of the civilized peoples (Persia bordered the Roman Empire and should be considered as a civilized state) of their regions. Outside their domains were only tribes and people who were considered to be barbarians. Other parts of the world were only dimly known to the civilized centers. This was even true for the knowledge of the two empires concerning each other and concerning the remaining leading civilized center, namely India.

It is thus not surprising that Rome as well as China considered themselves to be unique world states of eternal existence spreading law, civilization and peace all over the world. The Chinese spoke rather early of this empire as 't'ien hsia', 'what is under heaven' and Roman Emperor Valentinian III used the expression 'urbs aeterna', 'the eternal city' in a constitution he issued. The poet Virgil exclaimed some years before the birth of Christ "I set him neither a limitation to his borders, nor a time: I have given him a dominion without limits."[37]

According to Tertullian the Roman Empire was a sacrosanct society[37] and the Goth Athanaric, when led into the market-place of Constantinople, expressed the feelings of his barbarian nation: "Without doubt the Emperor is a God upon earth, and he who attacks him is guilty of his own blood."[37]

Excluding the wars with Persia, the Roman as well as the Chinese Empires were only threatened from time to time by barbarian tribes or by internal disorders. Several times during Chinese history the Empire was gravely endangered as for instance by the Huns or even overrun as by the Mongolians. Sometimes the Empire was split up either because the barbarians conquered only parts of it or because of internal strife among contenders for the imperial throne. But as we have seen before, the candidates for imperial power wanted to be emperors of the whole Chinese Empire. And the barbarian conquerors were soon civilized by the superior Chinese culture. They became emperors and very soon felt themselves to be Chinese. The Emperors were assimilated as were the barbarian people they had brought with them and who were only like drops in the Chinese sea surrounding them. The idea of a universal empire comprising all civilized men had taken deep roots and thus even defeated the conquerors. The unity of China was again and again restored, its dominion expanded with Chinese civilization, and the state lived on into modern times.

Roman history shows about the same pattern. Barbarian tribes like the Goths in Italy and Spain, the Vandals in Africa and the Franks in France tended to take up the superior civilization of the antique world. Like in China they soon preferred the language and religion of the defeated. They all became romanized. Their princes like Athanaric were over-awed by the splendour and might of the Roman Empire and soon strove to become either allies and generals of the Emperor or to make themselves Emperor and to restore the Universal Roman Empire. One of the ablest of the barbarian chieftains, Ataulf the Visigoth, brother and successor of Alaric, said:

It was at first my wish to destroy the Roman name, and erect in its place a Gothic empire, taking to myself the place and the powers of Caesar Augustus. But when experience taught me that the untameable barbarism of the Goths would not suffer them to live beneath the sway of law, and that to abolish the laws on which the state rests would destroy the state itself, I chose the glory of renewing and maintaining by Gothic strength the fame of Rome, deciding to go down to posterity as the restorer of that Roman power which I could not replace. Wherefore I avoid war and strive for peace.[38]

A remarkable statement. But the idea of Rome lived on for centuries even after the Roman Empire had definitely fallen as a universal state. Charlemagne and Otto I, kings of the Franks and of the Eastern Franks (Germany), respectively, tried to restore its glory and took up the Imperial Crown in Rome in 800 and after 900 A.D. So the Holy Roman Imperium was 'restored', following the noble idea of a Christian and peaceful universal empire, but without sufficient powers of fulfil this utopian dream. A late and convincing echo of the rationale of the empire can be found in the quotation from Dante's *De Monarchia* given above.

Having said all this one may wonder why the Roman in contrast to the Chinese Empire did break down given the forces working for its stability and even for its restauration. The successful invasions of the Germanic tribes cannot have been the decisive reason. For these tribes were easily assimilated by the superior Roman civilization and soon accepted the idea of a universal empire. Another possible reason which has been proposed is the deterioration of the Roman economy towards an over-taxed, inefficiently planned system, which finally turned slowly into the direction of feudalism. But this is a doubtful hypothesis, since the surrounding countries certainly could not boast of a more efficient economy.

It seems that the decisive reason for the final destruction of the Roman Empire was the appearance of the Islamic Religion. If the Arabians had conquered parts of or the whole empire without having had this religion they would probably have been assimilated like the Germanic tribes and the empire would have been restored. But now they had a religion which they considered to be superior to those of Rome and which gave a well-organized code of ethics and of rules of behavior. So they looked not to Roman or Hellenistic civilization as a superior one but just integrated the elements which seemed most valuable to them. They kept their different style of life, their different writing and their language and even assimilated the populations of the conquered provinces. Consequently the Islamic offensive was not like the feats of barbarian tribes as in the case of China. And this, I believe, explains the fateful end of the Roman Empire.

Did other universal empires besides Rome and China exist during human history? In a certain sense we may consider Hammurabi's Babylonian Empire in the eighteenth century B.C., the Persian Empire of about 600–300 B.C., Alexander the Great's short-lived Empire of about 330 B.C., the Mauryan Empire in India after 300 B.C. and the Aztec and the Inca Empires before Columbus' arrival in America to have been universal states. All of them were only surrounded by barbarian tribes (compared to the levels their civilization had reached) or by rather weak and more or less dependent neighbors. Only the Mauryan Empire had a strong neighbor in the west, namely the Seleucid kingdom. But this state was fighting with the other successor states of Alexander's Empire and therefore posed no danger for the Mauryan Emperor.

Still there exist reasons not to consider these empires as fully developed world states. The Aztec and Inca Empires were soon defeated by the sudden and unexpected advent of a superior outside power, Spain. Hammurabi's and Alexander's Empires were not consolidated enough during their lifetimes to survive the deaths of their founders. Thus these states had no chance to show the stability of universal empires extending over centuries which we have observed for Rome and China. The Persian Empire proved to be stable enough for two to three centuries. But it had one neighbor with a superior civilization and with superior military forces and tactics: the Greek city states. As a consequence it suffered a defeat when it tried to conquer Greece around 480 B.C., because most of the Greek states banded together in an alliance. Thus Persia never succeeded to combine all the superior civilizations of its region into its empire and to grow into a really universal state.

The Mauryan Empire in India existed for about three generations, and flourished especially under Chandragupta's grandson, Emperor Asoka, who favored the extension of Buddhist religion. Obviously, even this time-span was not sufficient to consolidate the empire. Parts of Southern India had never been subjugated and the empire split up and finally broke down under Asoka's heirs and successors.

We conclude that all of the empires mentioned were nascent universal empires which never quite developed. They either had not enough time to consolidate, did not succeed to include all superior civilizations in their regions or were destroyed in a rather early state by the advent of unexpected and strong outside powers. They had the potential to grow into truly universal empires but did not quite succeed because of some internal weaknesses, since they had not enough time to stabilize, because of clashes with far-removed superior civilizations or just because of historical accidents.

It has been stated that universal states have several attractive features. They show more stability and are more peaceful and well-ordered than other international systems composed of some or many independent states with about equal powers. Indeed, we may say that many of the present and past disorders like wars, trade warfare and international monetary and financial disturbances are nothing but flaws of a disorganized or unorganized international system relying on the fetishes of 'national independence' and 'sovereignty'.

It is true that despotism in a world state is a more appalling danger than in several but not all nation states. But should it not be possible to develop a universal state with internal characteristics preventing despotism as well as a stupid and boring equalization of all the different peoples, civilizations, religions and languages of the earth? If we take such a possibility into account, a world state certainly does appear to be a valuable aim for future development.

We have seen, however, that the hope for such a development is presently rather weak because of the stability of the bipolar system brought about by the balance of nuclear terror. There was perhaps only a short time immediately after World War II during which there would have been a chance to establish a world state. After 1945 the USA had for a few years monopoly of atomic weapons and would probably have been able to exploit this fact to gain world domination. Whether this would have been possible from the point of view of domestic policies is another question to which we have to turn later. A discussion of the possible further development of the present international political system and its prospects to develop into a world empire in spite of atomic armaments will also have to wait until the last chapter.

Table 2.3: The Spread of Different International Systems through Time and Space (not complete)

Type of System	Region	Period
Multipolar Systems	Mesopotamia: Sumerian (and Accadian) city states	2nd millennium B.C.
	Feudal states in China during 'Spring and Autumn'	722–481 B.C.
	Indian state system	Before 300 B.C.
	Greek, Phoenician, Etruscan and Latinian city states	Around 800–480 B.C.
	Feudal Medieval states in Europe	Around 900–1500 A.D.
	Italian city states	Around 1200–1400 A.D.
	Japanese feudal system	Around 1200–1600 A.D.

Table 2.3 (Continuation)

Type of System	Region	Period
Balance of Power Systems	Mesopotamia: Larsa, Eshnunna, Babylon, Qatna, Iamkhad, Assur	18th Century B.C.
	Near East: Egypt, Mitanni, Hittite Empire, Babylonia	Around 1600–1200 B.C.
	The 'Warring States' in China	481–221 B.C.
	The big Hellenistic states: Macedonia, Egypt and Syria. Possibly Rome, Carthage and Syracuse	323 – before 100 B.C.
	The 'big' Italian Renaissance states: Venice, Milan, Florence, Naples and the Holy See; in the beginning Verona, too.	14th and 15th Centuries A.C.
	The European Balance of Power, slowly extending, towards a world balance of power: Spain, France, Austria (-Hungary), Great Britain, Sweden, Russia, Prussia (Germany), USA, Japan, (Italy)	At least since 1648–1945 A.D.
Bipolar Systems	Athens and Sparta	4th Century B.C.
	Rome and Carthage (Western Mediterranean)	3rd and 2nd Centuries B.C.
	USA and Russia	Since 1945
Universal Empires which Nearly Succeeded	Mesopotamian Empires:	Around 2340–2200 B.C.
	Akkad (King Sargon)	Around 2050–1950 B.C.
	Ur III, Babylon (King Hammurabi)	Around 1800 B.C.
	Assyria	883–612 B.C.
	Persia	Around 600–450 B.C.
	Maurya Empire in India	3rd Century B.C.
	Aztec Empire in Mexico	Around 1430–1521 A.D.
	Inca Empire in South America	Around 1440–1531 A.D.

Table 2.3 (Continuation)

Type of System	Region	Period
Universal Empires	China	Since 221 B.C. – 17th Century A.D.
	Roman Empire	Around 100 B.C. – 500 A.D.
Expected Future World Balance of Power System*	USA, Soviet Union, Japan, China, Brazil, (European Community)	Beginning around 2000–2030 A.D.

* See Chapter 7.

Notes

[1] Carl von Clausewitz: *On War.* Edited with an Introduction by Anatol Rapoport. Penguin Books, Harmondsworth (Middlesex, England), 1968, p. 119. Original German Edition *Vom Kriege* published 1832.

[2] Kautilya, Artha-Sastra: Excerpts in: *A Source Book in Indian Philosophy*, edited by S. Radhakrishnan and Ch. A. Moore, Princeton University Press, Princeton (N.J.), 1957, pp. 208–209, Copyright (c) 1957 by Princeton University Press.

[3] Niccolo Machiavelli: *Der Fürst*, Alfred Kröner, Stuttgart 1963, p. 106.

[4] See William H. Riker: *The Theory of Political Coalitions.* Yale University Press, New Haven and London, 1962.

[5] Kautilya, op. cit., p. 206.

[6] Kautilya, op. cit., p. 209.

[7] Otto von Bismarck: *Gedanken und Erinnerungen*, W. Goldmann Verlag, München, without date, p. 309.

[8] Constantin Frantz: *Die Weltpolitik mit besonderer Bezugnahme auf Deutschland.* Reprint of the edition of 1882. Osnabrück, Biblio-Verlag, 1966, p. 3.

[9] See E. Kaeber: *Die Idee des europäischen Gleichgewichts in der publizistischen Literatur vom 16. bis zur Mitte des 18. Jahrhunderts*, Verlag Dr. H. A. Gerstenberg, Hildesheim, 1971, pp. 12–13.

[10] Compare J.I. Crump: *Intrigues: Studies of the Chan-kuo Ts'e.* Ann Arbor, Michigan, 1964.

[11] Quoted according to Quincy Wright: *A Study of War,* University of Chicago Press, 2nd edition, Chicago and London, 1965, p. 744.

[12] See also David Hume: *Of the Balance of Power.* Philosophical Works III, Boston, 1854.

[13] Henry Kissinger: *A World Restored. Castlereagh, Metternich and the Restoration of Peace 1812–1822.* Grosset and Dunlop, New York 1964.

[14] Klemens von Metternich: *Denkwürdikeiten, 1844* published 1859. Quoted from the excerpts in Walter Schätzel: Der Staat. Carl Schünemann Verlag. Bremen, without date, 2nd ed., p. 347.

[15] Friedrich der Grosse: *Der Antimachiavell,* 1739, Quoted from excerpts in Walter Schätzel, op. cit., p. 223.

[16]   Quoted according to Quincy Wright: op. cit., p. 744.
[17]   Morton A. Kaplan: "The Systems Approach to International Politics." In Morton A. Kaplan (ed.): *New Approaches to International Relations*, St. Martin's Press, New York, 1968, pp. 390–391. For other studies of the balance of power see: Dina A. Zinnes: "An Analytical Study of the Balance of Power Theories." *Journal of Peace Research*, vol. 4, 1967, pp. 270–328, and Gordon Tullock: *The Social Dilemma. The Economics of War and Revolution*, Center for Study of Public Choice, Blacksburg (Va.), 1974.
[18]   George Washington: "Farewell Address," quoted from Alexis de Tocqueville: Democracy in America. Vintage Book 1945, Vol. 1, p. 241.
[19]   Thomas Jefferson. "Inaugural Address" (first draft) of March 4, 1801. *The Writings of Thomas Jefferson*, Ed. by P.L. Ford. G.D. Putman's Sons, New York and London 1892–1897, vol. VIII, p. 4.
[20]   Friedrich der Grosse: *Das Politische Testament von 1752*. Reclam, Stuttgart, 1974, p. 101.
[21]   Constantin Frantz: op. cit., p. 51.
[22]   Alexis de Tocqueville: *Democracy in America*. Translated by Henry Reeve, revised by Francis Bowen and edited by Philipp Bradley. Copyright (c) Alfred A. Knopf, Inc., 1945. Vintage Book, Vol. 1, p. 452.
[23]   Friedrich Engels: "Introduction." In: Sigismund Borkheim, *Zur Erinnerung für die deutschen Mordspatrioten, 1806–1807*. Volksbuchhandlung, Hottingen-Zürich 1888, pp. 7–8.
[24]   Lewis F. Richardson: Generalized Foreign Politics. *British Journal of Psychology*: Monograph Supplements, vol. 23, Cambridge, 1939. For a more sophisticated development of Richardson's model with the help of optional control theory see: J.V. Gillespie, D.A. Zinnes, G.S. Tahim, P.S. Schrott and P.M. Rubison: "An Optimal Control Model of Arms Races," *American Political Science Review*, Vol. 71, 1977, pp. 226–244.
[25]   Patrick J. McGowen and Robert M. Rood: "Alliance Behavior in Balance of Power Systems: Applying a Poisson Model to Nineteenth Century Europe." *American Political Science Review*, vol. 69, 1975, pp. 859–870.
[26]   Morton A. Kaplan: op. cit., p. 397.
[27]   Anonymous (Lewis Einstein): "The United States and Anglo-German Rivalry." *The National Review*, vol. 60 (Sept. 1912 to Feb. 1913), January 1913, pp. 739–741. For a historical study of the reasons of World War I, see: Joachim Remak *The Origins of World War I, 1871–1914*, Holt, Rinehart and Winston, Hinsdale (Ill.), 1967. Compare also: A.J.P. Taylor: *The Struggle for Mastery in Europe 1848–1918*. Clarendon Press, Oxford 1954, especially ch. 22.
[28]   Lewis F. Richardson: *Statistics of Deadly Quarrels*. Pittsburgh and Chicago, 1960.
[29]   Lewis Einstein op. cit., pp. 749–750.
[30]   George F. Kennan: *American Diplomacy, 1900–1950*. Chicago and London, 1951, pp. 68–69.
[31]   George F. Kennan: op. cit., p. 73.
[32]   Jacques Bainville: *Les conséquences politiques de la paix*. Nouvelle Librairie Nationale, Paris, 1920, pp. 32–34, 81, 130, 150–151, 179–180.
[33]   Bruno S. Frey and Hannelore Weck: „Hat Arbeitslosigkeit den Anstieg des Nationalsozialismus bewirkt?" *Jahrbücher für Nationalökonomie und Statistik*, vol. 196, 1981, pp. 1–31.
[34]   Herman Kahn: "The Alternative World Futures Approach." In: Morton A. Kaplan (ed.): op. cit., pp. 131–132.
[35]   Dante Alighieri: *De Monarchia*. Houghton, Mifflin, Cambridge, Boston and New York, 1904, pp. 29–30.
[36]   Lewis F. Richardson: op. cit., ch. 12.
[37]   Compare Bryce: *The Holy Roman Empire*. London, 1904. First ed. 1873, pp. 17 and 20.
[38]   Quoted from Bryce: op. cit., pp. 18–19.

Chapter 3

Factors Determining the Power of States

The importance of the relative power of states for the working and the historical development of the international political system has been amply demonstrated in the preceding chapter. The relative power of a state first determines whether it is strong enough to be one of the essential actors of the system. Only essential actors are not dependent for their international political decisions and even for their very existence on the forbearance of one or several of the big powers.

Secondly, changes in the relative power position of states are responsible not only for their long-run fates, but also for the birth, growth and breakdown of the types of international systems we have discussed. The spectacular growth of Russia and the USA in territory, population and economic capacity foreshadowed their development into two superpowers and the end of the centuries-old European Balance of Power and its substitution by the present bipolar world system. The advances in nuclear physics and its application to atomic weapons stabilized this specific bipolar system, whereas its predecessors of the same type had been rather unstable in former times. Discerning the development of factors responsible for changes of the relative power of states, may facilitate highly impressive and astounding predictions about future development. This is what de Tocqueville did in 1835. It is therefore important to analyse the factors determining the power of states and this is the task to which we turn in the present chapter.

1. Military Power

One factor determining the relative power of states which is only too obvious is the size of the armed forces, the quality and amount of available arms and fortresses, the training of soldiers and the strategic and technical knowledge of leaders and staff of the military establishment. 'The art of war' and the available means to wage war have certainly been always an important factor determining international developments. It is trivial to state that weakly armed countries remain an easy prey for aggressive neighbors with stronger armed forces, even if they are bigger in terms of territory, population and economic capabilites. This is at the root of the armament dilemma leading to arms races and to a stalemate between the big powers able to afford the high and wasteful level of military expenditures necessary to preserve international equilibrium.

Because of these relationships expansionary states have a motivation to further developments which might enable them to break the stalemate. There seem to be several routes available for this purpose. Two of them are innovations creating new superior weapons and innovations leading to the development of superior strategies and military tactics. More peaceful states may also strive for innovation in these fields to defend their relative military positions, if they realize the potential threat of such policies undertaken by aggressive nations.

Historical examples of the importance of decisive innovations in military technology abound. It is perhaps instructive to consider just a few of them. The invention of horse-drawn chariots enabled the Indoeuropean people called Hittites to build up their powerful kingdom in Asia Minor, to defeat the Babylonians and to conquer their capital, Babylon (1531 B.C.). The Hyksos, too, used the newly invented chariots to defeat and to conquer the Middle Kingdom of Egypt around 1650 B.C. Note that in both these cases superior and more populous civilizations were overpowered by more or less barbarian tribes using a new military weapon.

The same happened when riding had been invented by the nomad tribes of Central Asia, Persia and Afghanistan, i.e. by tribes that bred horses. The impression of cavalry attacking for the first time infantry, who had perhaps never seen a horse before, must have been terrible. J. Bronowski tries to visualize the impression created by such attacks as follows:

For the rider is visible more than man: he is head-high above others, and he moves with bewildering power so that he bestrides the living world. . . . Mounting the horse was a more than human gesture, the symbolic act of dominance over the total creation. We know that this is so from the awe and fear that the horse created again in historical times when the mounted Spaniards overwhelmed the armies of Peru (who had never seen a horse) in 1532. So long before, the Scythians were a terror that swept over the countries that did not know the technique of riding. The Greeks when they saw the Scythian riders believed the horse and the rider to be one, that is how they invented the legend of the centaur. . . .
We cannot hope to recapture today the terror that the mounted horse struck into the Middle East and Eastern Europe when it first appeared. [1]

The technological advance creating this improvement of military technique had far-reaching consequences. It led to the successes of the Huns from China to Hungary and to their devastating intrusions into the Roman Empire under Attila, the 'scourge of God'. It enabled the heavy Gothic cavalry to impart to the Roman Legions their most terrible defeat since Hannibal beat them at Cannae (216 B.C.) in the Battle of Adrianople (378 A.D.). Gothic horsemen rode to Italy unimpededly, left it again by their own choice in 409 A.D. and moved to Spain nearly without finding any resistance.

Let us finally mention the successful cavalry of the Mongolian tribes united by Genghis Khan. Between 1200 and 1250 A.D. they overran the old civilizations of China and Central Asia, moved through Russia, which they dominated for centuries, and through Poland and Hungary to the Adriatic Sea and to Silesia. Europe was only saved because the Mongolian leader had to withdraw for reasons of domestic politics. In the Near East the Mongol forces conquered Persia and took Baghdad as well as Damascus, then leading centers of Arabic power.

It was only in the fourteenth century that infantry again reasserted itself against the mailed cavalry of feudal knights. This was the result of two military innovations made in different places, the English longbow and the Swiss pike. With a rain of arrows shot from a long distance the former prevented the approach of the feudal cavalry. It was nearly hopeless for the latter to force down a line of longbow-men by a mere frontal attack. The consequences of this military superiority soon showed themselves. The English kings were not only able to throw down the forces of Scotland but also the prime of French feudal aristocracy during the first half of the fourteenth century.

Swiss military supremacy stemmed mainly from the use of their pikes, which were ashen shafts eighteen feet long fitted with a head of steel which was another foot long. Used in a phalanx, a rectangle of enormous depth composed out of rapidly moving men, these pikes hit the knights murderously before they could use their own arms against the enemy. The Swiss succeeded with this military innovation against the feudal armies of the Habsburgian kings and dukes, who dominated parts of what is now Switzerland (they were of Swiss origin themselves) and who tried to reassert their authority in the remaining parts of Central Switzerland. After these victories the Swiss ruthlessly exploited their military superiority to conquer what is now French- and Italian-speaking as well as the north of German-speaking Switzerland and to sell their services as mercenaries. As C.W.C. Oman put it in his *The Art of War*:

Among each people [the Romans and the Swiss] the warlike pride generated by successful wars of independence led ere long to wars of conquest and plunder. As neighbors, both were rendered insufferable by their haughtiness and proneness to take offense on the slightest provocation. As enemies, both were distinguished for their deliberate and cold-blooded cruelty. The resolution to give no quarter, which appears almost pardonable in patriots defending their native soil, becomes brutal when retained in wars of aggression, but reaches the climax of fiendish inhumanity when the slayer is a mere mercenary. . . . Repulsive as was the blood-thirstiness of the Roman, it was far from equaling in moral guilt the needless ferocity displayed by the hired Swiss soldiery on many a battlefield of the sixteenth century.[2]

It was only with the end of their military superiority that the Swiss became the peace-loving people that they have been known as for about four centuries.

Other well-known innovations in military technology with important political consequences were the introduction of firearms, of tanks, planes and missiles and of atomic weapons. Let it suffice to mention that the availability of artillery was a final blow to the feudal military system, since castles could now be taken with the help of heavy cannon. The barons no longer had secure strongholds from which to start their military operations and where they could take refuge in case of emergency. The introduction of artillery was, moreover, one of the reasons for the decline of Swiss military supremacy. The Swiss phalanx was an especially good aim for artillery fire which led to great losses in these heavy concentrations of soldiers.

A second factor leading to military superiority is innovation in the fields of strategy and tactics. Let us just consider one example. With the defeat of Athens in the Peloponnesian War, Sparta became the dominating power in Greece (404 B.C.). But this predominance did not last long as a consequence of the strategic and tactical innovations introduced by one man, Epaminondas of Thebes. Thebes began to free herself from Sparta's grip by using the strategy of refusing battle in the open field. As a consequence, as the English military writer Lidell Hart puts it:

. . . Thebes [gained] time to develop a picked professional force, famous as the Sacred Band, which formed the spearhead of her forces subsequently . . . .
Thereupon Sparta turned eagerly to crush Thebes. But on advancing into Boeotia in 371 B.C., her army, traditionally superior in quality and actually superior in number (10,000 to 6,000) was decisively defeated at Leuctra by the new model army under Epaminondas.
He not only broke away from tactical methods established by the experience of centuries but in tactics, strategy and grand strategy alike laid the foundations on which subsequent masters built. For in tactics the 'oblique order' which Frederick [II of Prussia] made famous was only a slight elaboration of the method of Epaminondas. At Leuctra, reversing custom, Epaminondas placed not only his best men but the most on his left wing, and then, holding back his weak centre and right, developed a crushing superiority against one wing of the enemy – the wing where their leader stood, and thus the key of their will.[3]

2. Geographical Situation, Size and Population

Geographical situation, size and population of states are important factors determining their relative power. A situation at the periphery of a balance of power system is much more favorable than one in its very center, surrounded by other essential members of the system. Thus in the European Balance of Power System, Germany and Austria-Hungary were in a much more vulnerable position than France and especially Russia. After the weakening of Spain from the seventeenth century, France had no dangerous potential opponent left in the south and was even to a certain degree protected by the Channel against British intervention. Russia had to heed no strong power in the east and, after the deterioration of the Osman Empire, 'the sick man at the Bosporus', to the south.

Britain's splendid insular isolation shows the advantages of natural geographical frontiers. After having been successfully conquered by the Normans (Battle of Hastings, 1066) she suffered no other invasion of any importance. No doubt Napoleon and Hitler would have conquered Britain if it had not been an island. Compare this protected position to that of Germany where Danish and Swedish armies moved around freely during the Thirty Year's War, as did French troops during the invasions of Louis XIV and of Napoleon. Germany had no natural borders. The same is true for the eastern frontier of France and the western border of Russia, which both saw two deep invasions by German forces during the last decades. Napoleon was even able to move with his French forces to Moscow in 1812.

Another secure insular position has been enjoyed by Japan, which has never seen a successful invasion in all of its history until it was defeated in World War II by the United States. Finally, the USA are in a similarly isolated position. Protected by the wide reaches of the Atlantic and Pacific Oceans it has even today nothing to fear from traditional military forces, because no other big power exists on the American continent from the time the USA reasserted independence against the British in the War of Independence.

The central position of a state in the midst of other essential members of the prevailing international system should give rise to more occasions for confrontations and for more issues to quarrel about. As a consequence one would expect that a country would be involved the more often in wars the more numerous are its borders with neighboring states. At least this should be true for essential actors. Lewis F. Richardson has tested this hypothesis empirically and has found a correlation between the number of frontiers of states and the number of wars in which they were involved.[4]

The second of the factors to be mentioned in this section which is important for the power of states is territorial size. The size of territory is, first, one of the important determinants of the available natural resources, the growth potential of the population and of the economy. Size of population and economy are themselves causes responsible for the strength or weakness of a country. Second, the size of the territory of a state is sometimes a decisive factor for the success or failure of military operations. There can be no doubt that Britain would have been able to throw down the American Revolution, had the USA at that time been of about the territorial size of France, and, say, been composed of New England and the state of New York. As another example, Napoleon as well as Hitler would have succeeded with their military campaigns against Russia, had this country ended just behind Moscow and the river Don. World history would thus have taken a completely different course if the territories of these two states had been of about the same size as those of the other big powers.

If we take the influence of location, of natural boundaries and of territorial size together we find that the chances of success and even of survival of states in a balance of power system depend critically on the combination of these factors. A state of only moderate size, of no or scarcely any natural boundaries and of only moderate size has certainly a much lower possibility to expand and even to survive than other states suffering less of these disadvantages. It requires statesmen of exceptional quality to compensate for such disadvantages by forming adequate alliances and by laying the foundations to develop a strong economy able to sustain the heavy armaments necessary to keep up with all the strong neighbors. It would be surprising if such superior statesmanship would be available all the time, from generation to generation. Looking at the problems from this perspective it is not surprising that the European Balance of Power System broke down with the final defeat and dissolution of Austria-Hungary and Germany which had all the natural weaknesses referred to above.

The last factor to be discussed in this section is the size of the population of states. A strong military establishment can only be built up if enough soldiers are available or can be drafted and if the economy is big enough to support the army with the arms needed. Excluding the possibility of hiring foreign mercenaries, which is in any case a precarious means, the number of men available for military service is directly dependent on the size of the population. The potential capacities of the domestic economy are also related to this size.

What counts, however, if we look at the relative power of states, is not the absolute numbers of their populations, but their relative sizes. Now the relative sizes of the populations of states have often undergone rather drastic changes. If we compare for instance the population of Europe and Asiatic Russia taken together with that of the North American continent, we find that the former had 192 million inhabitants in 1800, the latter, however, only 6 million. This gives a relation of 32:1. In 1960 the population of Europe and Asiatic Russia had grown to 640 and that of North America to 200 million,[5] reducing the relation to 3.2:1, a tenfold increase in favor of the former, reflecting especially the increasing relative strength of the United States.

To be more specific, let us look at the figures given in Table 3.3. The upper figures refer to the size of the populations in millions, whereas the lower figures give their relations compared to the population of France. Thus the latter measure the relative sizes of the populations compared to that of France, which was around 1800 the strongest power in the world. The table shows two facts: First, the relative decline of French power as far as it is caused by population changes; secondly, the relative decline of all the big European states compared to Russia and the USA (see Figure 3.1). Thus the relative population of Great Britain increased from 1790/1801 to 1937 from 0.38 to 1.12, that of Prussia/German Reich from 0.32 to 1.61 (1.64 in 1913/14). But these changes are dwarfed by the relative growths of the populations of the USA (from 0.19 in 1790/1801 to 3.95 in 1970/72) and Russia (from 1.68 1838/39 to 4.69 1970/72); earlier figures would make the picture even more impressive.

We recall that Alexis de Tocqueville's prediction of 1835 was mainly based on the relative developments of populations as well as of the respective territories (Tables 3.2 and 3.3).

Table 3.1: Development of Prussian, Austrian-Hungarian and Russian Territories until 1800 (in square km)

Year	Austria-Hungary	Brandenburg/Prussia	Russia
1520	99 414	38 130	2 300 000
1550/90		39 413	12 400 000
1740	473 400	118 926	
1786		194 891	
1796		305 669	19 400 000
1815	537 640	278 042	

Table 3.1 shows clearly that whereas Brandenburg/Prussia and Austria-Hungary showed a significant growth of their territorries from 1520 to

1815, this was just not of a comparable magnitude to the gigantic growth of the Russian Empire. After 1815 all the traditional European powers had about reached the limits of their territorial expansion (see Table (3.2), as was clearly realized by de Tocqueville in 1835.

Only Prussia was able to grow to about the size of France by using the problematic means of annexing the greater part of the rest of Germany and by excluding the German provinces of Austria. After that it was 'satiated' as Bismarck put it. Only the USA and Russia were able to grow further nearly unopposedly. Russia from 36 times the size of France in 1796 to nearly 41 times its size in 1970, and the United States from 3.75 times France's size to 14 times its size during the same period. A truly staggering change of relative power as far as it is determined by population and territory.

One may object to the above analysis that other powers were able, too, to expand by acquiring bigger and bigger colonial empires. Thus the British Empire comprised in 1900 the incredible area of 29 million square kilometers and a population of 397 million. Both figures are even much bigger than the corresponding figures for Russia and the United States (see Tables 3.2 and 3.3). But the colonial empires were built on sand as the developments during the decades since 1914 have amply shown. They could not be integrated with the home country into a coherent whole like in Russia and the United States because they were separated from it by big distances and the sea. They were perhaps more of a drain on the military and economic recources of the mother country than a help to increase them. It is interesting that already de Tocqueville did not take into account the possible colonial expansion of the European countries when he made his famous predictions.

Looking at the facts concerning the relative growth of territories and populations one again has the somewhat depressing feeling that the breakdown of the European Balance of Power System and the rise of the present bipolar world system was nearly inescapable. Even the other fact that only the German Reich and Japan had some small chance to thwart this development, seems to follow from the figures, especially from those concerning the relative growth of populations. This impression will be strengthened when we look at the development of the economic power bases of the essential states. We are thus thrown back to the fundamental question, whether the course of history has in fact been predetermined, whatever the leading political actors and responsible or irresponsible statesmen may have done.

Finally the figures in Tables 3.2 and 3.3 for Austria-Hungary, Germany and to a certain degree for Japan (here only as far as territory is concerned) show the weakening of the relative power positions of these countries as a consequence of the two world wars. These figures, of course, do not take into account the consequences of the division of the former states.

Table 3.2: Territories of France, United Kingdom, Prussia/German Reich, Austria-Hungary, Japan, Russia and USA (Million square km)

Country	1790/96	1810/11	1825	1850/53	1870/72	1898	1913	1937	1970
France (without colonies)	0.538		0.538	0.538	0.5365	0.5365	0.5365	0.551	0.552
	1		1	1	1	1	1	1	1
Great Britain and Ireland (without colonies)	0.312	0.312	0.312	0.312	0.312	0.312	0.312	0.243[3]	0.243[3]
	0.58		0.58	0.58	0.598	0.598	0.598	0.44	0.44
Prussia/German Reich[1] (without colonies)	0.306		0.278	0.278	0.541	0.541	0.541	0.47	0.356
	0.569		0.517	0.517	1.01	1.01	1.01	0.853	0.645
Austria-Hungary[2]			0.538			0.582	0.582	0.177	0.177
			1			1.085	1.085	0.321	0.321
Russia	19.4		20.2			22.4		21.2[4]	22.4
	36.06		37.55			41.75			40.58
USA	2.019	3.093		5.121					7.828
	3.75			9.52					14.18
Japan						0.417[5]	0.635[6]	0.635[6]	0.37
						0.777	1.184	1.152	0.67

Upper figures: million sq km.
Lower figures: size of territory relative to that of France.

1 From 1870/72–1937 German Reich, 1970 territories of Federal Republic of Germany and of German Democratic Republic
2 1937, 1970 territories of Austria and Hungary
3 1937, 1970 figures are lower because of the loss of the territory of the Irish Republic

4 1939
5 With Taiwan
6 With Taiwan and Korea

Table 3.3: Populations of France, United Kingdom, Prussia/German Reich, Austria-Hungary, Japan, Russia and USA

Country	1790/1801	1825	1850/53	1870/72	1897/1901	1913/14	1937	1970/72
France (without colonies)	27.4	30.5	35.8	36.1	38.5	39.6	41	51.5
	1	1	1	1	1	1	1	1
Great Britain and Northern Ireland (Ulster)[1] (without colonies)	10.5[2]	14.4	22.3	26.0	38.2	40.05	46[3]	53.8
	0.38	0.47	0.62	0.72	0.99	1.02	1.12	1.04
Prussia/German Reich[4] (without colonies)	8.7	10.4	19.6	41.1	56.4	64.9[6]	66[7]	78.5
	0.32	0.38	0.72	1.14	1.46	1.64	1.61	1.52
Austria-Hungary		21.7[5]	35[8]	35.7	45.5	51.3	15.4[9]	17.2
		0.71	0.98	0.99	1.18	1.30	0.38	0.33
Russia	39.0		60[8]		128	180.7	170.5[10]	241.7
	1.42		1.68		3.32	4.56	4.16	4.69
USA	5.3	11.3	23.2	38.6	76	92[11]	131.7[12]	203.2
	0.19	0.41	0.85	1.07	1.97	2.32	3.21	3.95
Japan			27	31	46.5	49.1[11]	73.1[12]	103.7
			0.754	0.859	1.208	1.24	1.783	2.01

Upper figures: in millions
Lower figures: size of populations relative to that of France
1 The figures until 1913/14 are too low, since only the population of Southern Ireland is included.
2 Without Northern Ireland
3 Average of the 1931 and 1951 figures, without Northern Ireland
4 Prussia until 1850/53, 1970/72 populations of Federal Republic of Germany and German Democratic Republic.
5 1817/18, without Italian provinces
6 1910
7 1933
8 1838/39
9 From 1937: Populations of Austria and Hungary. Hungary: 1930; Austria: 1934
10 1939
11 1910
12 1940

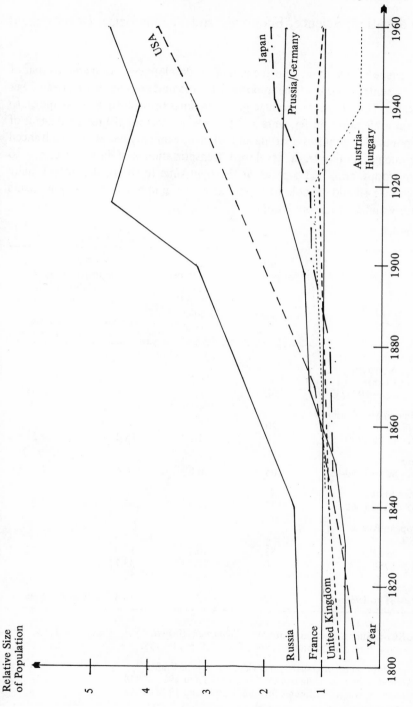

Figure 3.1: Relative Size of Population of Several Countries Compared to that of France (=1)

3. Education, Science, Economic and Technological Development

The degree of economic and technological development compared to that of other countries is one of the important factors determining the relative power of states. To be able to produce great amounts of sophisticated weapons, to sustain a big army during wars and to cater at least for the minimal needs of the population requires a strong and efficient economy based on an advanced technology. Moreover, a developed transportation system is necessary to carry troops, arms and supplies at the right time to the right places. Finally agriculture should be able to supply at least the minimal food requirements of army and civilian population.

Table 3.4

	Duration of period	Rate of growth per decade (%) of Total Product	Coefficient of multiplication of Total Product in a century	
			absolute	relative to France[1]
England and Wales/ United Kingdom				
1780 to 1881	101	28.2	12.0	
1855–59 to 1957/59	101	21.1	6.8	1.03
Germany/West Germany				
1851–55 to 1871–75	20	17.6		
1871–75 to 1960–62	88	31.1	15.0	2.27
France				
1841–60 to 1950–62	105.5	20.8	6.6	1
United States				
1839 to 1960–62	122	42.5	34.5	5.23
European Russia/ USSR				
1860–1913	53	30.2	14.0	2.12
1860–1958	98	32.73[2]	35.72[3]	5.41
Japan				
1879–81 to 1959–61	80	42	33.4	5.06

SOURCE: Simon Kuznets: *Modern Economic Growth*, Yale University Press, New Haven and London, 1967, Table 2.5, pp. 64–65.

[1] Absolute values of coefficient divided by that of France
[2] Weighted average of figures for 1860–1913 and 1913–1958
[3] Weighted average of figures for 1860–1913 and 1928–1958

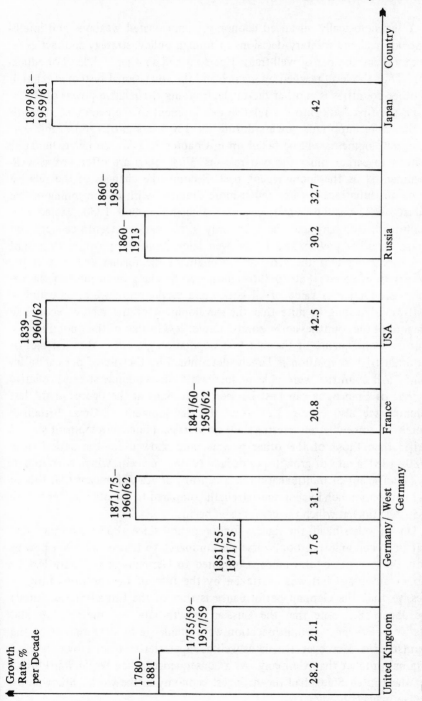

Figure 3.2: Growth Rates per Decade of Total Product of Several Countries

A technologically advanced economy, sophisticated weapons and intelligent political and military decisions in foreign policy, strategy and tactics require a great number of well-trained persons and a rather high level of education. Thus the level reached by science and the educational system in relation to other countries is another factor determining the relative power of states.

Let us first look into the relative development of the economic strength of the more important powers during the 130 years until 1960 (Table 3.4. Later developments will be taken up in Chapter 7.2). We do not extend our analysis to earlier times for two reasons: First, they are often not as well-documented as the more recent past. Second, the changes of the relative economic situations became much more dramatic with the beginning of the Industrial Revolution, which began in England around 1750, gained momentum in Germany and the USA only in the mid-nineteenth century and spread to other powers like Japan even later. Table 3.4 provides an insight into the changes of the economic strength of the former and present big powers from about 1850 to 1960, measured by the growth rates of the national products, the value of all goods and services produced in a country.

It is interesting to note that the development of the relative economic strength of the countries corresponds more or less to that of their populations. This is a consequence of the fact that population growth in the first part of the Industrial Revolution is largely determined by the rise of per capita incomes. All countries were able to increase their economic strength relative to that of France, as can best be seen by looking at the figures in the last column (see also Figure 3.2). Here the development of Great Britain is moreover, somewhat underestimated, since its economic development started earlier than those of the other powers, and showed for the period from 1780–1881 a rate of growth per decade of 18,2 percent, which corresponds to a coefficient of multiplication in a century of 12. This means that Britain had won very much in economic strength compared to the other states before 1850, the time at which the comparison begins.

On the other hand, the figures for the period since 1855 show that Great Britain's economic position worsened compared to that of all other powers with the exception of France. Compared to Germany it not only lost its former advantage but was overtaken by the turn of the century. More impressive than the German performance is that of the United States, Russia and Japan. But note that the Russian growth rate and the absolute and relative coefficients of multiplication were smaller until 1913 than were the German ones. Moreover, Russia as well as Japan started from a lower level of national product than Germany. As a consequence, when World War I broke out the United States had the strongest economy in the world, followed by the German economy.

Table 3.5: Production of Pig-Iron and Crude Steel in Several Countries: (1) Production of Pig-Iron (1000) metric tons)

Country	1870	1890	1900	1902	1938	1950	1966
France	1178 / 1	1962 / 1	2699 / 1	2427 / 1	6012 / 1	7767 / 1	15584 / 1
Great Britain	6059 / 5,14	8031 / 4,09	9052 / 3,35	8645 / 3,56	6870 / 1,14	9789 / 1,26	15561 / 0,999
Germany/West Germany	1341 / 1,18	4658 / 2,37	8521 / 3,16	8530 / 3,51	18046 / 3,0	11157 / 1,44	25413[2] / 1,63
Russia	358 / 0,304	746 / 0,38	2878 / 1,07	2493 / 1,03			70000 / 4,49
United States	1693 / 1,44	9348 / 4,76	14010 / 5,19	18106 / 7,46	19474 / 3,24	60217 / 7,75	83604 / 5,36
Austria-Hungary[1]	403 / 0,342	965 / 0,492	1312 / 0,486	1450 / 0,6	886 / 0,147	1383 / 0,172	3835 / 0,246
Japan					2677 / 0,445	2299 / 0,296	32018 / 2,05
China, People's Republic							14000 / 0,9

Table 3.5 (Continuation) (2) Production of Crude Steel (1000 metric tons)

Country	1938	1950	1966	1972
France	6216	8650	19591	23773[4]
	1	1	1	1
Great Britain	10565	16554	24704	25321
	1,67	1,91	1,26	1,065
Germany/West	22656	14020	35316	45040[3] [4]
Germany	3,64	1,62	1,8	1,895
Russia			96900	120700[5]
			4,95	5,08
United States	28805	87848	121632	120443[5]
	4,63	10,16	6,21	5,07
Japan	6472	4839	47770	93000[4]
	1,04	0,559	2,44	3,91
China, People's			12000	21000[5]
Republic			0,613	0,883

[1]   From 1938 combined production of Austria and Hungary
[2]   27861 together with production in German Democratic Republic
[3]   1966: 39397 and 1971: 50390 together with production in the German Democratic
       Republic
[4]   1970
[5]   1971

The second figures for each country and year give the production of pig-iron and crude steel relative to that of France.

The conclusions just drawn are confirmed if we look at the development of the production of pig-iron and steel in the different countries (Table 3.5 and Figure 3.3). The iron and steel industry has been selected because of the importance of iron and steel for the war industries, for construction and transportation.

There are several remarkable facts to be mentioned. The relative economic weakness of Russia and expecially of Austria-Hungary at the outbreak of World War I is reflected by their low relative pig-iron productions in 1902. Note, moreover that Germany produced more pig-iron and steel as France and Britain together in 1938. The low relative figures for Japan in 1938 show the economic weakness of this country when it entered World War II. The impressive increases in its pig-iron and steel production occured only after this war. Finally, the development of the productions of the United States (since 1870) and of the Soviet Union (after World

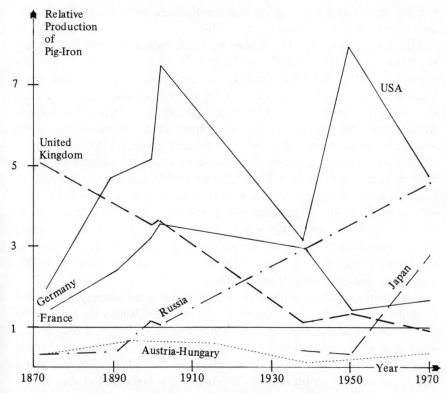

Figure 3.3: Relative Production of Pig-Iron in Several Countries Compared to that in France (=1)

Table 3.6: Percentage Share of Various Countries in Total Industrial Output of Market Economies (Without Centrally Planned Socialist Economies), 1938–1973

Country	1938	1950	1960	1973
United States	35,7	51,2	43,8	29,8
Great Britain	11,1	8,9	7,5	4,8
West Germany	10,6	5,8	9,1	14,1
France	6,2	4,3	4,9	7,5
Italy	2,8	2,0	2,9	3,6
Japan	4,2		ca. 4,2	ca. 10,0

SOURCE: Lars Anell: Recession – The Western Economies and the Changing World Order, London 1981.

War II) again dwarf those of the European states, even if the USA show a decline of their relative position after 1950.

The restrengthening of the relative economic position of (West) Germany and Japan since World War II (see Tables 3.5 and 3.6) raises the interesting question, whether these and possibly other countries with a medium-sized population (compared to that of the USA and Russia) and a relatively small territory may have a chance to reenter one day the group of big powers. We return to this question in the last chapter when we have to discuss the possible future development of the present world system.

Before leaving the economic situations of countries as a factor determining their relative powers we have to turn to the problem of economic autarchy. Even a highly developed economy is vulnerable if it depends on foreign sources for its food, raw material and energy needs. This is especially true in case of war, if the enemy is in a position to hinder the inflow of the scarce goods from abroad But as will be discussed in chapter 5, when we look at the means of foreign policy, the dependence may also be used by foreign powers for economic pressures and economic warfare.

The problems related with such a dependence were severely felt by the Central Powers during both World Wars when the British (later with the help of the Americans) set up an efficient blockade. Thus not only a food shortage developed in Germany and for its Allies, but also a shortage of goods of strategic importance for military purposes like salpeter (during World War I) and oil and gas (during World War II). The Japanese had similar problems during World War II, and Great Britain, too, experienced some problems for a time during which German submarines were successful.

Today Western Europe still finds itself in a rather precarious position since it is not self-sufficient for many goods. In 1974 it had to import 23 million metric tons of grain and 712 million metric tons of oil. Even the USA had to import 194 million metric tons of oil in the same year. Japan was, relatively speaking, even more dependent. We will return to the problems following from this lack of self-suffiency of several countries in chapters 5 and 7.

In the beginning of this section we have already mentioned the importance of the development of science and of the educational system of a country for its relative international power. It is, of course, difficult to measure the level reached by science and the educational system in any reliable way.

For this level is not only determined, say, by the number of scientists or the percentage of the population having attended university or high school. It depends, too, on the quality of the scientists and of the education. Still, some impression of the performance may be gained by looking at the number of Nobel prize winners from different countries). As can be seen from Table

3.7, Nobel prize winners were heavily concentrated in the leading western countries. It is interesting to note that the economic, political and scientific climate must have changed since the 1930s in favor of the USA, since the number of Nobel prizes awarded to citizens of this country increased strongly in the second period. This points to a well-known fact, namely, that the relative scientific importance of Germany, of France and of the whole Western Europe (only Great Britain is a notable exception) declined over the years, whereas the opposite was true for the United States. This is a fact which again points to reasons for the change of relative power between these countries.

Table 3.7: Number of Nobel Prize Winners from Some More Important Countries, 1901—1979 (According to citizenship at the time of award, only natural sciences and medicine)

Country	1901—1939	1940—1974
Austria	6	1
Denmark	4	3
France	16	5
Italy	3	2
Netherlands	8	2
Sweden	6	5
Germany	34	15
Switzerland	6	5
United Kingdom	23	36
Western Europe[1]	109	79
China	0	2
Japan	0	3
Russia/USSR	2	7
USA	14	104
All Other Countries	6	15

[1] Including Austria, Switzerland, Germany and Scandinavia without Finland.

SOURCES: *Encyclopaedia Britannica* 15th edition. Helen H. Benton, Publishers, Chicago and London, "Micropaedia", vol. VII, 1976 pp. 369—372 and *Grosser Brockhaus*, 18th edition, vol. 8, 1979.

4. Social and Political Organization

A final factor which is of great importance in determining the relative
power of states is their social and political organizations. The traditional
outlook and ideas of a people as conditioned by cultural heritage, religion
and historical experience, social and political institutions and organizations
all bear upon the shaping of its international aims, the determination and
persistance with which they can be followed and upon the morale, self-
reliance or obedience of its population. Even the images formed about
foreign countries and about international relations depend heavily on these
cultural patterns and on the social and political environment.

A few examples will make this clear. For the believer in Islam war against
unbelievers is a holy war and death in such a war brings with it heavenly
rewards. The famous islamic scholar Ibn Khaldûn wrote in his book *The
Muqaddimah* in the fourteenth century:

The first [kind of war] usually occurs between neighboring tribes and competing families.

The second [kind of war] − war caused by hostility − is usually found among savage
nations living in the desert. . . .

The third [kind of war] is the one the religious law calls 'the holy war'.

The fourth [kind of war], finally, is dynastic war against seceders and those who refuse
obedience.

These are the four kinds of war. The first two are unjust and lawless, the other two are
holy and just wars.[6]

It is obvious that if most of the population truly believe in such ideas,
this will not only shape their images of the enemy, of the unbelievers. But
the morale of the warriors during holy wars will also be strengthened. Moreover, foreign policy will be influenced by this idea of rightfully converting
the unbelievers by force and will tend to be rather expansionary. That such
a tendency can reassert itself has been proved by the first hundreds of years
of Islamic history, when the faithful warriors swept victoriously from Arabia
through North Africa to Spain and through Persia to India and Central Asia.

Morale is strengthened not only by the fact that men killed in the battles
of a holy war are considered to be martyrs, but also by the believe that

[the help of God] explains Muhammad's victory with small numbers over the polytheists
during his lifetime, and the victories of the Muslims during the Muslim conquests after
[Muhammad's death]. God took care of his Prophet. He threw terror into the hearts of
the unbelievers. [That terror,] eventually, seized control over their hearts, and they fled.
[This, then, was] a miracle wrought by god's messenger. Terror in the hearts of their
enemies was why there were so many routs during the Muslim conquests. . . .[7]

Finally, in the divine revelation to Muhammad (reported in the Quran), it is said:

God loves those who fight in His behalf in a line as if they were a strongly constructed building.[8]

Similar religious beliefs can be found during the Christian crusades to the Holy Land in the Middle Ages as well as in other periods. No doubt that they strengthen the military power of a state and allow it to follow, because of broad popular support, a more cohesive and permanent foreign policy bent towards aggression and expansion.

Assume, on the other hand, that sects like Jehovah's Witnesses, who consider it sinful to hurt or kill in war and are rather prepared to endure imprisonment or even to die than to fight 'enemies', are widespread in a country. Then the military, and as a consequence, the political and diplomatic power of a state is seriously weakened. The situation may even tempt potential aggressors, who were otherwise not in position to go to war or to apply war threats.

Similar effects can be brought about by a bad conscience arising from an unpopular war in the population, especially if the mass media of a modern state are — as in democracies — allowed to take up freely the issue of a 'dirty and unjust war' and to direct the attention of broad segments of the people to the ideas of the opponents of the war. Dissatisfaction and resentment may spread rapidly and soon undermine the war effort. All this happened in the United States as a consequence of the Vietnam War a few years ago. One recalls that this war was finally considered no longer to be a defensive war against communist aggressors, but was felt to be an unwarranted, unjust, dirty and bloody intervention into the affairs of a small country, perhaps even caused by capitalist forces wanting to extend or to preserve their profitable markets. Thus a conflict arose between the American's image of the war and the perception of his own country as the country of freedom and democracy, which should only wage war either against foreign aggression or to help to make democracy and peace more secure in the world. Remember the title of General Eisenhower's book about World War II, *Crusade in Europe* to get a feeling of the identity crisis, which arose from the fact that the United States was now, as a World Power, involved in the dirty international power business, in which countries could not be nicely separated into free countries and dictatorships and wars not into just and unjust wars.

The weakening of American power resulting from the identity crisis in the wake of the Vietnam War would probably not have happened, if the government had tightly controlled — like in Nazi Germany or in the Soviet Union — the mass media and not have allowed free speech and free expression of political ideas. Moreover, it is doubtful whether the USA would have reacted in the way they did, that is to end the war as soon as possible and at nearly any cost, if President and Congress had been independent of popular majorities. We have thus to conclude that the kind of organization of a country has a strong influence on its relative power and on its policies in international affairs, and that free democratic states have certain disadvantages compared to repressive oligarchies and dictatorships in conducting their foreign policies.

The latter fact has been recognised early by de Tocqueville in 1835. This is the more surprising, since the United States, which he studied as a democracy, was at that time still enjoying its isolated position on the American continent, following the advice given by Washington and Jefferson, to keep out of the quarrels of the European Balance of Power System. Let us quote here from de Tocqueville's work:

Since the Union does not mix into European affairs, it has as it were no foreign issues to debate, for it has not yet any powerful neighbors in America. . . .

It is, therefore, difficult to know presently which capabilities American democracy will develop in the conduct of foreign affairs of the state . . . .

As far as I am concerned I have no difficulty to say: it is in directing the foreign interests of society that democratic governments seem to me decidedly inferior to others . . . .

Foreign policy does not need any of the qualities which belong to democracy and demands by contrast the development of nearly all which it lacks. Democracy furthers the growth of the internal resources of the state; . . . it develops the public spirit, strengthens the respect for law in the different classes of society; all things which have only an indirect influence on the position of a people compared to another. But democracy can only with difficulty coordinate the details of a great enterprise, stick to a design and follow it obstinately through all obstacles. It is scarcely able to combine measures in secrecy and to wait for their result patiently. These are qualities belonging especially to one man or to an aristocracy. But these are precisely the qualities which lead a people as well as an individual towards domination. . . .

The inclination of a democracy to obey in politics feelings more than reasons, and to give up longterm designs for the satisfaction of a momentary passion, could be well observed in America when the French Revolution broke out. . . .

The sympathies of the people in favor of France declared themselves . . . with so much violence that it needed no less than the inflexible character of Washington and the immense popularity he enjoyed to prevent war being declared on England. . . .

If the constitution and the public favor had not given to Washington direction of the external affairs of the state, it is certain that the nation then would have done precisely what it condemns today.

Nearly all people, who have strongly influenced the world, have conceived, followed and executed grand designs, from the Romans to the British, have been directed by an aristocracy, and how should this be astonishing?

Of all things of the world it is aristocracy which is most fixed in its views. The mass of the people can be reduced by its passions; one can misuse the spirit of a king and let him vacillate between his projects; and, moreover, a king is not immortal. But an aristocratic body is too numerous to be captivated, but not numerous enough to give in easily to the intoxication of unreasoned passions. An aristocratic body is a firm and enlightened man who never dies.[9]

Here we find all the main elements, stemming from the political organization of states, which influence their relative power. Free democratic societies encourage innovation and the growth of the economy, both long-term factors able to strengthen the external powers of nations. But in democracies politicians are dependent on majorities to be elected or reelected, on majorities, who are ill-informed about and inexperienced in foreign affairs. Democracies are thus influenced by often changing popular passions and prejudices and, therefore, are scarcely able to follow clear-cut long-term designs in their foreign policies. This situation is made worse by the numerous personality changes characteristic of democracies, which bring again and again inexperienced politicians into office and make them responsible for the conduct of foreign affairs.

Aristocracies have all advantages in planning, following and executing long-term foreign policy goals. They usually lack however, the free environment necessary for internal innovation and development, a fact which often leads to long-term problems for the relative powers of their states. Kingdoms as well as dictatorships may from time to time have leaders, who are very capable and experienced in directing foreign affairs. But these leaders have often, like Louis XIV, Frederick II, or Bismarck no able successors, sometimes even as a consequence of their own overpowering stature. Other kings or dictators may vacillate more or less among the different advice given by several members of their favored entourage. Or, if they are stubborn, fanatic and not open to advice, they may like Hitler, ruin their countries with their misdeeds and blunders. Strictly controlled dictatorships or oligarchies — like modern planned economies of the Soviet type — show, moreover, a tendency to stifle initiative, innovation and efficient growth, and thus to erode the future relative power of their states.

Notes

[1] J. Bronowski: *The Ascent of Man*. Little, Brown & Co., Boston/Toronto 1973, pp. 79–80
[2] C.W.C. Oman: *The Art of War in the Middle Ages*. Revised and edited by John H. Beeler, Copyright 1953 by Cornell University Press. Great Seal Books, Ithaca, New York, 1963. First Ed. 1885. pp. 75–76.

[3] B.L. Lidell Hart: *Strategy*. Signet Book, New American Library, 1967, p. 14.
[4] Lewis F. Richardson: op. cit., pp. 177–183.
[5] The figures are taken from Simon Kuznets: *Modern Economic Growth*. Yale University Press, New Haven and London, 1967, p. 38.
[6] Ibn Khaldun: *The Muqaddimah, An Introduction to History*. Translated by Franz Rosenthal, Copyright (c) 1958 and 1967 by Princeton University Press, Princeton (N.J.), 1967, Vol. 11, p. 74.
[7] Ibn Khaldun: op cit., Vol. II, p. 86.
[8] Quran 61.4(4).
[9] Alexis de Tocqueville: *De la Democratie en Amerique*. Michel Lévy Frères, Paris, 1868. Vol. II, pp. 102–106.

Chapter 4

Aims of International Politics

It is often assumed without much thinking that states in their foreign policies have definite and specific aims like human beings. Now a state is nothing but an organization of a group of people living on a certain territory, whose representatives claim for it the monopoly of physical power. But an organization cannot have wishes or aims, it cannot feel or think, it cannot act like a person. Only its members can pursue certain ends and formulate compromises, which may be considered by many of them to be 'the ends' of their state. Other members, however, of this entity may have different ideas about the right aims of the same state and strongly oppose the execution of the compromises reached by their representatives, the government.

Looked at from this perspective, the state is no longer a real actor. For only people decide and only people act. True, the very existence of a given nation, its kind of organizational structure and its situation in the middle of other states, in an international system, may well influence the kinds of decisions taken by its members as well as those by members of other states. Restrictions created by the existence of states for human decisions concerning international politics may even be such that there is not much room left for an independent choice as to which aims should be followed by the state. If other states follow, for instance, an expansionary policy there may not be any choice but to reinforce the power of the actor's own state, to rearm, to form and to change alliances if the population wants to preserve its own national organization.

Moreover, the very existence of states and nations usually causes an identification of its members with this organization. Most people feel themselves to be, say, Swiss, Chinese or Americans. Not only their perceptions of the world, of other nations, of 'foreigners' and of 'compatriots' is shaped by the loyalty engendered by this identification, but also the kind of national goals which are arrived at in internal political processes.

Problems also arise because decisions taken by the government as representative of the state in international affairs are mostly an outflow of the choices made by several people. Everybody who can influence these decisions may have a quite rational and consistent set of preferences concerning the foreign policies to be followed. But the outcome of the collective decision process and, as a consequence, foreign policy may, in spite of this private rationality, be irrational and inconsistent. To make clear what is meant, let us consider an example:

Recall the situation just before the outbreak of World War I. The Crown Prince of Austria-Hungary, Archduke Ferdinand, had been murdered by Serbian nationalists. Austria-Hungary sent an ultimatum to Serbia to demand the extradition of the assassins. The government in Belgrade proved to be stubborn and depended for its attitude on Russia's decision whether to honor its alliance with Serbia, in case war with Austria-Hungary should break out because of non-compliance with the ultimatum.

For Germany the situation looked as follows. First, it had an alliance with Austria-Hungary. Second, there existed an alliance between France and Russia. Finally the German General Staff had years before prepared a plan (under General Schlieffen) to attack and to throw down first France and then to turn against Russia in case of war. The reason for this plan had been the fact that the Russian railway system was less developed than the German and it thus took the Russians a longer time than the Germans to bring their armies into position. The Schlieffen plan sought to use this extra time to defeat France before Russia could employ her full forces on the Eastern Front.

The Germans had thus roughly speaking three options:

A. Preserve peace even at the cost of breaking the alliance with Austria-Hungary.
B. Enter the war as required by the treaty, if Russia should declare war on Austria-Hungary, but do not declare war on France.
C. If Russia makes war with Austria-Hungary declare war on both Russia and France to be able to use the Schlieffen plan.

Now assume that, contrary to historical fact, only three persons, the German Emperor, the Chancellor and the Chief of the General Staff, had to make the German decision and that they had the following preferences concerning the three alternatives:

Emperor	Chancellor	Chief of Staff
A	B	C
B	C	A
C	A	B

The most preferred alternative is on top and the least preferred at the bottom of the three columns. The Emperor is peace-loving and prepared to violate even the treaty with Austria-Hungary. The Chancellor thinks that treaties must be kept at all cost not to undermine the credibility of German foreign policy. But he wants to limit the war as far as possible and not to declare war on France. The Chief of the General Staff agrees with the Chancellor as far as the credibility of Germany as an alliance partner is concerned. But he is convinced that France will honor its alliance with Russia to regain Alsace-Lorraine. And he thinks that there is no hope for the German army to win the war if the Schlieffen plan is not exacted. Thus he wants to declare war on Russia and France or otherwise to preserve peace.

The Emperor does not have a very strong character and is, therefore, prepared to follow the advice of the Chief of Staff and the Chancellor if both of them have the same opinion. Given this situation, the outcome of the decision depends more or less on chance. Let us assume that the Emperor proposes that they should first decide whether to keep peace or to have war only with Russia, and then secondly to put the alternative chosen in their first decision against the third alternative, a general war with both Russia and France. Now, if the three follow this procedure, a general war with Russia and France would be chosen, since two of the three prefer first A to B, and then C to A. The outcome would be different, however, if the Emperor wanted first to decide the question, whether a general war or peace were better, and then to compare the ensuing alternative with the remaining one, limited war with Russia only. In this case a majority of them would first prefer C to A, and then another one B to C. Thus limited war would be selected. Finally, if they would first decide whether in case of war limited or general war should be waged, and only then decide between the winner among these two alternatives and the peace alternative, then peace would be preserved. For Emperor and Chancellor both prefer war against Russia (B) to war against Russia and France (C), whereas Emperor and Chief of Staff prefer peace (A) to a limited war (B).

The outcome of the example obviously depends on the question among which pair of the three alternatives the first of the two decisions is taken. It depends thus either on chance or on some clever person understanding the relationship sketched above, who arranges the sequence of the decisions according to his own preferences.

The relationship illustrated by the example is the simplest case of a very general relationship called cyclical and, therefore, inconsistent group preferences. It can happen in each case in which three or more people have to choose between three or more alternatives. For three alternatives we have from the above example:

$$A \; P \; B \; P \; C \; P \; A \; ,$$

where P means 'preferred by a majority of the decisionmaking group'. It follows from the relationship that A is indirectly preferred to itself by the group, which means that the preferences of the group are inconsistent. As a consequence, in all cases in which at least three persons have to decide between at least three alternatives, either contradictory decisions may be taken by 'the state' over time or the decisions taken may be determined more or less by chance. It is, therefore, highly improbable that states always follow a coherent and consistent foreign policy, even if all the people involved act perfectly rational. This tendency is, of course, reinforced by the fact that the composition of the body of people participating in foreign policy changes over time.

Things are easier if there is only one person deciding foreign policy for a long period. This is the case if a king, absolute monarch, a dictator or a very dominant Prime Minister rule. Examples were Frederick II of Prussia, Louis XIV of France, Napoleon, Metternich, Bismarck and Stalin. 'L'état c'est moi', 'I am the state', a sentence attributed to Louis XIV illustrates this situation. But things are different, if the kings and dictators are weak or stupid. And even the capable ones have no eternal lives. Thus consistent policies may have a better chance in an aristocracy, where inconsistencies and contradictions are not as probable as in a democracy, first because of the greater similarity of the preferences of the people belonging to such a group and, secondly because of its smaller number.

We have seen that the state as an organization cannot decide and act on its own but only 'through' human beings. It can thus be considered not to be an actor at all in international politics. From this perception it is only a small step to the idea that other more or less organized human groups, classes or even superhuman entities like Multinational Corporations, Unions, The Churches, The Jews, International Finance, God and The Devil, The Proletariat and Capitalism are the real actors on the international stage. In this case The State is only used by them as an instrument to promote the work of The Devil or of Capitalism. It is obvious that when such a view of reality is taken, the aims of foreign policy are seen from a quite different perspective. There may even exist no aims of this kind. Nations may just be impelled by these forces into certain directions of foreign policy, and even into wars, without anybody having planned or foreseen the consequences. We will have to keep these as well as the other problems mentioned above in mind when we discuss different aims of foreign policy in the following sections.

1. Limited Aims: The Nation State

The aims of most states have been rather limited during long periods of human history. States often just strived to preserve their own independence and their own territory, and perhaps to get some neighboring provinces by marriage or inheritance (this was quite common when princes still ruled as absolute monarchs), or by war, if this could be done without too much risk.

We have already discussed Bismarck's policy to strengthen Prussia by territorial expansion (mainly at the cost of some smaller German states) and by 'unifying' Germany without risking a protracted war in which an alliance could be formed against Prussia. After reaching these aims Bismarck thought Prussia/Germany to be satiated and pursued a course of utmost restriction.

Another good example of limited foreign policy objectives is provided by the secret testament of King Frederick II of Prussia in 1752. Under the heading 'Political Reveries' Frederick writes:

... Politicians, too, are allowed to promenade in the infinite fields of phantasmic designs. For they may become reality from time to time, if one does not lose sight of them and if several generations striving towards the same aim, are skilful enough to hide their intentions thoroughly against the curious and sharp-sighted eyes of the European powers.

Machiavelli says that an altruistic power which is situated between ambitious powers will finally perish. Unfortunately I have to concede that Machiavelli is right. Princes must of necessity be ambitious, but this ambition must be sagacious, moderate and enlightened by reason...

The House of Brandenburg has undisputable rights of succession in the principalities of Ansbach and Bayreuth ....

Our claims on the dukedom of Mecklenburg are as clear ....

Of all countries in Europe Saxony, Polish Prussia and Swedish Pommerania have to be taken most into consideration [for annexation], for all three would round off the state.

Saxony would be the most useful ....

Next to Saxony, Polish Prussia would be the most advantageous. It now divides Pommerania from East Prussia and hinders to defend this province first because of the barrier of the Vistula river and secondly because of the threat of a landing of Russian troops in the harbour of Danzig ....

I do not think it appropriate to conquer this province by arms; ... Poland is a kingdom where the king is elected [by the aristocracy]; at the death of each king it is torn apart by factional struggles. This fact has to be exploited and one has to acquire once another town, once another region for the price of keeping neutral, until everything has been swallowed. ...

Acquisitions with the pen are always preferable to those with the sword. One is less exposed to contingencies and neither harms one's purse nor one's army. . . .

Next to the two countries mentioned, Swedish Pommerania would be the most advantageous for us. Its acquisition could only be reached by treaties.[1]

The Prussian kings and governments obviously followed the limited ends set by Frederick. He himself succeeded to gain Western (Polish) Prussia without the cities of Danzig and Thorn during his lifetime. The latter two cities were acquired in 1793. Swedish Pommerania and about one half of Saxony were seceded to Prussia at the Vienna Peace Congress in 1815.

If one looks at the periods of history during which limited aims of states dominated, one gets the impression that they were usually periods in which multi-polar or balance of power systems were present. In multi-polar systems no state is strong enough to follow very ambitious expansionary goals. At least for a limited time-span ends have to be rather modest to prevent the formation of too strong a coalition against the aggressive state. The same is even more important in a balance of power system, where alliances against too expansionary and too strong essential members are easily formed. Thus statesmen have to learn in time to limit their aims or they run a great risk of ruining instead of expanding their states, a fact clearly seen by Frederick II, and by Bismarck. In cases in which this knowledge was no longer present, defeat or even ruin of the nation followed as in the cases of Napoleon and Hitler.

We conclude that there is a strong feedback of the prevailing international system on foreign policy aims of states. Since too ambitious plans (too ambitious at least in terms of time) end usually in defeat, a kind of selection process is at work in multipolar and balance of power systems furthering states and statesmen who are prepared to pursue limited aims only and to move very cautiously in doing so. Limited aims lead to a limitation of means, including a limitation of warfare in time and space.

This does not imply, however, that the ends followed remain limited if one of the states gains slowly more and more relative power over time. This is especially true in cases in which the growth of power has scarcely been noticed by the other essential actors, like in the cases of Ch'in, Rome, Russia and the USA. Then such a nation may change its aims and embark on an outright policy of universal domination. Or it may be slowly dragged – as in the case of the USA – into world power politics, because it cannot help but do so as the only other remaining power in a bipolar system.

Let us conclude by pointing out that in rare cases a breakdown of a given international system may result just because the aims of states have been changed to quite a different dimension from the ends of preserving independence or to acquiring this or that province. These more 'exciting' goals may be the 'winning of the world for democracy', 'delivering it from the scourge of capitalism' or by 'converting it to the true belief into the One God, Allah'. We will turn to these 'unlimited aims' in section 3.

2. Expansionist Aims: The Nation State and Economic Interests

Some states may follow a policy of cautious, others of reckless expansion (with all the dangers implied by the latter policy for themselves). As a con-

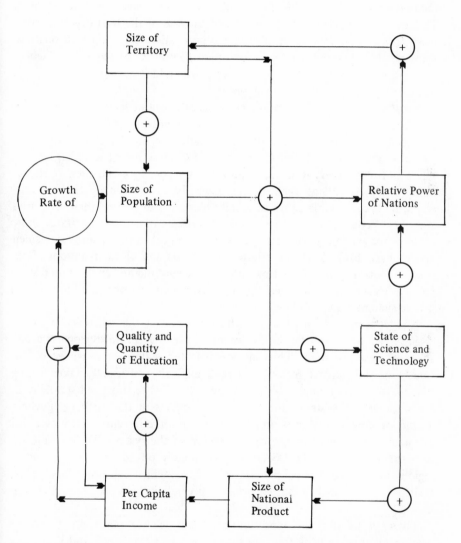

Figure 4.1: Interrelationships between Territory, Population, National Product, Education, Science and Technology and Relative Power

sequence more peaceful states have to heed against the possible threats resulting from such a policy not only for the present but also for the future.
Their future relative power positions are mainly determined by their strength
as measured by size of territory and population, economic development
and the level of education, science and technology. The latter have usually
a positive influence on the state of the economy, which is itself one of the
factors responsible for the quality of education, science and technology.
The level of economic development and the size of the territory are, moreover, factors determining the size of the population. The supposed relationships are described in Figure 4.1. Note that the positive or negative influences
assumed correspond to the empirical facts which have been usually observed,
but that they are not theoretically necessary.

Because of these relationships even peaceful states have to strive for an
expansion at least of their economies and, if possible, of their territories,
just to keep up their relative future strength compared to the nations with
expansionary aims. It follows, that not only states aiming to enlarge themselves but also others wanting to preserve independence and their territory,
have to try to enlarge their future power bases to keep up their relative
strength. They are able to do so mainly by trying to expand their territories
and their economies. As a consequence systems of competing states show
an inherent tendency for power to become a goal in itself, since statesmen
always have to look at the relative future position of their nations. Thus
original aims may recede in time into the background and an unlimited striving for extending power may gain predominance in the thinking of the
people shaping foreign policy.

Now it is very difficult to gain territory against the resistance of other
essential actors, a resistance always present in the central region of a balance of power system. Thus all sophisticated statesmen move very cautiously in this central region, and it is difficult and usually takes a long
time — if it is not impossible — to increase one's territory substantially in
the core of the system. But often other regions of the earth exist where
a kind of power vacuum is present and where other essential actors are not
as much interested as in the central region of the system. We have already
seen that Russia and the USA expanded mainly outside the system and in
regions in which either people and tribes lived, which enjoyed a less sophisticated level of civilization, or where only relatively weak countries were
present.

There exists thus an opportunity to gain relative power by trying to
acquire territory outside the core system of competing states and in regions
where a relative power vacuum prevails. This route has been followed several
times in history, and explains at least partly the colonial imperialism followed

by European powers from the sixteenth up to the early twentieth century. The acquisition of colonial empires meant not only more territory, but also additional population and often − at least in the perception of many politicians and civilians − secure markets for the products of their industries and raw materials needed by them as inputs.

From this it is easy to understand that the aim to increase or to preserve relative power drove statesmen towards overseas colonial expansion, for this expansion went on in regions where a relative power vacuum prevailed. Such an expansion held, therefore, less risk of involving states in severe conflicts with other essential members of the system. This does not mean that no such conflicts ever happened. But it is true that they became numerous only towards the end of the period, when nearly all easily available territories on the globe had been bought, conquered or annexed by the big powers. And even then the conflicts arising over colonial territories were not as vital as conflicts over expansions in the core region.

Colonial imperialism can be promoted because of other reasons. Some people have claimed that all foreign policies, including colonial expansion and wars are nothing but an outflow, a consequence of economic interests. Especially Marxists see all political developments only from this perspective. According to them states are not independent actors but just instruments used by the class dominating at a given time to pursue its own economic interests. The political ideas followed in foreign policies as well as the organizational forms applied are just a consequence of the economic forces at work. The capitalist class dominates modern industrialized countries at least since about 1800. It is involved in a class struggle with the proletarian class, the workers, and has itself defeated the feudal class, which dominated the state before.

In the course of further economic development the proletarian class will gain power in a series of economic crises and revolutions, and remove the outdated modes of production instituted by the capitalist class striving for profit. The ensuing socialist society will need no longer the instrument 'state' to oppress other classes as soon as it has established communism everywhere in the world. States will wither away and with them the age-old scourge of imperialism and war.

What are the forces driving foreign policy according to this theory? It is well-known that the labor theory of value is the basis of Marx's system. This theory asserts that socially necessary labor determines the value of all goods including that of labor and the worker (labor force) itself. In a capitalist society, workers have no ownership of the means of production. These belong to the capitalists, to whom they have, therefore, to sell their labor. But capitalists pay less for labor than the value of the goods produced by a worker during a working day. The difference, the surplus value, is kept by them as their profit. This exploitation of workers is possible because the value of the goods needed by them for their reproduction (including their own and their children's food, housing, clothing and education) is lower than that of the goods produced by them. But how is it possible that capitalists have to pay lower wages than the value of what workers produce? Would not their competition for labor drive up wages? Such a development is prevented by several factors. First, the worker has to sell his labor since it is his only source of income. Second, capitalists use their profits mainly for investments to increase their capital stock, that is their machinery and plants. But the use of more machines puts workers out of jobs, creates an industrial reserve army and leads through the competition of the unemployed to the low level of wages corresponding to the value necessary for the reproduction of labor.

What is the relevance of all this for foreign policy, imperialism and imperialistic wars among capitalistic states? It follows from the above arguments that the total income and therefore the total expenditures of workers are lower than the value of the products produced. Thus there must be an excess production of goods leading with the accumulation of capital in the course of time to more and more severe crises, since the workers cannot buy all the consumer goods produced. The situation of the proletariat becomes worse and worse, leading to an awareness by more and more workers of their class situation and of capitalist exploitation. Unrest and revolutions spread following deeper and deeper crises and lead finally to the overthrow of capitalism and the victory of socialism.

But before this can happen imperialism helps the capitalistic class to gain some breathing time. For outside the industrialized states exist underdeveloped regions in a pre-capitalistic condition. It is thus possible to get rid of the surplus production of the capitalist countries in these less advanced parts of the world. Moreover, since these regions pay with raw materials, inputs become cheaper in industrialized countries. The impoverishment of the working masses in the capitalist states is retarded. There may be even an increase of the standard of living of the domestic proletariat. The accumulation of capital goes on, for some time even without crises. An inflow of population may take place, which allows the creation of a greater surplus value and of higher profits.

But in time colonial regions will be more and more integrated into the capitalistic process, and their populations become proletarianized. Crises recur with increasing severity. Even before this happens, national imperialism by the capitalistic states has followed the economic penetration of underdeveloped countries. This political and militaristic imperialism increases the danger of war since it leads to a confrontation of capitalist states in the colonial regions.

To protect the home markets so important to capitalists because of excess production, import duties are introduced and increased. Because of these new obstacles to international trade, competition for the unprotected colonial markets becomes stronger, strengthening in turn the tendencies to gain colonies and to close them to imports from other capitalist countries. This then, is the Marxist explanation of colonial expansion, of the tendencies to limit free trade, of the increased danger of wars and of the final outbreak of imperialistic wars between capitalist nations. To quote Lenin:

The question of imperialistic wars, of the international policy of the finance capital dominating today all over the world, which inevitably causes new imperialistic wars, brings about inevitably an incredible strengthening of national suppression, of the plundering, exploitation and choking of the weak, retarded, small peoples by a few 'advanced' powers – this question has become a cornerstone of the policy of all countries of the globe since 1914. It is for dozens of millions of men a question of life or death.[2]

It follows, according to Marxist theory, that foreign policy is an outflow of the inevitable historical process driving world history towards the final destruction of class society, of capitalism and towards socialism and communism, the final state of socialism, in which the state has withered away, and in which all oppression, exploitation and wars come to an end.

Marxist analysis has fascinated many people. But is it correct? We believe not. It certainly contains some partial truths, but the general theory and its results have been disproved by the empirical facts. Labor is not the only factor determining the value of goods. Everybody looking at the prices of scarce natural resources like oil realizes at once that they are higher than the labor costs necessary to produce them. Thus there are other scarce original factors of production besides labor determining the value of goods. The labor theory of value is wrong and with it all conclusions about the surplus value flowing to capitalists as profits. Second, there has been no increasing impoverishment of workers, but real wages have risen incredibly during the last hundred years in developed countries. As a consequence the purchasing power of the population has risen strongly and no surplus production which has been increasing all the time has been observed. But if this is true, then the necessity of colonial expansion as an indispensable outlet for surplus production in pre-capitalistic countries does not follow. The same is true for the increasing probability of war as a consequence of confrontations following from colonial expansion and for the need to protect home markets against foreign surplus production. Other facts corroborate this criticism of Marxist theory. Why were the colonial powers able and willing to give up their colonial empires after World War II and why did they not suffer terrible economic crises as a consequence, but were able to increase their wealth beyond the wildest dreams of everybody?

Probably to explain some of these discrepancies of the Marxist theory of imperialism from real developments, some Marxist thinkers have developed a theory of neo-colonialism during the last decades. To present this adapted version of Marxism, it is perhaps best to quote one of its proponents, James Petras:[3]

In the neoclassical phase, national independence and the formation of the nation state [in developing countries] led to the creation of social strata between imperial capitalism [coming from developed capitalist countries] and the labor force. Drawn from a variety of sources, including political movements, the university, the army, the civil service, this social strata is representative of the propertyless 'intermediary' groups; rooted in the state bureaucracy, it has access to powers of the state, including revenues and expenditures. The impulse to personal property ownership and affluence through derivative 'ownership' via association with metropolitan enterprises [i.e. from developed capitalist countries] or through directorships in state enterprises creates the basis for negotiated conflict between imperial/nationalist social strata on the one hand and on the other hand by enlarging the scope of the class relationship, heightening tension within the periphery between these intermediary strata and the labor force. Imperial capital exploitation mediated by internal class forces creates and multiplies contradictions and disguises them. Imperial policy [of developed capitalist countries] is oriented toward manipulating national 'intermediaries' as a protective covering, whereas the dominant national strata struggle to increase their social preponderance, vis-à-vis their own labor force. (p. 41)

The post-independence national regime can choose among at least three strategies or types of class alliances for capital accumulation. In the first instance, it can join with imperial firms and regimes in intensifying surplus extraction from the labor force through a variety of . . . working relationships outlined under the . . . rubric of dependent neo-colonialism. An alternative strategy for the national regime involves extracting the surplus from the labor force and limiting or eliminating the share going to imperial firms, thus concentrating it in the hands of state and/or private national entrepreneurs. This approach, which can be referred to as national developmentalism without redistribution, leads to concentration of income within the national class hierarchy. A third alternative is for the national regime to ally itself with the laboring population, extend the areas of national control (through nationalization), reinvest the surplus of the national economy, or promote a redistribution of income within the national class structure.

The type of class alliance on which the national regime rests and the strategy for capital accumulation directly affect the distribution of income. Capital accumulation from above and outside (what can be called the 'neocolonial model') results in an income structure that resembles an inverted pyramid – with wealth and power concentrated in the hands of foreign capital. The national bourgeois developmental approach, which capitalizes on the foreign elite and the national labor force, concentrates income among the intermediary strata (in the form of the governing elite . . .), leading to income distribution in the shape of a diamond.

The alliance between national intermediaries and the labor force, which can be referred to as a 'national-popular' strategy, leads to a broader based society in which income is more diversified, spreading downward and taking the shape of a pyramid. (pp. 43–44)

It is obvious that this way of analysis has moved far away from traditional Marxist theory. True, it does cling to the Marxist labor theory of value and its theory of exploitation, which has been rejected above. But now a new group of people, the governing elite controlling the developing nation, are seen as a decisive actor. They are able to determine to a smaller or greater degree the relations with capitalist centers and can appropriate and distribute part or nearly the total of the surplus value produced by domestic labor. This is certainly a picture contrasting with the traditional Marxist pattern, for the new and partly decisive elite is not a class in the sense of Marxist tradition, a fact explicitly mentioned by Petras. But if this is true, then parts of his analysis may be accepted after the remaining Marxist background has been removed. In fact, the reader will find that there are some resemblances of our approach (compare section 3) concerning the relations between developed capitalist and developing countries to that taken by Petras.

A Marxist theory should be able to explain, as pointed out before, why developed capitalist countries were prepared to give up their colonial empires after World War II, i.e. why the forces of imperialism pictured by traditional Marxist theory did not work any longer. Moreover, such an approach should point out why the capitalist retreat was not followed in the newly independent countries by socialist regimes, by the dominance of the proletariat, but by that of a small group of nationalist leaders.

There seems to be no adequate Marxist answer to the first question, which will, however, be answered by our approach (in the remaining part of this section). For the second question some answer is available:

Nationalism emerged largely as a result of the low degree of social differentiation within the colonies, leading to the amalgamation of various class and preclass forces. The existence of subsistence farmers and their general isolation from political life contributed to making the land question less pressing than the national question. As a result, political organization was confined to the urban petty bourgeoisie, products of commercial and administrative expansion. The predominance of the petty bourgeoisie, the small size of the proletariat and its relative isolation from the peasantry created circumstances in which the tradition of class struggle was much weaker than nationalist politics. The large concentrations of urban petty capitalists and state employees over and against the industrial proletariat set the tone and direction of independence politics. (Petras, p. 42)

I leave it to the reader whether he is satisfied with this explanation. But it certainly does not contribute much to explain the withdrawal of the former colonial powers from their empires.

Let us return to our critique of the Marxist theory of imperialism. According to this theory wars are just a consequence of class struggles and will end with the final victory of socialism and the demise of capitalism. Thus tensions and wars should not arise between socialist nations. But this is exactly what happened after World War II.

Tensions and even border-fighting arose among 'socialist' countries like China and Russia or China and Vietnam; war was waged between Vietnam and Cambodia, both socialist states; and insurrections against the hard-line communist regimes arose in East Germany, Hungary, Czechoslovakia and were only suppressed by Russian military forces in the 1950s and 1960s. Who would believe that all these problems were just brought about by the hidden capitalistic class enemy? But if this critique and the interpretation of facts presented are true then Marxism can neither explain foreign policy including colonial expansion, imperialism and war, nor is it able to take into account the tensions, insurrections and wars happening between and in 'socialist' nations.

Having drawn this conclusion it is important to ask whether our critique of Marxism implies that economic factors do not influence the aims of foreign policy, colonial expansion, imperialism and the outbreak of wars. The answer to this question is certainly 'no'. For, there exists, as has already been shown, a strong tendency in a system of competing states to increase not only territory and population, but also to strengthen their relative economic position. This may lead to colonial imperialism, which may in its turn, because of the confrontation arising from it, involve the big powers in international tensions and wars, especially when nearly all easily accessible countries have already been annexed.

But this is not all. There exist certainly domestic economic interests trying to promote colonial expansion through internal political processes which are more or less independent of considerations of preserving or enlarging the relative international power of their country.

To understand the working of these internal political forces, we have to look at countries with a specified political and economic system. Thus let us assume that a given industrialized country enjoys a growing economy and a free market system combined with a democratic political process. Because of the latter, politicians and thus government parties and opposition parties have to try to win the support of at least a majority of votes during the next elections to preserve or to win governmental powers. They will, therefore, as government parties enact and as opposition parties propose policies attracting enough voter support to reach this aim, which is a precondition for pursuing any other goals the politicians and their parties may have.

In a growing market economy there are always some industries which are under pressure. These are usually sectors of the economy which have flourished in earlier times but for whose products demand has been saturated in the course of time. The first such industry has been agriculture, then textiles, coal and steel, and nowadays the automobile industry. The reasons for these developments are easy to understand. Technical, organizational and institutional developments lead to increasing productivity which brings about higher real wages and incomes. Now people do not want to spend all their additional incomes on food, but prefer to buy more textiles and better housing. Thus the textile and housing industries expand, whereas agriculture stagnates. Later, with further real income increases, the additional demand turns to automobiles, to radio and television sets, to travelling, etc. The textile and later the automobile and television industries begin to stagnate, whereas the computer industry flourishes. This process goes on as long as innovation and economic growth takes place.

The stagnating and sometimes even shrinking industries have to pay about the same increasing real wages as the other sectors of the economy. To be able to do so they have, because of lagging demand, to raise their productivities. Or, to put it in other words, they have to produce the same amounts of goods with less workers and, given the stagnating demand for their products, to reduce their work-force. Taken together, the following picture emerges. In a growing economy, one industry after the other enters a period of stagnation with lagging demand and increasing labor costs. Because of the former it cannot increase the prices of its products much so that its profits come under pressure and may even turn to losses. To decrease costs it has to lay off workers. Some may leave on their own, too, because real wages are somewhat lagging in this sector, and look for employment in the new, rapidly expanding industries. Thus, incomes and profits are under pressure and job security is threatened.

The situation just sketched is not without consequences for the political process. Workers, managers and capitalists of the lagging industries will hold the government responsible for their situations and vote together with their families against government parties, if the ruling politicians do not take measures against the plight of the lagging industry. The politicians of the opposition party will realize their chances to make proposals for adequate help. As a consequence the government parties have to propose measures themselves so as not to lose the upcoming elections.

The best way to help export industries is obviously to promote exports, whereas import-competing industries can be assisted by increasing import duties or by introducing import quota. This will in both cases keep up or increase domestic prices for the products of these industries and lead to bigger sales because of higher exports or of lower competing imports. The foreign firms and their workers hurt by these policies have no right to vote in the respective country and can, therefore, be neglected by politicians.

But what about domestic consumers who suffer from the higher prices and who are more numerous than the people benefitting from them? Will they not vote against the government parties introducing the export promoting and import reducing measures? In a developed industrialized country this has not to be expected. For there exists a very large number of consumer goods and the expenditures on each of them amount only to a small fraction of household budgets. Thus consumers have scarcely an incentive to inform themselves about the reasons of higher prices, especially since their influence on political decisions as one among millions of voters is very small, indeed. It just does not pay to be well-informed as long as the higher expenditures are rather small and are smaller than the rise of real disposable income following from the growth of the economy. If this is true, consumers feel better off in spite of the price increases, which they scarcely notice or of which they at least do not know the reasons. Thus politicians have not to be afraid to lose the votes of consumers as long as the consequences of their actions do not lead to a substantial increase of household expenditures.

What have all these relationships to do with foreign policy? Well, as long as there are underdeveloped countries which can be annexed and dominated with rather low cost for military expenditures, colonization and administration, it is possible to promote exports by subjugating colonies and by closing them through duties at least partly to foreign competitors. Moreover, cheaper imports in the form of raw materials may be preferably exported from the colonies to the industries in the home country. The extra jobs created for administrators and military personnel lead to additional demand in the labor market, and the more secure chances for profitable capital investment attract domestic capital owners. All these groups as well as exporters and workers employed by the respective industries gain from the colonial expansion and are prepared to vote for parties proposing and introducing it. It follows that there are in fact forces in democratic market economies working towards nationalistic imperialism.

It is, however, important to realize that these forces are rather weak. For if the costs of acquiring and keeping colonies become high enough to be felt by domestic taxpayers, then colonial imperialism will be ended and the colonies be abolished. For in this case politicians can win the votes of taxpayers, that is of a majority of voters by giving up the colonies and by reducing taxes, since the difference will now be felt by taxpayers and lead to a reaction at the voting booth. In a situation, moreover, in which people in the colonies become restless and turn to subversive actions or even a guerilla war against the colonial administration, the costs to the imperialistic power increase drastically. As a consequence there exists a big chance that the colonial state will withdraw and grant independence to its former colonies. It is obvious that this theory allows not only an explanation of colonial imperialism, but in contrast to Marxist theory is also able to explain why colonial empires like the British, French and Portuguese have given up their colonies after World War II.

3. Economic Relations between State and Non-State Actors

It has been shown in the last section that economically developed democratic countries tend, because of internal economic interests and the response of politicians, to hinder imports and to further exports of goods produced by lagging or shrinking sectors of the economy. On the other hand, imports of goods which are not competing palpably with domestic industries but are important as inputs or as consumption goods (measured as a percentage of consumers' expenditures) will be encouraged and, if necessary, safeguarded as far as possible by the state. For in this case either the profitability of the respective branches of the economy and the employment offered by them may be at stake; or consumers would feel badly hurt by sizable price increases or a scarcity of these imports. Since the politicians of the governing parties would be held responsible for such developments and be blamed by the opposition, they are interested in encouraging and protecting the unhindered flow of these goods into the country.

These tendencies may be strengthened by organized interest groups formed by concerned industries and (or) unions. For these are sometimes able to influence the governing parties by threatening with or by using strikes and boycotts, by promising or withholding financial help to parties, by not providing information relevant to the government or by trying to influence voters. In so far as the governing parties are afraid to lose votes by such activities they may be prepared to change their policies in response to the wishes of these groups provided the political leaders do not expect to lose more voters than they can win as a consequence of the measures to be taken.

Whereas the discouragement of imports and, to a lesser degree, the encouragement of exports of goods produced by lagging or shrinking sectors of the economy are widespread in developed countries, this is not true for the encouragement of imports. This can be easily explained by the highly diversified nature of developed economies. In such countries only a few import goods, namely some raw materials and perhaps some highly modern equipment produced only in even more advanced nations can be not easily substituted by domestic products. As far as consumers' goods are concerned, scarcely one exists which cannot easily be replaced by home products and which at the same time amounts to a sizable percentage of household budgets. One exception is gas and oil. It is thus not surprising that foreign economic policies of developed market-oriented democracies are usually biased (with a few exceptions like those mentioned) against imports and in favor of exports.

These tendencies lead to several consequences. First, developed democracies 'prefer' an export surplus to an import surplus. But if they are successful in these efforts, the export surplus has to be financed by credits or grants to foreign debtors. For the income foreign countries receive from their exports is under these conditions not sufficient to cover the necessary expenditures for imports. It follows that nations showing export surpluses are usually interested in extending loans, in the safety of credits granted and the interest payments due on them, since politicians have to take into account the political influence of domestic creditors and those industries whose additional exports they finance.

Second, a foreign economic policy protecting lagging import-competing industries and furthering certain exports must necessarily collide with the same policies of other countries. Thus international tensions over these problems or even trade wars may follow, like those between the USA and the European Community over restrictive agricultural policies of the latter and those between the USA, the Community and Japan over steel and car imports from the latter two to the USA. Note that the economic sectors mentioned are all lagging or shrinking. History has shown that trade wars can result in stronger and stronger restrictions on imports like higher tariffs, import quotas, foreign exchange controls, etc., as witnessed by the development in the 1930s after the Great Depression.

It is obvious that such beggar-my-neighbor policies are not in the interest of anybody including the industries furthered by domestic, but restricted by foreign measures. As a consequence, sooner or later during this development, politicians, may on balance, be able to win or preserve votes by changing the course of their trade and foreign exchange policies. This can, however, only be done by international, preferably by multilateral agreements, since the removal of restrictions on foreign trade is only helpful if other countries take the same action. Examples are the General Agreement on Tariffs and Trade (GATT) and the Bretton Woods Agreement creating the International Monetary Fund (IMF), both founded in the wake of World War II. The latter was created to help to return to general convertibility of currencies, that is to the removal of exchange controls, at fixed exchange rates. For this purpose the IMF was empowered to extend credits, usually given with certain conditions, to prevent the return to exchange controls because of passing balance of payments deficits. After the abolishment of fixed exchange rates by major countries in 1973, the IMF has maintained its function as a credit institute; moreover, it is used to prevent competitive devaluations of exchange rates by participating countries to further exports.

The GATT has served well to promote free trade with its rules and agreements to lower tariffs and to abolish import quotas for non-agricultural products. It was less successful in preventing non-tariff restrictions and treaties between governments limiting the export of certain goods like textiles from one of them to the other. These tendencies which are again a consequence of the biases of developed capitalist countries to further lagging industries have been strengthened by the two recessions in 1974 and 1980/81, which increased the number of such industries or worsened their already precarious situations.

Socialist countries with more or less planned economies and countries of the so-called Third World are distinguished by different internal environments and by dissimilar economic and political organizations. It is not surprising that these differences are reflected in tendencies of their foreign economic policies strongly contrasting with those of developed market economies. Let us first discuss the socialist countries. Nearly all of them try to steer their economies with centrally administered plans and state property of the means of production. This has several important consequences. First, international economic relations have to be subordinated to the exigencies of the plan. Second, because plans have to be constructed and executed with very incomplete information and since profit or income motivation of individuals linked to the success of firms is largely missing, shortages and inadequate qualities of goods and services are everyday experiences. Thus a strong demand exists for imports to fill the gaps left by domestic production, whereas exports often suffer from lack of competitiveness, quality, reliability and availability. The need to import is strengthened, since the recently developed high-technology products are often badly needed by planned economies. For, because of the rigidities of planning and the lack of motivation to innovate, the economies of these countries are typically not at the top of technological development. We conclude that socialist economies show a tendency to develop deficits of their trade balances, since they encourage imports and are weak in developing exports. Now, it is obvious from the above, that this tendency implies a certain complementarity with developed market-oriented democracies 'preferring' export surpluses and prepared to finance them with the help of loans.

This complementarity does, however, not mean that no conflicts between these countries can arise. First, what happens if socialist countries incur more and more debts without being able or willing to repay them? Second, since their imports and exports are subordinated to the requirements of the plan demand and supply may change in a way obnoxious to their trade partners. Moreover, the prices of exports can be set by planned economies without a definite relationship to the costs, thus endangering competitors in market-oriented countries. Finally, the planned economy may further its military capabilities and thus its relative power by importing the most recent technological innovations related to this field. In this case internal conflicts may arise within the exporting democratic country between politicians, the military and segments of the public interested in adequate defence and the export industry and the people employed in it. Similarly, conflicts may burden the relationships between developed market-oriented democracies, if they participate to a different degree in these exports or weigh the issues at stake differently in their domestic political processes. The Reagan embargo concerning the supply of steel tubes for the Siberian natural gas pipeline and the ensuing controversy and conflict with some Western European countries have highlighted these possibilities in the early 1980s.

The economic policy biases of socialist countries show, moreover, a tendency to lead to conflicts with other socialist nations. If several socialist countries plan their economies the question arises how these plans can be coordinated; for without any coordination either chaotic or anarchic economic relations must result among these nations. On the other hand, it is difficult to reach one coordinated plan by negotiations between equals. Thus with one strong or dominating country present, its government will be tempted to subordinate the plans of the other socialist countries to the exigencies of its own plan; a behavior which will be strongly resented by the other countries, their leaders and/or population. If, however, two or more strong countries exist, then it will be nearly impossible to prevent conflicting demands and strong tendencies of becoming independent of each other will arise. We conclude by pointing out that a separation of foreign policy and foreign economic policy is even less conceivable for socialist than for developed capitalist countries, since politicians and functionaries plan and control all aspects of life including the economy. But this means that 'economic' conflicts can more easily deteriorate into general political conflict.

We turn to the countries of the Third World. These nations are, of course, very different from each other, but some general traits are common to most of them. The underdevelopment usually implies the existence of a relatively large agricultural and of a small industrial sector. Agriculture is often mainly subsistence farming; other parts of agriculture like plantations may be highly developed and oriented toward the world market. If an industry has already developed, it is, with the exception of mining, restricted to traditional eco-

nomic sectors like textiles or steel, since poor countries do not have the capabilities for innovative breakthroughs in technologically sophisticated fields.
A broadly based educational system, the necessary economic resources,
modern entrepreneurship and efficient organization, in short, the preconditions of such innovations are mostly missing.

In developing nations the segment of the population, from which the
political, military and bureaucratic leadership originate, is usually rather
small. Most of these people belong to a strata of intellectuals educated in
developed countries or at least at institutions structured according to ideas
prevalent in these countries. They come from small bourgeois or even from
peasant families, and mostly do not enjoy independent property income
of great importance.

All these factors work together to shape the economies of many underdeveloped countries and their relationships with other nations in a specific
way. The governing people owe their power, status and income only to their
control of the state. They have thus to look for sufficient public revenue
to secure their salaries and possibly for other income sources for themselves.
But income and property taxes are scarcely available because of the low development of the economy, of widespread illiteracy and poverty. Thus high
tariffs on imports, taxes or royalties on foreign-owned profitable firms
or plantations or their outright nationalization must provide the necessary
revenue, which is usually augmented with the help of public borrowing
abroad and inflationary financing of deficits by creating money. Additional
income sources are tapped by the governing elite by restricting imports, by
import quotas and by exchange controls. These measures lead to higher
domestic than world market prices and thus make importers willing to pay a
premium to get import licences and foreign exchange. The decision-making
politicians or bureaucrats are thus able to ask for bribes or to become partners
in the favored importing firms.

These tendencies are furthered by the underlying economic situation.
We observed already that developing countries are often exporting raw
materials, agricultural and tropical products. Moreover, if they have already
developed some export industry, traditional goods like textiles and steel
are produced and exported. But the demand for these goods is not income
elastic, that is, it grows at a lower pace than per capita incomes in developed
capitalist countries. This follows because first, consumers spend additional
incomes mainly on new goods and services: they do not want to buy more
and more traditional goods. Second, the inelasticity is a consequence of the
better and better substitution of raw materials in the process of technological
development. We conclude that the demand for exports from developing
countries lags behind the growth of real per capita income in rich capitalist

countries. This tendency is strengthened by the fact that developed market-oriented democracies restrict imports competing with their own lagging traditional industries. But such measures hurt just such products like textiles and steel which are produced by the new industrial sectors of developing nations.

The situation looks quite different for the goods imported by countries of the Third World. Here the population, too, wants to buy more sophisticated goods if the country succeeds in embarking on a path of economic growth with increasing per capita income. Even if the latter is not true, then the small rich segment of the population including the governing intellectual elite are strongly demanding these products produced abroad. We can thus conclude that whereas exports are lagging behind development abroad, the opposite is true for import demand especially as a consequence of domestic development. It follows that the balance of trade tends to show deficits and that underdeveloped countries show a strong demand for foreign credits. This tendency is reinforced by the inflationary bias mentioned above and the demand for foreign imports and loans because of the investment demands of poor countries, often exacerbated by an ambitious leadership who wants to enforce a rapid industrialization. It is thus not surprising that these factors encourage quotas and exchange controls for reducing the consumption of 'inessential' goods, to protect weak domestic industries, to reduce the balance of trade deficit and to postpone the devaluation of the national currency.

It is obvious that a corresponding situation of Third World countries can lead to many tensions and conflicts with developed capitalist countries. This is not to deny that a certain harmony of interests exists, since capitalist nations 'prefer' trade surpluses and are prepared to grant credit.

But tensions arise as soon as too many loans have been given so that interest payments and the repayment of debts are threatened. In these circumstances capitalist governments and banks are only inclined to grant moratoria and to extend new credits to solve the payments crisis, if the debtor country is prepared to fulfill certain conditions usually requiring more restrictive domestic economic policies. The same is true for international organizations like the International Monetary Fund which is controlled by the developed capitalist countries. But restrictive fiscal and monetary measures hurt the well-being of broad segments of the population and lead to even higher unemployment, at least temporarily and thus threaten the position of the governing elite.

Other sources of tension and conflict arise from tax or royalty increases for or by regulations and nationalizations of foreign-owned business firms by the developing country. The same is true of import restrictions introduced by capitalist nations. Conflicts arise, too, as a consequence of worsening relative prices for the goods exported by many Third World countries resulting from the low income elasticity of their export goods.

Developing nations often stimulate the development of new industries by encouraging foreign and especially multinational corporations to invest in the domestic economy. For these corporations combine the required capital resources, know-how and organization to build up new industries. Foreign firms are, moreover, attracted first because of low labour costs and secondly by low tax rates. Moreover, they establish plants at least in bigger developing countries since the import of their products is hindered by high tariffs, import quotas and exchange controls. To repeat, the governments of the respective countries encourage the investments and the development projects undertaken by foreign multinational firms. But they resent their growing influence on economic life and the governing elite want to participate in the fruits of these developments. Moreover, they may be convinced that they are able to run the plants themselves, once they have been established. So the political leadership may increase taxes, royalties or even nationalize these firms. Tensions and conflicts arise, especially if these plants belong to multinational corporations or foreign firms having some influence with their governments because jobs or incomes are threatened at home.

In such cases multinational firms may behave like independent international actors. Besides being perhaps able to cause their government to take economic or other sanctions against the country in question, they may boycott the sale of the goods produced in their (former) plants if they control or influence the distribution system in the world market. Foreign banks may be caused by them to withhold loans. Or if the developing country is weak they can even try to bribe government officials, finance a coup d'état or mercenaries to topple the government with the purpose of reversing the unwanted measures.

Let us conclude this section by looking at the possible relations of Third World countries to socialist states. From the factors analyzed above, several conclusions can be derived. First, socialist as well as Third World countries show a tendency to run into balance of trade deficits and to look for loans. Thus developing countries cannot hope to get more goods than they export and to receive substantial credits from socialist nations which usually have similar problems. Their demands for products will, moreover, be subordinated to the exigencies of the socialist plan; exceptions will only be granted if the leadership of the socialist state considers this to be of political importance. Finally, since planned economies are rather weak concerning innovative activities, they will usually not be able and willing to respond to demands for technologically sophisticated goods. It is thus not surprising to see Third World countries turn again and again to Western nations, even if they have experienced a 'socialist' revolution before and are governed by a socialist leadership.

4. Holy and Unholy Imperialism

We have seen how economic forces stemming from private interests can be a reason for imperialistic expansion of nations. This cause of imperialism, which has probably been at work together with other reasons during the last decades before World War I, is, however, very different from the forces driving a state towards establishing a universal empire. In democracies voters can only be burdened with the costs of colonial expansion, if these costs are small enough not to be felt because of information costs. But costs are high, if the expansion hits the determined resistance of other essential actors. Thus, with a democratic system and other essential states in the international community, economic imperialism will never reach for a world empire.

If, on the other hand, a state is dominated by a dictator or an oligarchy, either the state will be in outright command of a planned economy, or dictator and oligarchy will be able to intervene at their own convenience into a private market economy. In both cases the state and its policies will be dominated by the dictator or the oligarchy and thus follow their aims. Should these aims amount to narrow economic interests of dictator or oligarchy, then it is again doubtful whether the state will embark on a route towards universal empire. For a simple calculation would show that the risks and costs involved in a confrontation with other essential states are usually quite out of proportion with the narrow economic gains which could be won by the ruling elite, who have already a big share of the resources of the state at their disposal.

The roots of unlimited imperialism striving for universal empire in a world containing more than one essential actor are thus quite different from the possible economic causes of limited colonial imperialism. One of them is the outright pursuit of power. Another, as important reason for unlimited imperialism are the forces let loose by religious or non-religious beliefs. Such beliefs drive individuals not only to self-negating efforts but also to self-sacrifice for a 'higher cause' and fill their leaders with the absolute certainty of being destined by God, Fate or Historical Necessity to spread the true gospel, creed or truth all over the globe. In such a mood all narrow calculations of costs and benefits, all selfish interests are abhorred. In view of the all-importance of the aims pursued no sacrifice can be too burdensome, no effort too big for the glorious task to lead believers and non-believers to the best of all worlds to come, may it be the Promised Land, Heaven or an Earthly Paradise.

The power and influence of religious or quasi-religious movements on national and international politics can scarcely be exaggerated. We have already seen that Islam considers all wars against unbelievers as 'Holy Wars' and that the expansion of the Arab Empire from Spain to India and to Central Asia within two to three centuries, can only be explained by the conviction of Mohammed, his successors and followers to follow a divine command to bring the right creed to the whole world. A conviction which was coupled with an unshakable belief that Allah would help to gain final victory and that death on the battlefield would be compensated by eternal rewards in Paradise.

During the last years we have witnessed another revival of Islam as a political power,[4] culminating in the resurrection of an Islamic Republic with Ayatollah Khomeini as charismatic leader in Iran. Khomeini has been quite frank about the kind of state he and his followers want:

Each secular power, in whichever form it is maintained, is necessarily an atheistic power, the work of Satan. The Islamic government, however, is subject to the law of Islam, which is derived neither from the people nor from its representatives, but directly from Allah and His Divine Will. The law of the Koran, which is nothing else than the Divine law, is the whole of each Islamic government and rules infallibly above all individuals.

If a destined man embodying these highest virtues reveals himself to the public with the intent to form a truly Islamic government, then he has been endowed by the Almighty with the same message as once the prophet: he has to lead the people. In this case it is the absolute duty of the people to obey him. All military and civil power, which has been transferred by the Almighty to the Prophet is also at the disposal of the Islamic government of today.[5]

Let us now turn to the international aims of orthodox Islamic revival. In a radio broadcast of Radio Teheran, Khomeini said in a speech on November 22, 1979:

Muslims have to arise in this fight, a fight which is more a fight between Islam and the world of believers than a fight between Iran and the USA. The muslims shall triumph in this fight.

Somewhat earlier the Ayatollah from Qum had already revealed what the future might bring:

The Holy War means a conquering of territories which are not yet dominated by Islam. Precondition for the declaration of Holy War is the formation of a truly Islamic government . . . . The final aim of the Holy War is the subjugation of the world under the law of the Koran. . . . But the whole world shall know that the universal predominance of Islam is fundamentally different from the claim for power by ordinary conquerers. Guarantor of the difference is the authority of the Imam, the man of faith. He does not wage an unjust or tyrannical war of conquest.[6]

It follows that Islam has been and still is one of the religions providing stimulus for unlimited imperialism striving for universal empire. Christianity, too, had the possibilities to grow into a similar movement, as shown by the crusades and the conquests of the Teutonic Knights in Prussia in the Middle Ages. The religious wars between Catholics and Protestants culminating in the Thirty Years War (1618–1648), which devastated Germany and obliterated about two thirds of the population, were in the same direction. Finally, the whole idea of the Holy Roman Empire cannot be understood without this Christian background. It is true that this empire was seen as successor to the Roman Empire. But it was also strongly influenced by the Christian idea that it existence derived directly from God's divine will and that it had to provide an opportunity to all mankind to follow the right path to Heaven. These ideas clearly show up in the following sentences from Dante's *De Monarchia*:[7]

Temporal Monarchy, called also the Empire, we define as a single principality extending over all peoples in time, . . . (p. 5)

Consequently we perceive the nearest way through which may be reached that universal peace toward which all our efforts are directed as their ultimate end, and which is to be assumed as the basic principle of subsequent reasoning . . . . (p. 17)

We are now agreed that the whole human race is ordered for one end, as already shown. It is meet, therefore, that the leader and lord be called Monarch, or Emperor. Thus it becomes obvious that for the well-being of the world there is needed a Monarchy, or Empire. (p. 21)

It is obvious that these ideas could have been the driving force of universal imperialism, had historical conditions only been more favorable. For the emperors would have done nothing but to follow divine orders had they restored the one Christian empire all over the world. In fact these were the ideas leading the medieval emperors again and again to Italy and Rome, and which dominated a last time the thinking and deeds of Emperor Charles V, who combined during the fifteenth century as Emperor the Habsburgian and Spanish dominions all over the world and strove for imperial rule over the rest of Europe.

Religious fervor to lead people to their salvation can be, but need not be, a cause of unlimited imperialism. A good example for the lack of imperialism is provided by the history of the Jewish people. The Jews believed that they were God's chosen people. As a consequence there was no need to spread their creed to other people: and because of this there was no tendency towards unlimited imperialism, but only towards limited nationalistic aims, as witnessed first by Solomon's kingdom. Nevertheless, Jewish religion proved to be of the utmost political importance for the survival of the Jewish people. Consider only the incredible historical fact, that the Jews succeeded to found a new state after 1945, nearly nineteen hundred years after their capital Jerusalem had been conquered by Titus, the later Roman Emperor, and they themselves had been spread all over the world. Thus one could observe the astounding spectacle of more and more Jews with different languages and cultures flocking back from a score of countries to the country of their ancestors and reestablishing a Jewish state. Who would doubt that this feat was only possible because their religion had kept alive a feeling of belonging together and of sharing the same manifest destiny to be one of God's chosen people?

In modern times quasi-religious believes have often taken the place of religions as causes of unlimited imperialism. Here we have to mention the belief entertained by National Socialists (Nazis) in the superiority of the Germanic or Indoeuropean (Aryan) race and the conviction of Marxists in the final victory of the proletarian class bringing about a kind of paradise on earth after the establishment of communism. Both quasi-religious beliefs led or lead to imperialistic tendencies, as can be seen from the following quotations. Let us begin with Hitler's *Mein Kampf*:[8]

Everything we admire on this earth today – sciences and arts, technology and inventions – is only the creative product of a few people and perhaps originally of one race. The existence of this whole civilization, too, depends on them. If they perish, then the beauty of this earth sinks into its grave with them. (p. 316)

What we see today in front of us in the form of human culture, of the results of art, science and technology, is nearly without exception a creative product of the Aryan. (p. 317)

With this the path to be followed by the Aryan had been clearly predetermined. He subjugated as conqueror the inferior races and then ordered their practical work under his command, according to his wishes and for his aims. But by leading them to a useful, though hard activity, he not only saved the life of the subjects, but perhaps even gave them a better lot than their earlier so-called 'freedom'. As long as he recklessly adhered to his point of view as a master, he not only remained in fact the master, but also preserved and augmented civilization. (p. 324)

The foreign policy of a nation state has to secure the existence on this planet of the race brought together by the state. To do so it has to create a sound, viable and natural relation between the number and growth of the people and of the magnitude and quality of land and soil.

As a sound relation can only be considered a situation in which the food supply of a people is secured by its own land and soil. (p. 728)

It would appear from the last passage that Hitler planned only a limited expansion of German territory to provide for a self-sufficient food supply for the present and future needs of a growing master race. There remains no doubt from his writings that he wanted to gain this territory in thinly settled Eastern Europe, especially in Russia. This was certainly an important imperialistic aim, but it would not have led to unlimited imperialism. But the earlier passages quoted show clearly on the other hand, that Hitler would not have stopped had he reached these limited goals. The Aryan race is a much broader concept than the Germanic race. It is spread far over the world. Moreover, since this race creates and promotes civilization by subjugating and leading inferior races, there would have been ample justification to enter a course leading to universal empire from the underlying ideology.

Marxism, at least as conceived by Lenin, is even more outspoken in its quest for eventual world domination. But here another idea is added: Communism will spread all over the globe by historical necessity. The final victory of the proletarians in the class war against capitalism as well as their dictatorship and the final withering-away of the state are all believed to be inevitable. As a consequence, wars, oppression, alienation and, of course, foreign policy will all come to an end in this final earthly paradise. Thus everybody working for socialism as well as for the socialist state will by necessity belong to the finally victorious cause. This is certainly a powerful ideology promoting strong forces striving towards universal empire. But let me quote from Lenin's writings:

The essential thing in the question of concessions is from a political point of view . . . that one has to make use of the antagonisms and contradictions between . . . two systems of capitalistic states and that one has to incite them against each other. As long as we have not conquered the whole world, as long as we are weaker economically and militarily than the capitalistic rest of the world, so long one has to follow the rule that one has to understand to make use of the differences and contradictions among the Imperialists.[9]

He who wants a lasting and democratic peace has to be in favour of civil war against government and Bourgeoisie . . . Marxism is not pacifism. It is necessary to fight for the quickest end of the war. But the demand for 'peace' has only a proletarian meaning if it is continued with a summons to revolutionary fight. So-called democratic peace remains a Philistine utopia without a series of revolutions.[10]

These are revealing sentences. They show how the political activist brought up in the Marxist creed has turned this system into a means to strive for universal domination.

Nazism and Marxism have not been the only modern quasi-religious ideologies furthering a tendency of unlimited imperialism. Only the revolutionary belief in the world-saving secular aims of 'Freedom, Equality and Fraternity' leading to the French Revolution of 1789 made the imperialistic policy of Napoleon possible. Even American intervention into the two world wars was strongly influenced by the popular belief of fighting for freedom and democracy, to promote final peace all over the world by a 'Crusade for Democracy' against the dark forces of oppression.

5. The Aims of Universal States

It is interesting to note that religious or quasi-religious belief-systems or ideologies leading to unlimited imperialism never succeeded in establishing a true universal empire. The Roman as well as the Chinese empires were built by Rome and Ch'in without the use of an imperialistic religious or quasi-religious belief system, a fact which probably did not occur by accident. The fervor of ideological movements often hinders a sober rational analysis of the expected advantages and disadvantages of different courses of action in the field of international analysis. The political leaders may themselves become convinced that they have been selected by fate and may thus be blinded by their very successes. This was probably the case with Napoleon and Hitler and accounts for the severe blunders and mistakes they committed in their later careers.

Statesmen, on the other hand, who are only trying to expand the power of their states, are usually open to rational calculation and thus able to escape the risks of rash actions. It follows that states pursuing pure power politics for an extended period have usually a higher chance to move towards universal empire than those driven by the forces of religions, or ideological believes. There may be cases, however, where the politicians in an ideological system free themselves from the fetters of ideology and follow a rational course of action to expand their own powers and that of their states. Religion and ideology are then only used as a means for internal and foreign policies and thus do not hinder but help to attain their aims. It is possible that this was true for Stalin and his policies and that a corresponding policy is still followed by the present political oligarchy of Soviet Russia.

It follows from the above that religious and ideological beliefs have played at best a minor role in the foundation of universal empires during the course of history. This does, however, not imply that universal empires did not create their own ideologies after they had been established. We have already seen that Rome was considered by its citizens a guarantor of universal peace, of justice and of civilization and that its existence was believed to last forever. Lactantius, a christian contemporary of Emperor Constantine, wrote:

When Rome the head of the world shall have fallen, who can doubt that the end has come of human things, aye, of the earth itself. She, she alone is the state by which all things are upheld even until now; wherefore let us make progress and supplications to the God of Heaven, if indeed His decrees and His purposes can be delayed, that hateful tyrant [the Antichrist] come not sooner than we look for, he for whom are reserved fearful deeds, who shall pluck out that eye in whose extinction the world itself shall perish.[11]

The quotation shows that Lactantius and the early Christians had taken up the proud belief of Virgil in the manifest destiny of the Roman Empire. And much later, while the Western Empire had already fallen eight hundred years ago, Dante expressed his belief.

That in subduing the world the Roman people had in view the aforesaid good [the rule of law for the benefit of those under the laws], their deeds declare. We behold them as a nation holy, pious and full of glory, putting aside all avarice, which is even adverse to the general welfare, cherishing universal peace and liberty, and disregarding private profit to guard the public weal of humanity. Rightly was it written, then, that 'The Roman Empire takes its rise in the fountain of pity!'[12]

Now, nobody will think that these as well as similar statements are true descriptions of Roman reality. But the religious ideological beliefs expressed by them lay bare some of the forces helping to keep together and to maintain universal empires.

What were the real aims of such empires as Rome and China? This is a question difficult to answer. But it is at least obvious, that a universal empire has to preserve its unity and to defend its borders against 'barbarian' invasions. Moreover, if the leading politicians strive for power, prestige and income, they will certainly favor such a policy. It follows from this that the preservation of internal peace, of a functioning administration and economy, of a workable system of law must be among their aims. Since they are interested in the unity of the state to preserve the domain of their powers, the spread of the dominating civilization and languages will be furthered. All of this seems to have been true for Rome and China and can be expected for possible universal empires in the future. But peace, the rule of law and the spread of a universal common civilization do not guarantee the absence of despotism and the existence of the just law of a free society, as witnessed by the historical experiences of the Roman and Chinese Empires. For power-hungry leaders may, from time to time, try successfully to extend their powers by removing constitutional democratic controls, if they did indeed exist before; or they may use the very emergencies arising during the fights leading to universal empire to introduce a despotic regime.

Notes

1 Friedrich der Grosse: *Das politische Testament von 1752*. Reclam, Stuttgart 1974, pp. 82–87.
2 Wladimir I. Lenin: *Zum vierten Jahrestag der Oktoberrevolution*. Published October 18, 1921. Compare W.I. Lenin: Ausgewählte Werke in zwei Bänden. Vol. 2, Moskau 1947, p. 887.

3 James Petras: *Critical Perspectives on Imperialism and Social Class in the Third World*. Monthy Review Press, New York and London, 1978.
4 The roots of the modern revival of Islam go back to Al-Din Al-Afghani (1838–1897), compare Bernhard Dahen: "Muslime zwischen Mobilisierung und Modernisierung." In: Hartmut Boockmann, Kurt Jürgensen and Gerhard Stoltenberg (eds.): *Geschichte und Gegenwart*. Karl Wachholz, Neumünster 1980, pp. 541–555. Compare also the special report: "Islam," In: *Time*, vol. 113(16), April 16, 1979, p. 24 sq.
5 Quoted from Gerhard Konzelmann: *Die islamische Herausforderung*. Hoffmann und Campe, Hamburg 1980, pp. 43 and 47.
6 Gerhard Konzelmann: op. cit., p. 38.
7 Dante Alighieri: *De Monarchia*. Ed. with a trans. and notes by Aurelia Henry. Houghton, Mifflin, Riverside Press, Cambridge, Boston, New York 1904.
8 Adolf Hitler: *Mein Kampf*. Franz Eher Nachfolger, München 1933.
9 Wladimir I. Lenin: "Speech to Cell Secretaries in Moscow on November 26, 1920." In: *Sämtliche Werke*, 2nd ed., vol. 18, Vienna and Berlin 1929, pp. 293–294.
10 Wladimir I. Lenin and Sinovjew: "Sozialismus und Krieg", August 1915. In: W.I. Lenin: *Sämtliche Werke* 2nd ed., vol. 18, Vienna and Berlin 1929, pp. 267 and 284.
11 Quoted from Bryce: *The Holy Roman Empire*, London 1904, pp. 20–21.
12 Dante Alighieri: op. cit., p. 90.

Chapter 5

The Means of Foreign Policy

The means of foreign policy are numerous and varied. They reach from outright military warfare to guerilla war, terrorism, infiltration and internal destruction; from diplomacy to economic pressure and warfare and to the use of ideological beliefs to win even the population of potential enemies. Given this multitude of different means it is one of the most difficult tasks of statesmanship to coordinate their use and to apply them or to threaten their application at the right time. If we take a broad definition one may consider the art of foreign policy to be the correct coordination and application of these different means including the threat to use them, given the aims to be followed. But foreign policy is not limited to this. It has, moreover, the task of bringing together or of preventing alliances with or of foreign countries with the purpose of using the power of other states for its own goals.

In this chapter the different means available to foreign policy will be discussed. In doing so we will, however, exclude traditional warfare, which has already been discussed several times, especially in Chapter 3.

1. Economic Pressure and Warfare

There are quite a number of economic measures available for use in foreign policy. Very often, as is true for other means of foreign policy, it may even be sufficient to threaten with the use of such measures. For example, Saudi-Arabia may threaten to cut off the delivery of crude oil to Western Europe, if these countries do not take a favorable position towards the Palestinian Liberation Organization (PLO).

The available economic measures can be grouped into four groups:

(a) Measures limiting or prohibiting the export of certain goods to the state in question;
(b) measures limiting or prohibiting the import of certain goods from this state;

(c) using credit relationships with the target state;

(d) undermining and weakening the economic order of this state.

All these measures can also be used in reverse to strengthen a potential ally.

Let us first discuss point (a). If the leaders of a country want to weaken another state or if they want to get certain concessions from it, then one of the measures available is the limitation or interruption of some or all important imports of this nation. An obvious precondition for such a move is the need by the target state to import certain goods. The resulting decrease of the imports must at least lead to a severe inconvenience, better to serious difficulties for the importing country. Such difficulties would, for instance, arise, if the food or oil supply would be decreased or cut off to countries, which are net food or oil importers and whose internal food or oil supplies amount only to less than, say, 60 or 70 per cent of their needs for foodstuffs and energy. Another example would be a reduction or stop of the delivery of machines, automobiles, tanks and airplanes and of the spare parts to repair them in the case of countries which are not themselves producers of these goods.

The success of a policy to limit critical exports to a certain state can be prevented by the possible competition of other countries. If the leaders of other states are able and willing to supply the necessary foodstuffs, the crude oil, the machines or automobiles instead of the country which has limited or stopped their delivery, then the target state will only be slightly hurt because of the different types and qualities of the goods supplied and perhaps because of somewhat higher prices. The people living in the acting nation, on the other hand, may be hurt much more by the measures of their own, since the demand for own products is reduced, which may even, if it is widespread, result in a recession, an increase of unemployment, in lower incomes and lower tax revenues.

It follows from this that a successful limitation or interruption of critical imports to the target state can only be reached if either the acting country is the only or by far the most important supplier; or if its government acts together with other states supplying the goods in question, so that they together are the major suppliers; or that it is able to control by force or by threat of force the flow of the respective goods to the target state.

In history it has been a rare fact that one country had a monopoly of some important good or was even its main supplier. Chile had a monopoly of salpeter, which was necessary for the production of explosives, until World War I, when Germany succeeded in producing it artificially. Saudi Arabia's importance as a supplier of crude oil is today so great that a cutting-off of its deliveries would lead to severe economic and political problems in Western Europe. The USA are now the major net grain exporter and a severe shortage on the world markets would possibly arise if it stopped its exports especially in years of bad harvests in other countries.

We conclude that only very few countries are in a position to inflict severe damage on other countries by limiting or stopping their exports of certain goods. Even then the countries which can be hurt may not be those in which they are most interested. Moreover, the cost of such a policy to the government may appear to be more important than the advantages to be gained. The danger of losing the political support of farmers may, for instance, well prevent the American government from stopping the export of wheat to Russia for an extended period. Saudi-Arabia may hesitate to interrupt the crude oil supply of Western Europe even if these countries would not support the position of the PLO against Israel, because its leaders are afraid that the resulting weakening of the West may lead to an erosion of the internal position of the Royal House as a consequence of a lack of Western military support.

A cartel between the most important suppliers of critical goods is always difficult to forge and to maintain, even if its sole purpose is higher prices. For to keep up higher prices permanently, supplies have to be cut. It is, therefore, profitable to act as an outsider enjoying the higher prices fixed by the cartel by slightly undercutting them and thus increasing one's own sales. Thus there exists a strong motivation for members to leave cartels and to act as independent outsiders. Moreover, the importance of already existing outsiders grows with the passage of time, since they can increase their exports whereas cartel members have to cut down their sales.

The difficulties increase if one or several states want to use the cartel for their foreign policies. Not all cartel members may share these aims and some states may even prefer to follow contradictory goals. Thus it is hard to find examples for successful cartels used for specific foreign policy purposes. In recent years even the boycott of a small country like Rhodesia – now Zimbabwe – has not been successful. OPEC comes to mind as another possible example. But its partial success has probably only been possible because it was able to combine the purely economic aims of the non-Arab with the mixed economic-political ends of the Arab members. Moreover, the strategic position of major members like Saudi Arabia for the existence and the policies followed by the oil cartel should not be overlooked. Finally the specific embargo against the Netherlands and the USA in the early seventies proved to be a failure, since the free flow of crude oil from one developed country to the other could not be prevented.

A final possibility of limiting or interrupting the flow of goods to the target state is through control of routes of transportation. A country with superior sea forces can, for instance, control the transportation of goods by ships and thus interrupt the imports from other continents and the cheaper sea-borne transportation from harbors on the same continent. Great Britain with its naval superiority has often used this method in times of crises or war, for instance, against France during the Napoleonic Wars and against Germany during the two World Wars. With the development of air traffic the interruption of sea transportation has become less effective, and has to be supplemented, if possible, by control of air-borne imports.

The method to control the routes of transportation has its limitations, too.

First, superior forces have to be available to control the access to the respective state. Second, the countries exporting the goods to the target state will not take the measures with equanimity, except if they are allies. Thus the nation beginning a blockade not only risks tensions and war with the importing, but also with the exporting country or countries. As a consequence there must be good reasons and a high chance of success before the leadership of a nation enters this course of action. It is, therefore, not surprising that the method has usually been used only in times of war.

Let us turn now to the measures limiting or prohibiting the export of certain goods from the target state, that is, its exports to other nations especially to the acting country. Again, the effectiveness of such measures depends on several conditions. First, the amount imported from the country must be sizable. Second, the state restricting its imports from this nation must not be hurt so much that the costs of its actions outweigh the intended benefits in reaching the foreign policy aims. A favorable situation is for instance given, if a certain commodity like coffee, cocoa, sugar or bananas is one of the major export articles of the target country and if a big proportion of these supplies is consumed in the state which wants to take action. For example, the USA consumes a lot of coffee, cocoa and bananas and could probably hurt strongly the economies of Brazil, Colombia and Costa Rica by forbidding the import of these goods. The same is true, if the import of motor cars and of other durable goods from Japan would be stopped by the US government, especially since the USA has a strong import surplus with Japan. In all these cases the target state would be severely hit, and not only the profits of the respective industries, but also employment, growth of gross national product and tax revenues of the government would suffer.

Even in the favorable examples just mentioned, a democratic government may find it difficult to pursue a corresponding path of action. For consumers may not be willing to forego the consumption of coffee, cocoa or bananas and react accordingly as voters. They may resent the higher prices brought about by limiting or ending the import of cars and other durable goods, and vote against the government party (parties) in the upcoming election. This shows again the problems faced by democratic governments in pursuing a foreign policy which is not appreciated or understood by a majority of voters, even if it should be in their own long-term interests.

A limitation or interruption of exports of some or all goods from a given country is, of course, more effective if a cartel of as many as possible of the more important countries importing from the target state can be formed. The difficulties of such a policy are again given by diverging foreign policy aims of the potential cartel members and by possible benefits they can derive from the cartel as outsiders because of lower prices of the respective goods.

Exports as well as imports of goods of the target country can most effectively be limited by a blockade. The preconditions and the difficulties are the same in both cases. There is thus no need to repeat what has been said above. Blockades will usually be limited to times of war and then to interrupting not only all exports but also all imports of the enemy.

If a target state is not dependent on the acting country and its potential allies for any of its exports or imports, then the latter can try to build up such a dependence. For instance, the Soviet Union has in the late 1970s proposed to supply big amounts of natural gas to Western European nations in exchange for their help to build up the necessary pipelines to bring the gas from Siberia to the west. These plans have been accepted and the deal has been completed. Now, if the natural gas supplied should in later years amount to a substantial percentage of the energy needs of the respective states, then a dependence on deliveries from the USSR would have been created. There is no doubt that such a dependence could be used for either weakening the economies of these countries or for the purpose of gaining political advantages by cutting off the supply of natural gas. It is even possible that just a threat to stop the flow of natural gas would be sufficient to reach the compliance of these states. The government of the United States has in fact warned the respective countries against such a possibility. But they have denied that such a danger exists, perhaps since they do not intend to let the dependence on natural gas from the Soviet Union to increase to a high proportion of their energy needs.

A further possibility to exert economic pressure on a given state for foreign policy purposes is the use of credit relationships. A credit can be granted or withheld to reach the compliance of the target state. Again certain preconditions have to be fulfilled. First, the terms of the credit have to be more favorable than those available from other creditors in the national or international markets. Second, the aims pursued by the government of the acting state have to be such that the disadvantages to the target state are overcompensated by the more favorable credit conditions. In some cases it may be necessary that, given these aims, an outright grant has to be offered instead of a favorable credit. In other cases even a big grant may not be sufficient to reach the aims. Finally the disadvantages caused by the grant or the more favorable credit conditions must not be more costly to the leaders of the acting state than the value of the possible benefits resulting from a realization of the foreign policy goals.

The granting of credits has another peculiarity. Once credits have been given they can be used by the debtor country as a weapon against the creditor. For the former can threaten not to repay its debts, if the creditor country does not comply with its foreign policy aims. The only negative consequence of such a threat would be the loss of credit-worthiness in the future and possible further sanctions by the creditor country.

A final group of measures out of the arsenal of economic warfare are actions able to undermine and to weaken the economic order and the economic processes of a state. Lenin once mentioned that the economic and social fabric of a state can be shaken by destroying the value of its money. But how could this be done by an outside nation? Several possibilities could at least be tried. One of them would be to print substantial amounts of bank notes of the target state, to bring them into circulation and thus to cause an inflation. This would, of course, presuppose that the forgeries could be detected only with great difficulties. But a state certainly has better chances than individuals with limited resources.

Next, most of modern money like checking accounts is just a claim against a bank in the form of an entry in the bank's ledgers or, nowadays, even of an electromagnetic signal on a tape. The bank only keeps a limited percentage of these outstanding liabilities in the form of bank notes or of claims against the central bank which can be easily converted into bank notes. But each customer has the right to turn the balance on his checking account into bank notes at any time.

This system of credit money is extremely vulnerable to panics and a rapid and substantial withdrawal of assets. Let us assume that some agencies of the acting country have deposited big amounts on a checking account at one of the major banks of the target country. After some time the agents of the acting state spread rumours that the respective bank is in a bad liquidity position and may have difficulties honoring its obligations. Then it suddenly withdraws its balances with the bank, thus in fact dealing a blow to its liquidity. It is then quite possible that the bank may not be liquid enough to provide the bank notes demanded or the claims against the central bank necessary to cover the transfers to other banks. This is especially true if many of its clients withdraw their accounts before or together with the foreign country. Other banks may suddenly find themselves in difficulties, too. First, the endangered bank may withdraw the deposits it has with them. Second, the public may become suspicious because of the problems of the first bank. As a consequence a severe liquidity crisis may arise, leading to a financial breakdown and a depression in the real sector of the economy. Of course, the central bank could stem the tide by providing help to the endangered bank or banks. But this could lead to a strong increase of the money supply and may strengthen inflationary forces. It should be noted, that in pursuing the said operations, the government of the acting country will usually prefer not to act openly itself but through foreign banks owned by it or dependent on it.

Another measure to bring the money and credit system of the target state into difficulties would be the following. The leaders of the acting country first order the taking up of substantial credits with the banks of this state and then declare later that their nation is unable to repay the debts. In this case the creditor banks may well be driven into bankruptcy and their financial difficulties may spread in a chain reaction to other banks and finally to the whole economy. It is true, the central bank can help in this case, too, but this again leads to the problems mentioned above.

There are other possible measures to weaken the economic order of a country. To mention just one of them, strikes in the target country can be encouraged and financially supported whenever possible, to decrease production and the supply of goods to the population. Thus dissatisfaction and unrest can be spread and perhaps even an unfavorable government can be driven out of power.[1]

2. Infiltration, Internal Destruction and Terrorism

The last remarks of the preceding section refer implicitly to the possibility of infiltrating a target state with the purpose of accomplishing a given objective, namely to instigate workers to strike in certain industries.

Some of the means of infiltration, of internal destruction and of terrorism, which can be used against a target state have long been known to experts. Kautilya already mentions around 300 B.C.:

... or I can destroy the works of my enemy by employing spies and other secret means; or by holding out such inducements as a happy dwelling, rewards, remission of taxes, little work and large profits and wages, I can empty my enemy's country of its population, with which he has been able to carry his own works; ...[2]

Infiltration can be used for several purposes. First, espionage can help to get the necessary information about the situation in the target state and about the actions planned by its government and other internal groups and organizations like parties, unions, interest groups, business firms, military units, etc. The spy net can also be used to supply wrong information about the acting country and its plans to the government of the target state, for instance by employing double agents.

But agents can be employed for quite different purposes, too. They can try to kindle smouldering dissatisfaction into strikes, demonstrations, civil unrest, use of violence against police and armed forces, internal destruction and even coups d'etat. It is important for them to provide an organizational structure which can be put at the disposal of dissatisfied groups of the population to reach their purposes apparently or in fact, as long as this amounts to a weakening of the government of the target country or of its social fabric, or as long as there is hope to slowly direct the dissatisfied group into the wanted direction.

The kind of dissatisfaction and the reasons for unrest are themselves usually unimportant. Whether workers are dissatisfied with their wages or working conditions or because they feel their jobs are threatened, whether people are hurt by an inadequate housing situation or by increasing rents, whether they are concerned for peace, or whether students worry about their examinations, all this really does not matter. All that counts is that the agents are able to use the feelings of dissatisfaction and the spreading unrest to organize people into action. Again, what kind of action results is unimportant, provided that it weakens the economy, brings about additional unrest, increases the chances to topple a government resisting the aims of the acting country, or decreases the determination of police and armed forces to resist violent internal opposition groups.

Modern industrial societies are highly vulnerable against sabotage. This is especially true for the transportation and power supply networks, as witnessed by several blackouts in New York and other places and by the chaos created even by simple accidents or repairs on highways. Thus agents can cause heavy damages to the economy and spread a lot of dissatisfaction in the population by causing a limited amount of destruction, for instance by exploding a major power line, a central railway station, an airport or highway.

With these remarks we have moved on to terrorism.[3] In a world in which a kind of stalemate has developed between the two super-powers because of the introduction of nuclear weapons carried by missiles, political leaders bent on expansion of their states will by necessity look for other means to reach their ends. Among these means, terrorism and guerilla warfare will probably have to play a more and more important role. Both of them take place inside the target state or inside the territory of its allies. It is thus not possible to get rid of terrorism and guerilla warfare by using atomic weapons, since terrorists and guerilla armies mingle with the population of their own country or with that of the allied state. Otherwise, the population would have to be destroyed together with the enemy or terrorists.

It follows that it is very hard to fight terrorism, if the terrorists belong to the population itself and if the latter is not prepared to identify them to the security organs of the government. Foreigners can, of course, usually be more easily identified. It is, therefore, of great importance to the acting state to be able to use nationals for terroristic acts. Further, the domestic population should at least have enough sympathy for the terrorists or their pretended cause, or enough indifference, ill-feeling, or hatred for its own government, that it does not notify the authorities of suspicious actions or persons. To fulfill both these preconditions it is very helpful for the acting state to have a 'higher idea' available, a religious or quasi-religious system able to attract the sympathies or even the enthusiastic support of as many foreigners as possible. We have to return to this point in the next section.

Terrorism can apply different measures. One of them is outright killing and destruction, which has been discussed above. But these methods are only adequate, if a general weakening or destruction of the economy and the political system, a discouragement of the armed forces or the spread of unrest and dissatisfaction are intended. They are not useful, if specific concessions by the government, by unions, firms, individuals, etc. are sought for. For instance, a release of imprisoned guerillas or terrorists or the delivery of a certain sum of money can not be reached by destroying a power plant or by killing a cabinet member.

Thus, to accomplish ends requiring the collaboration of the enemy, a threat to kill certain persons or to destroy certain objects has to be applied. It is true that the threat itself has to be credible and that credibility may be reached by killing some people or by destroying some objects before using a threat. But the threat cannot itself use these measures. For it is the very aim of a threat not to be executed. The threatening party wants to forego the execution in exchange for a concession by the government or other organized groups or by individuals. It wants to reach the release of prisoners, the withdrawal of the police, an armistice or an amount of money or arms. True, the threat may still be executed after the concessions have been granted. But this may be rather costly, since a promise not to execute a threat would not be believed in later cases, a fact which would make future threats ineffective.

The credibility of a threat by terrorist movements is severely weakened, if they announce that they will destroy *specific* objects or kill *specific* persons should their demands not be met. For then the government is able to take action to protect the very objects and persons threatened. There is one exception to this rule, namely that the terrorists bring the objects or persons under their control before transmitting their demands together with their threats. It is because of this fact that taking hostages and air piracy are so appealing to terrorists.

A terrorist threat can only be successful if the concessions demanded can be granted and if they are less valuable to the organization or individual concerned than is the threatened damage. Moreover, the latter have to be convinced that the disadvantages brought about for the terrorists by executing their threats are less important to them than the concessions asked for. This fact makes some threats rather questionable. Assume for instance that a group of ten terrorists kidnaps an airplane without passengers and crew to ask for the release of one of their fellow terrorists. In this case they would be in danger of being killed if they resisted an attack by armed forces. Would they be prepared to do so for the dismissal of just one prisoner?

Finally, the threatened organization or individual has to take into consideration the possibility of future threats. For if a threat is never complied with, then later threats become less and less probable, since the terrorists know with increasing certainty that such threats shall be ineffective. It may, therefore, be more promising from a long-run perspective to refuse to comply with a threat and to accept the loss of life and property implied. For the number of lives and the value of goods saved in the future may be greater than that lost in the beginning. But it is obvious that such decisions are very hard to take. Still, the government of Israel has (with one exception when it released a number of terrorists to get back one of its airplanes) consistently refused to be blackmailed by terrorist demands.

We conclude by stating that infiltration, internal destruction and terrorism are liable to be more and more widely used by states bent on expansion in times of a stalemate produced by nuclear weapons. The increasing vulnerability of economically advanced nations created by technological, economic and organizational progress enhances the chances of such measures. If wide sympathy or even support exists for the agents and terrorists in the population, then the domestic government may have a hard time to resist the slow erosion of its power.

3. Ideology and Religion

The best way to defeat enemies or opponents is to convince them of one's own ideas and aims. This can be achieved by spreading an attractive or tempting system of ideas, an ideology or religion to as many people as possible, especially to the populations of states which are the immediate targets of the acting government.

We have seen in Chapter 4 that ideologies and religions can become aims leading state power towards universal imperialism. We have now to realize that they can at the same time serve as means for expansionist goals and that they can help infiltration, destruction and terrorism directed against a target state. They may even provide the means to weaken its resistance, to bring about 'peaceful' take-overs of the government or to kindle guerilla wars and revolutions. This is at least possible, if a large segment of the population can be turned into adherents of the new creed. The spread of the new set of ideas to a target state undermines, as it were, the monolithic unity of this nation. It turns most of the population into opposite or warring factions, one of which have turned into more or less fanatic agents of the aggressor state, even if they believe they are following the good cause of fighting for divine aims or a future paradise on earth.

We have already seen, how much religious or quasi-religious systems have strengthened the forces of aggressive governments in history. But there are enough examples, too, how such ideas have influenced outside states and weakened their power of resistance and even their will of independence. China and Rome often defeated their barbarian enemies and conquerors not with their arms but with the superior ideas of their civilizations. The ideas of the French Revolution spread to other countries and helped France to win predominance in Europe. The racist ideology of the Nazis was taken up by several movements in European countries, which sometimes provided puppet governments after German occupation. Communist parties are present all over the globe and are working for the 'proletarian revolution' and the final demise of capitalism, mostly in close cooperation with Russian or Chinese communists and their governments.

What are the preconditions for a profitable use of ideological beliefs in international politics? First of all, the belief system has to be attractive for as many people as possible. It has therefore, not to be restricted to a limited group of people, and it has to give the impression of being able to solve problems which are important to many. Even better still is a system which can additionally arouse the attention of many others who have not previously been aware of these problems although they share them with others.

The more limited the group of potential followers of a belief system, the more restricted is its use for imperialistic expansion. The Jewish religion traditionally only spoke of the Jews as the chosen people. Its appeal is, therefore, limited to a small group of humanity and can only be used for limited nationalistic expansion. The messages of Christianity, Buddhism and Islam, on the other hand, are directed to all human beings and can thus create much broader support. The same is true for the belief systems of freedom, rule of law and democracy. Finally, to turn to more recent developments, the doctrine of a superior Germanic or Aryan race created by National Socialism has certainly a more comprehensive group of potential converts than Judaism, since the people considering themselves Aryan are more widespread and more populous than the Jewish people. But the potential membership of this doctrine is still much smaller than that of the communist creed which addresses itself to the whole proletariat and to the 'exploited masses' all over the globe.

But the number of potential addressees is only one aspect of the power of belief systems as instruments of international policies. Another one is their capability to convince people that they have problems which can only or best be solved by the promises held out by their specific system. Only then will they be able to make converts. Now, problems may either be objectively existent, or they may be only subjectively felt or both. A deep depression like in the 1930s with millions of unemployed people, or the destruction and suffering of a major war certainly provide fertile ground for the success of ideologies and of religions which seem to explain convincingly the reasons of these catastrophical events and to offer a solution to the difficulties and suffering related to them. Only World War I allowed the success of the Bolshevik October Revolution in Russia. Only the Great Depression enabled Hitler and the Nazi party to grab power in Germany in 1933. In fact, it has been convincingly shown that the number of votes won by the National Socialist and the Communist parties in Germany during the late 1920s and early 1930s was strongly correlated with unemployment.[4]

These relationships were clearly recognized by Lenin:[5]

And the main difficulties we faced during the four years, were caused by the fact that the Western European capitalists had succeeded to end the war and to adjourn the revolution. We all have observed very clearly here in Russia, that the situation of the Bourgoisie was most insecure during the imperialistic war.

From here it is only a small step to conclude that one can further or even bring about the objective conditions favorable for the spread of a belief system, in this case communism. As Lenin put it:[6]

... that one has to use the tensions and contradictions ... between two systems of capitalistic states and to incite them against each other.

To use and to further a favorable situation is, however, not sufficient to convince people of the advantages of an ideology or religion. Missionary work has to be done to convince people of the ability of the belief system to solve the very problems they encounter and to lead them out of their predicament. But even missionary work will only be successful if the system itself seems to be capable of accomplishing such a feat. To do so it has usually to offer some appealing reasons and remedies for the present plight and to provide goals which make the lives of converts meaningful again. Thus the devil, capitalism or Jewish conspiracy and plutocracy have to be responsible for war or for depression and unemployment. A way out of the crisis will be found with certainty, if the people only turn to the Kingdom of God, give up their sinful lives, if the Jews are driven out and are obliterated or if the proletariat finally defeats capitalism and leads the way towards a communist paradise. Thus the belief systems have to offer a coherent system explaining the roots of the present plight and the path towards a better future. Even better, if the final victory can be depicted to be inevitable, like the victory of socialism and communism which, according to Marxism, shall approach with the same necessity as the final judgment of Christian religion.

A fertile ground for the spread of ideologies and religions can be but need not be prepared by an objectively bad economic or social situation of broad segments of the population. It can also develop if many people feel a lack of meaning in their lives even when they live in unprecedented prosperity. This feeling may be strengthened, if the political and social system seems not to be able to cope with many present and future problems which do not immediately reduce the well-being of the people concerned. During the last fifteen years we have observed several waves of dissatisfaction especially among the younger generation. The Vietnam War, the danger of a lethal nuclear war, hunger and poverty in underdeveloped countries, energy dependency, the risk of atomic energy and the pollution of the environment have all been taken up as issues. But each of these problems has existed before and seems to enjoy a changing appeal over time. Many young people try to find a more meaningful life by experimenting with drugs and narcotics or by turning towards several, mostly oriental religions or sects. It is, therefore, doubtful whether the issues are really responsible for the unrest and dissatisfaction and whether the real causes have not to be sought in the erosion of family life and a loss of meaning in individual life. But whatever the reasons of recent dissatisfaction and unrest, they have certainly brought about some moderate success not only for religious groups but also for communist and left-wing socialist ideologies in several Western industrialized countries.

We have now discussed some preconditions for a general success of belief systems. But the ability of such systems to win a wide range of followers, possibly all over the world, is only a first condition for their use as instruments of foreign policy. A second condition for a successful belief system is its capability to be used flexibly as an instrument in international politics. Here, however, several obstacles may be present, to which we now have to turn our attention.

It seems very difficult to create an ideology or religion artificially, that is without believing in it oneself. All important ideologies and religions in history seem to have been created by charismatic leaders and spread by apostles and disciples who strongly believed in the truths and prescriptions revealed to them by God, fate or historical necessity or passed on to them by their prophets. We know for certain that this has been true for the founders of the great religions. But it seems that Marx and Hitler were also strongly convinced of the truth of their ideologies. Marx probably believed that he had found strictly scientific propositions, but his belief in the *absolute* necessity of the movement of world history towards communism seems to be a strangely unscientific conviction. His followers behave towards his, Engels' and Lenin's teachings as if they were holy sriptures containing only absolute truths. Marx, Engels and Lenin are treated as if they were prophets of a metaphysical religion.

It is perhaps inevitable that the founders of belief systems are themselves strongly convinced of the truths they profess. Nothing helps more to attract people to a new ideology or religion than the exaltation and emotional engagement of personalities of an overpowering stature, that is of charismatic leaders. To convince people of 'truths' which one does not believe oneself seems to be very difficult, indeed. But if this is true, then certain problems arise for the use of belief systems as instruments of foreign policy. For since the leaders believe themselves in the truth of the religions or ideological system, their aims will be the spread of the belief system but not of the state they happen to dominate. Thus the state and its power become an instrument rather to spread the system than the other way round. Of course, this does not mean that the power, the territory and population of the state do not grow in the course of the expansion of the religion or ideology. But it follows from the fact that the organization of the state will only be used as an instrument, that its expansion will usually not take place mainly as a consequence of rational calculations and premeditated actions. The leaders are concerned with the spread of their creed and may even be prepared to sacrifice the survival of the unworthy instrument, the state. Moreover, they are mostly convinced that God, fate or historical necessity will help to reach the inevitable and final success of their just cause. Finally, the leaders have often built up their following with the help of a broad emotional appeal. The followers will, therefore, often be people whose talents are stronger in the field of emotional than of intellectual forces. It is obvious that all these factors weaken a careful calculation of the relative powers of states, of the kinds of actions to be taken and of the chances of success. We have already pointed out that it was probably not by chance that the only universal empires of history, Rome and China, were not founded by people adhering to strong ideologies or beliefs. The blunders and mistakes committed by Napoleon and Hitler were at least partly a consequence of their conviction that they were chosen by destiny. The forces unfettered by a belief system may thus not be sufficient in the end to overcome the drawbacks of an insufficient reliance on rational calculation.

The disadvantages of belief systems in the field of foreign relations just sketched may recede when the second or third generation of leaders has followed the original founders. Lenin and Stalin were certainly prepared to sacrifice the world revolution at least for some time for the survival of the Soviet Union. It must be doubtful whether at least Stalin still believed in the communist creed. But even Lenin was already pragmatically oriented and prepared to take a few steps back before advancing again. The present-day leaders of the Soviet Union seem to be highly pragmatic and one may doubt whether they still believe their communist ideology or whether they only use it to cement and to expand their empire. Thus the second or third generation may be less fettered by the original belief system, more able to subjugate the religious or quasi-religious fervor to rational deliberation and prepared to use the belief system for the promotion of a universal empire.

This does not mean that no drawbacks are connected with this change of attitude. The leaders themselves often become rather colorless people, lacking any emotional appeal and charismatic qualities to kindle the spirits of the masses. This factor is certainly weakening the attraction of the ideology or religion. If some of the 'truths' of the belief system become, moreover, doubtful because experience seems to show that they contradict reality, then the ideology or religion may become a much less powerful instrument of foreign and even of domestic policy. For instance, if the plentiful supply of goods expected by communism does not materialize even after more than sixty years of socialism have passed, if people are exploited more rigorously by socialist functionaries and bureaucrats than formerly by capitalists and if the state is found to be oppressive and hostile to all liberties instead of withering away, then people have a hard time believing Marxist ideology against their own experiences. It is, therefore, not surprising that Marxism seems to have been discredited now for a broad majority of people in Eastern Europe and in Russia who have had a long and intimate experience with this kind of socialism. Still, communist ideology can nevertheless be used in Western industrialized and in underdeveloped countries as a tool of foreign policy by a pragmatic soviet leadership, since most people in these countries lack the immediate experience with real communism as practiced in Eastern Europe and Russia.

Not all ideologies or religions are equally suitable for foreign policy purposes. Christianity with its command to love one's enemy is certainly less adequate for this purpose than Islam. The same is true for Buddhism with its prescription not to kill any living being and its understanding of the world as a delusion of the senses and the brain. All religions with their metaphysical aims of a blessed, eternal life after death in heaven for the righteous or a reaching of Nirvana are probably less useful as instruments of foreign policy than a quasi-religion like communism which promises a future earthly paradise. It thus depends very much on the nature and the aims of belief systems and on the methods proposed to reach them, whether the specific system can be more or less useful as an instrument of foreign policy.

We conclude this section with some remarks concerning the direction of missionary work most fruitful for expansionary foreign policies. In target states it will be usually the leading elite directing government and politics, the economy, the army and the social institutions of a country, who are most resistent against new belief systems, especially if these are closely connected with foreign states. They are, moreover, usually the least dissatisfied with their economic and social positions. As a consequence the missionary work will have to be concentrated mainly on the more dissatisfied groups of the population. Still, it is of great importance to win as many followers as possible in key political, military and economic positions. This can be done either by converting some of the leaders, which is difficult, or by motivating converts who have been won in other groups of the population to start a corresponding career. In this way critical positions can be occupied in the course of time by people adhering to the belief system of the aggressor state and sympathetic to its ideological goals.

The biggest chances to win converts are given in countries with unstable economic and social conditions. This is usually true for poor, underdeveloped countries, especially if these countries are in a self-identity crisis due to their contact with superior Western civilization shaking traditional ideas of old near-subsistence economies. Here many people are rootless and dissatisfied because of the transformation of the economy and the new expectations of a higher standard of living spread by oral propaganda, mass media and immediate acquaintance. Thus many people are unemployed, are out of their original jobs in agriculture, lack an adequate education for the skills required in new jobs and have moved hopefully from their rural homelands to the restlessly growing major cities. But, the hopes of most of them must by necessity be disappointed by the few opportunites open to them in the poor countries and the shanty towns in which they settle in their slum dwellings. This situation is often worsened by the plight of the rural population, which is in many countries exploited by big landed proprietors. It is not surprising that all these people provide a fertile ground for the explanations and hopes provided by an adequate ideology. It is, therefore, interesting to note that communism has mainly concentrated its efforts with more or less success on underdeveloped countries during the last decades.

4. Guerilla War

We have seen that the advent of atomic weapons has severely limited traditional warfare, especially between the countries which are in possession of such weapons and which can threaten each other with mutual destruction. It follows that a big power with expansionary goals has often to use other means than traditional warfare to reach its ends. One of these means is guerilla warfare, which has won increasing importance since World War II.

What are the preconditions for a successful guerilla war and its use as an instrument of foreign policy? A concise list of the conditions of a successful guerilla war has been put together by Sebastian Haffner in his introductory essay on Mao Tse-tung's writings on guerilla war: [7]

Besides the two general basic conditions for a total guerilla war of the Mao kind, a population ready for revolution and a revolutionary party capable of forming a state, three special preconditions have to be fulfilled, which are only present in 'underdeveloped' countries. All three are connected with each other.
The first is a poor, wretched, desperate mass of population, who have scarcely anything or nothing to lose and for whom there is only a relatively small difference between a permanent war and the kind of life, which is available to them in the existing peace order.
The second is a mainly self-sufficient agrarian economy, which cannot be made totally unworkable through permanent war and which allows the feeding of a peasant army of partisans having no food supply of their own.
The third is a country only scarcely opened up to transportation, which is inaccessible in wide parts; a country in which the organization of state power leaks away and from which it is just as possible to escape into inaccessible regions as to surprisingly concentrate [the guerilla forces]. . . .
The more, however, a country has been developed technically, the more its countryside and its conditions of life take a city style, the more is a mechanized and motorized force of the state favored against partisans independently whether it is that of the government, or that of an invading power. In Europe there remain only a few potential countries for partisans; it is characteristic that the subsidiary partisan war of World War II has been most successful in the 'underdeveloped' European South and East; the only European country, in which a total guerilla war of the Mao style could develop was Yugoslavia, and here again mainly in its least developed parts, Bosnia and Montenegro.

The importance of the three specific conditions mentioned by Haffner seem to be obvious. The population in a developed country with a high per capita income would not be prepared to lose all or nearly all their belongings to endure a protracted war and its miseries against the superior forces of an enemy only with hope in an uncertain better future. This is quite different from the situation of a wretchedly poor peasant population exploited by big landowners. If a land-reform has taken place in their favor – as was the case during the Communist revolution in China in the 1920s and 30s – then these poor peasants may well be prepared to endure a not much harsher situation in a protracted guerilla war for the benefits offered to them by the land reform.

The second condition also refers to the state of the economy. An industrialized country would suffer a nearly total breakdown of its economy in the case of a long-lasting war. It would become impossible after some time to feed the population and even the partisans, especially if the country has been a net food importer. Under these conditions the guerillas would experience increasing difficulties and the population might be well-prepared to accept even the repressive order of a tyrannical government if it could only secure again the sheer necessities of life.

The third point mentioned by Haffner is a condition for effective warfare. Since the regular troops of the government and the invader are in the beginning stronger in arms and often in numbers than the guerilla forces – otherwise no guerilla warfare would be necessary – the partisans have to follow a strategy of hit, run and hide. They have to run away from superior enemy forces and to hide themselves in different inaccessible regions in which they are supported by the population. But when the enemy forces have dispersed and exhausted themselves in the pursuit of and the search for the guerillas, then the latter have to be able to concentrate rapidly and unexpectedly to be able to deal annihilating blows to inferior and possibly encircled enemy troops. By following this strategy they can not only secure their arms supply by taking weapons and ammunition from the enemy, but can slowly erode the total superiority of the enemy's army and undermine its morale. In the end they will thus be able to turn from guerilla to open warfare and to sweep away the remaining enemy forces. But again, the condition for such a strategy is the availability of inaccessible support regions and the possibility to concentrate forces hidden from the enemy to turn the defence into a counter-attack.

The three conditions stated by Haffner seem thus to be persuasive. Still, one may doubt whether they must always be fulfilled. For in Northern Ireland a guerilla war already drags on for years in a developed and industrialized country which is easily accessible in all of its parts. Thus all three conditions are not fulfilled. Perhaps a guerilla warfare can nevertheless be entertained, if a small group of fanatical people can easily hide themselves in a sympathetic, but passive population, and if they are so convinced of their aims that they are prepared to sacrifice their own well-being as well as that of other people.

Until now we have not discussed the main general conditions for successful guerilla warfare: "a population ready for revolution and a revolutionary party capable of forming a state, . . ." Without a large section of the population ready for revolution the guerillas would not be able to hide from the enemy, to get sufficient food supplies and to recruit new enthusiastic partisans. They would be betrayed by the people to the enemy and food supplies would be hidden from them as far as possible. Guerillas pressed into service would try to escape as soon as possible and would have a very bad morale. Without an organization capable of forming a new government no long-lasting guerilla war could be organized, no steps taken to secure the support of the people, for instance by land reforms, instruction and individual help, and there could be no possibility to set up a reliable order in the support regions held by the partisans in more or less inaccessible regions.

How can the population be prepared for revolution? In a sense we have already dealt with this problem in section 3. There has to be a feeling of widespread dissatisfaction with the existing political, social and economic order. The problems of a bad economic or social situation have to be felt personally. In such a situation an adequate ideology able to explain the causes of the bad plight and promising a total change to the better following a revolution against a repressive government and its supporters can possibly kindle a widespread revolution. The chances for such a development are especially great, if the 'repressive' group, class and government are foreigners, invading or colonial forces, or if they can at least be depicted as the domestic lackeys of forces in other countries, for instance of Western capitalists.

A revolutionary organization capable of forming a government can, too, best be formed, if an adequate ideology and if perceived problems are present. Many disenchanted people can then be convinced of the truths of the ideology and are prepared to serve as willing and fanatical instruments of the leaders constructing the organization.

These are then the preconditions for guerilla warfare. But how can guerilla war be used as an instrument of foreign policy? Did we not just mention that guerilla activities can best be kindled against *foreign* aggressors, against *colonial* or *invading* powers and their puppet regimes, because in such cases hate against foreign oppression and revolutionary fervor can be combined into one cohesive whole? True, this question points to limitations in the use of guerilla warfare for foreign policy. It does, however, not prevent it. The solution to this seeming paradox is again given by the influence of belief systems. If, for instance, the ideas of communism or Islam can be successfully offered to the people who feel themselves in a bad situation and who are totally dissatisfied, then this ideology will spread, its aims and the directing communist or Islamic organization will all be accepted. The arms and money flowing from foreign supporting communist or Islamic states will be considered as brotherly help. But the leading elite of the aggressor state may be able to control and to direct the revolutionary organization in the target states. This is especially true if the guerilla war is supported by sending military advisors or armed troops. Note that in doing so it is preferable to camouflage the help as much as possible and to bring in troops from other minor states of one's ideological camp.

By providing this assistance and by keeping a close ideological control the aggressor state may even be able to maintain its dominating influence after the final success of the guerilla forces, especially if the target states are weaker neighbors. In this case the aggressor state may be able to add these countries to its sphere of influence.

Such a development need not happen, however. The successful revolutionary leadership may resent the control by the leading country. It may risk falling in disgrace, if it is strong enough and (or) is removed far enough. Then the leadership of the target state may even develop its own brand of the successful ideology, its own 'heresy', to differentiate its product as the true creed more clearly from that of the leading country. This would not only help its domestic political problems but also further all efforts to spread its power to other countries by exporting its own belief system, revolution and guerilla war to other states. It is well known that Tito's Yugoslavia and Mao's China have successfully followed such a path by creating their own versions of communism and by severing their ties with the Soviet Union.

5. Diplomacy

Diplomacy is the art of reaching the aims of a government by using hidden or open threats or promises, by forming offensive or defensive alliances, by concluding or breaking treaties and diplomatic relations. If the aggressive or defensive goals of the political leaders can be reached with these means instead of applying war, economic measures, terrorism or guerilla war, this is preferable because of the substantially lower costs of diplomacy.

To be effective, diplomacy needs skilful, patient and discreet politicians with definite goals and a long-term perspective. For it may not be possible to reach ends within a few years or even a decade due to the resistance of competing states. It may be easier to get concessions from the target country if threats or promises are made secretively, so that no internal public opposition is aroused in this state or in third countries. And nothing is more pernicious to the success of foreign policy than to vacillate between different and possibly vague goals. Domestically such behavior leads to a feeling of insecurity and is apt to undermine the bases of power on which successful diplomacy depends. Externally it causes the mistrust and contempt of able foreign politicians, who can find no reliable pattern and thus distrust the offers, promises and threats of such a policy, since they may be withdrawn or changed at any time. Consequently a first ingredient of diplomacy — and, for that matter, of successful foreign policy — is to educate high quality personnel and to maintain and replace it adequately over generations. A second ingredient is the formulation of meaningful goals which can be pursued, if necessary, for several decades. To create these preconditions a certain tradition has to be built up not only in the Foreign Office but also within the present and future leading elite of the country.

To accomplish its purposes diplomacy needs, moreover, a power base. Offers, threats and promises, whether they are of a military, ideological or economic nature, have to be credible. It must, therefore, be possible to execute them. What is more important, it may even be necessary from time to time to apply the respective means to convince future enemies or allies that the promises and threats can and will be applied if necessary. As Quincy Wright puts it in his *A Study of War*:[8]

Diplomacy under the balance of power has always concealed a mailed first under a velvet glove, but if the glove was cast off war was usually near.

It should not be overlooked, however, that even a weak state may sometimes use diplomacy successfully to gain certain advantages or to resist stronger potential enemies by joining or forming the right coalitions. In these cases the superior strength of the allies is, as it were, used as a diplomatic weapon. A precondition for such a policy is the existence of some common interest with the powerful allies. A good example of such a situation is offered by several buffer states which have been able to preserve their independence by forming the right alliances and this sometimes in spite of the fact that they have been defeated and occupied during wars. The Netherlands and Belgium were threatened or even defeated and occupied several times by French King Louis XIV, by the French revolutionary armies and by Germany in the two World Wars. But they were always saved or reconstituted afterwards because of the help of their powerful allies. Especially

England was very much interested to help them against France and Germany for the sake of the balance of power.

Another example is Denmark, which had been neutral in World War I but succeeded to gain the province of Northern Schleswig from Germany with the help of the Western Allies after the German defeat. Finland was the only Eastern European country able to keep, partly with the help of the Western powers, a degree of independence from its Russian neighbor after World War II, due to the skilful diplomacy of its leaders, especially of President Kekkonen.

Even a big power may be relatively weak and therefore in need of supporting its strength by skilfully using the tool of alliances. This was done by Austria-Hungary during the last phase of the Napoleonic wars. Its foreign minister Metternich first led his country slowly out of a formal alliance with France into a new one with Russia, Prussia and Great Britain, without causing the impression of breaking the agreement with France, by enticing Napoleon to commit diplomatic mistakes. But when victory against France came closer and closer, he concluded a kind of understanding with Britain's foreign minister Lord Castlereagh to contain Russian power and to prevent for that purpose a further weakening of France and to keep it as a big power. With this diplomatic masterpiece he suceeded to restore the European Balance of Power in spite of the relative weakness of Austria-Hungary.[9]

Our examples show that diplomacy which has to rely on alliances because of lack of adequate means can usually only be used for defensive purposes and for keeping or for re-establishing the balance of power. Sometimes it can succeed to gain some limited territories. The reason for this fact should be obvious. A weak state with aggressive aims can rarely find allies willing to support its expansionary aims. It thus follows that a relatively weak state can at best slowly extend in a very limited measure. A country which wants to reach bigger aims has to build up its own power, especially its military and economic power not only as a base for possible wars but also for an expansionary diplomacy.

Let us review some of the means which can be used as offers, threats and promises by diplomacy. We can be brief in doing so, since the military, economic and ideological means, which have already been discussed above, are also the means available for offers, promises and threats.

Economic threats can be threats to cut off certain exports and imports, to refuse credits or not to pay interest or not to repay the capital. They can be strengthened by preparing boycotts, embargoes or blockades. Sometimes these threats may even be executed to make other stronger threats, like military intervention, more credible. Threats can only be successful if they are believed, which implies that the aims followed are less costly to the target state than an execution of the announced measure.

The offering of credits, of economic help, the removal of trade barriers, of boycotts and blockades, the granting of better prices, of investment opportunities and of secure supplies or markets can also be promised in exchange for certain actions taken by the target state, which are favorable to the foreign policy aims of the acting country.

Stronger threats like reprisals against nationals or property of the target state, of limited military expeditions and of outright invasion and war may also be applied. One recalls that the latter measures were successfully used by Hitler first to gain German-speaking Sudetenland from Czechoslovakia in 1938, and then to dissolve the rest of this state and to annex the Czech part of it as a protectorate in 1939, without having to resort to war.

Sometimes military displays are helpful in making military threats credible. Maneuvers of large armies near the frontiers of a country or of naval forces near its seaboard are examples which have often been used by colonial powers. The recent build-up of Russian forces in and around Poland in 1980—1981 has certainly served the larger policy aims of the Soviet Union to keep their communist puppet regime in a rather shaky power position in this country. The earlier Russian invasions in Hungary in 1956 and in Czechoslovakia in 1968 lent even more credibility to such a threat of imminent military action.

A very effective threat may be used if a weapons system endangering the whole population of a country has been created, like nuclear bombs or warheads combined with long-distance missiles or bombers. In this case a whole people may be intimidated if no counterthreat of a similar kind is available.

In several cases incidents can be exploited or even engineered to provide a pretext for a threat against a target state. This may happen, if a citizen or a diplomat of the acting country or their property have been maltreated or if the territory of the acting country has been allegedly violated. By using such incidents the government may be able to justify its aggressive behavior in third states and make it acceptable to the population of the target country or at least to its own population.

The tactics of peaceful nations wanting to thwart the expansionary plans of an aggressor can use the same promises and threats. The use of these instruments will, however, often be somewhat different. To contain aggressive governments it is sometimes important to isolate them from other countries and, if possible, from their own people. To reach these goals it may be advisable to convince other governments of the approaching dangers and thus prevent them from becoming allies of the aggressive state. But it may be better not to form a formal counteralliance which would consolidate the support of the hostile government by its own people. Also, the economic collaboration with the people can be helpful to prevent them from identifying with the government. No threats of a preventive war should be applied and the press, television and radio should be used to make a clear-cut difference between the aggressive government and the people. All taken together, the government of the target state should firmly resist all threats of the aggressive country, try to win the quiet support of other states and to isolate its population from the government. This mollifying attitude should, however, not prevent the peace-loving country from applying strong counterthreats and from keeping the balance of military power whenever necessary.

The use of promises and threats is not confined to economic and military instruments. Weak threats are threats to break diplomatic relations with the respective country or to make the entry of its citizens more difficult. Another threat would be to exclude a country from international institutions like the UNO or its suborganizations, or to prohibit its participation in international fairs, exhibitions or sports events. Several of these measures have been applied against South Africa in recent years and some Western states boycotted the Moscow Olympic Games of 1980 because of the Soviet invasion of Afghanistan. But one realizes the weakness of these threats from the very fact that they had to be executed and did not lead the South African government to a revision of its racist policies, nor the Soviet Union to a withdrawal of its troops.

For minor problems between states diplomacy may successfully use international arbitration by third states, decisions by the International Court in The Hague or the European Court, or decisions of international organizations like the Security Council of the United Nations. The latter is even able to solve more important problems between smaller or medium-sized states as long as the big powers can agree on the issues in question. For the big powers are by definition able to make credible threats. On the other hand, the Soviet Union, the USA, France, Britain and China have the right to veto any decision of the Security Council. Thus no UN actions or threats can be taken against them or against any country they want to protect.

In specific historical circumstances even ideological and propaganda threats can be used to force a target state to take certain actions. In medieval times a Papal interdict could be more powerful than a big army. It is well known that Pope Gregory VII cast an interdict against Emperor Heinrich I of the Holy Roman Empire which was sufficient to deprive Heinrich of nearly all his support. The emperor had to make a pilgrimage to Canossa in 1077 and to repent on his knees in front of the Pope to obtain the removal of the interdict as a precondition for regaining a substantial part of his political power. Similarly, if the Soviet Politbureau denounces a leading figure in

Eastern Europe as a bad communist or worse, as a capitalist, he will not be able to stay in power much longer. Since 1979, we have seen how the Ayatollah Khomeini has shaped the fate of Iran for better or worse with a few words directed to the masses of his fanatical religious followers at the right time. There can be no doubt then that threats to use interdictions and sanctions of a religious or ideological nature can be very effective political weapons and that their application can be used as threats, if an adequate ideology or religion exists or has been built up in the target state.

In concluding this section we have to point out that different political systems are not similarly suited to the use of diplomacy. Threats and promises are more credible if they seem to be supported by the whole population and if no different opinions are pronounced by the mass media of the acting country or by its opposition parties. Negotiations are often more successful if they, together with the threats and promises applied, are not conducted in the open. Ideological or religious interdicts and sanctions are more effectively used in foreign countries if the whole domestic population is convinced of their rightfulness, too. All these factors concur to limit the effective use of diplomacy by democracies but to make their application easier for dictatorships, theocracies and oligarchies. To quote Quincy Wright again:[10]

Democracies normally require that important decisions be made only after wide participation of the public and deliberate procedures which assure respect for law and freedom of criticism before and after the decision is made. They are, therefore, ill adapted to the successful use of threats and violence as instruments of foreign policy. Autocracies, on the other hand, are accustomed to rule by authority at home and are able to make rapid decisions which will appear to be accepted because adverse opinion is suppressed. Consequently, in the game of power diplomacy, democracies pitted against autocracies are at a disadvantage. They cannot make effective threats until they really mean war; they can seldom convince either themselves or the potential enemy that they really do mean war; and they are always vulnerable to the dissensions of internal oppositions, capable of stimulation by the potential enemy, whatever decision is made.

A good example of the problems thus faced by democracy is the recent NATO decision to install missiles with atomic warheads in Western Europe able to attack Soviet territory. This decision has allegedly been taken to counter the Soviet build-up of SS20 intermediate missiles directed against Western Europe. The decision has been coupled with a proposal to begin disarmament talks to reduce the number of the missiles to be installed together with that of the SS20s. Even a reduction to zero has been envisioned by the NATO partners.

Now, if the underlying assessment of the military situation was correct and if the intentions were sincere, then the bargaining power of NATO could have been severely eroded by the so-called European Peace Movement which started in 1981 and was strongly supported or sometimes even instigated by communist parties. The mass rallies of 100—300,000 people which have been brought together mainly against the NATO decisions may well have caused the Soviet leadership to drag their feet during the disarmament talks in the hope that the 'Peace Movement' would grow strong enough to prevent the installation of NATO missiles. This is the more probable since the movement had been joined by substantial factions of governing parties like the German Social Democrats, which were the senior partner in the former West German government. In case of success the Soviet Union would have been able to keep its SS20s without having to fear the installation of similar NATO missiles.

Notes

[1] For a more comprehensive discussion of the means of economic warfare compare: Peter Bernholz: *Aussenpolitik und internationale Wirtschaftsbeziehungen*. V. Klostermann, Frankfurt a.M. 1966, und Henry York Wan, Jr.: *A Contribution to the Theory of Trade Warfare*, Massachusetts Institute of Technology Thesis, Cambridge (Mass.), 1961.

[2] Kautilya: Artha-Sastra: "Excerpts" in: Sarvepelli Radhakrishnan and Charles A. Moore (eds.): *A Sourcebook in Indian Philosophy*. Princeton University Press, Princeton (N.Y.), 1957, p. 210.

[3] For a detailed study of terrorism see Lester A. Sobel (ed.): *Political Terrorism*. Clio Press, Oxford, 2 vols., 1975 and 1978.

[4] Bruno Frey and Hannelore Weck: Hat Arbeitslosigkeit den Aufstieg des Nationalsozialismus bewirkt? *Jahrbuch für Nationalökonomie und Statistik*, vol. 196(1), 1981, pp. 1—31.

[5] From Lenin's "Speech to Representatives of Textile Workers on February 6, 1921." In W.J. Lenin: *Sämtliche Werke*, 3rd ed., vol. 26, Moscow 1940, p. 184.

[6] From Lenin's "Speech to Moscow Cell Secretaries on November 26, 1920," op. cit., pp. 293—294.

[7] Sebastian Haffner: "Introductory Essay" to *Mao Tse-tung: Theorie des Guerrilla-Krieges*. Rowohlt Taschenbuch, Reinbek (Hamburg), 1966, pp. 28—29.

[8] Quincy Wright: *A Study of War*. University of Chicago Press, Chicago and London, 1965, p. 693.

[9] See Henry Kissinger: *A World Restored*. Grosset and Dunlop, New York 1964.

[10] Quincy Wright: op. cit., p. 842.

Chapter 6

Contradictions and Dilemmas of International Politics

The reader has probably asked himself several times during the discussions of the preceding chapters, whether there are not problems related with international policy which seem to lead to unsolvable contradictions or dilemmas with other aspects of human life or of national politics. Already in the first chapter the dilemma of the international armament race was mentioned. But this is not the only problem we have encountered. A free, democratic society seems to make foreign policy less effective, the design and execution of foreign policy appears (with what we have called 'the law of minimal international morality') to contradict widely accepted rules of ethics and morality, and the general disorders and upheavals of the international system with its vehement acts of bloodshed and sanctioned violence are in strong contrast to the rule of law followed within the borders of civilized states. It seems absurd that a soldier is not only allowed, but ordered to kill unknown people, perhaps even foreign friends, during a patriotic war, but punished for killing a dangerous enemy in civilian life, even if he is attacked himself; and it is a patriotic duty, and has even been called a crusade to kill tens of thousands of civilians by bombing their cities or by driving them away from their homelands.

It is the task of this chapter to discuss these and other problems before we turn to an assessment of the present international situation and of possible future developments. In doing so we will begin with some specific and then move on to more general problems.

1. The Armaments Race

The nature and origins of the armaments race have already been discussed in the second chapter with the help of a simple example (see section 1). Let us recall the fundamental relationships. If there is a danger that one or more states arm to get a preponderant military position which can be used for threats through diplomacy or for outright war, then other nations have to rearm, too, to prevent aggression and to preserve their integrity. Thus, if there exists even only one aggressive state, others have to respond with similar rearmament efforts. The first state may then react with a more extensive arms program, the others may respond again, and so on. The spiral of an arms race has been entered. Given these relationships, it is even possible that all states mistakenly suspect each other of having aggressive intentions and rearm because of unfounded fears. Then, observing that the other state is strengthening its military establishment they believe that their mistrust has been well-founded, and the armament race goes on.

How far can an arms race be pursued? An extreme limit is given by the economic capacities of the weaker powers participating. The economic well-being of the population can be reduced to a mere subsistence level and for a limited period even below that and the whole remaining economic potential directed towards the production of arms and military equipment. No doubt that exactly this has been done by some of the major belligerents during the two World Wars. In peacetime such a behavior has, to my knowledge, not been observed, but it is true that the industrialized countries are presently spending incredible amounts on armaments. Even worse, there are poor underdeveloped countries where many people still die from starvation, which spend vast sums on their military establishments and, like Pakistan and India, even try to build atomic bombs and long-range missiles.

The United States have presently the biggest economic capacity of all states in the world. Judged only by this capacity it would be able to out-maneuver all other nations including the Soviet Union by just driving up military expenditures to the point at which all other countries would be turned to starvation and be forced to forego the most pressing civilian needs if they wanted to follow the United States. The US would thus be in a position to build up a military strength far superior to that of any other power in the world. By looking at this extreme case, which is certainly economically feasible, we see at once that it could never happen politically, at least not in a democracy like that enjoyed by the US. The necessary reduction of per capita income would never be tolerated by voters except in obvious national emergencies like wars not openly brought about by the country itself. The government would be defeated at least at the next elections, and excessive rearmament plans would probably not get a majority in Congress even before that, since its members would be concerned too much for their reelection. Thus an arms race beyond the limits of the economic capacities of the weaker big powers is not possible for democracies if it implies a sizable reduction of per capita income except in case of a national emergency perceivable by everybody.

Political limits to an arms race up to economic capacities exist probably even in dictatorships and oligarchies. First, a danger of a revolution or a coup d'etat of dissatisfied groups of the population may be present. Second, even if dictator or oligarchy are, perhaps with the help of the military, in tight control so that no such danger exists, there may be other reasons preventing a corresponding course of action. The drastic reduction of the standard of living implied will motivate people to work less and to turn to out-of-job activities to get more food and clothing. Cultivating crops in their own small garden plots, searching for goods on black markets and in the countryside are just a few examples. In this case the leadership may get a lower arms output if it reduces civilian supplies below a certain threshold. Further, if the industry is directed too much towards arms production this may lead to a reduction of net investments and the innovations necessary for future economic growth of the country, leading to a future weakening of its relative power position.

It follows that there are several reasons able to explain why an arms race up to economic capacities seems not easily to happen during peace-time. This, of course, does not prevent that dictatorships or oligarchies like those of Hitler and Stalin were in a better position to rearm than democracies. But such a policy can even for aggressive regimes only be rational if they hope to achieve their expansionist aims within a relatively short time. Otherwise the chances of their plans would be diminished by the worsening future relative economic power of their states.

Considering these facts it cannot be surprising that increasing military expenditures of states have often been limited by economic growth. Economic growth provided the means to raise outlays on arms without running into internal political problems, since they left room for higher disposable per capita incomes of the members of society and for extending social welfare programs. No wonder that several states have been and are still favoring economic growth just to be able to increase their military power.

Given the underlying dilemma of the arms race and its negative influence on human well-being, what can be done to limit or to get rid of it? No doubt, not many alternatives exist as long as one remains within the system of sovereign states competing for power. True, if no country wants expansion it may be possible to find ways to slowly weaken mutual distrust, to come to an agreement to limit and to reduce arms and to find ways for an adequate control of the mutual reduction of arsenals. In situations like the present one, for instance, between the USSR and the USA, there seems to be no other alternative than first to preserve the balance of power, but, secondly, to try hard to come to a disarmament agreement which can be controlled by both sides. No doubt that this is a very difficult job not only because of the mutual distrust, but also because of the difficulties of an adequate control, of determining what is meant by military equilibrium given different arms systems, and the different perceptions of reality by the participants because of ideological reasons. But it is perhaps the only path which may save humanity from the unbelievable horrors of an unintended atomic war or from the destructions of a carefully designed and executed 'limited' war, whether it may get out of control or not.

2. The Preservation of Knowledge and the Continuity of Foreign Policy

Even individuals sometimes have problems in preserving a long-time consistency of their actions, and are likely to change their aims or preferences slowly and sometimes even rapidly during the course of their lives. A state is not a person, not even an organism, but an organization of people with a changing membership resulting from births and deaths, emigration and immigration. The organs of the state including its government have to cope with an even more rapid turnover of personnel. But a change of personnel often means a change in methods and goals, even if everybody involved has unchanged preferences and acts consistently. On top of this, even without a change in membership, non-dictatorial decision-making can lead to inconsistent behavior of collectivities like state agencies in spite of rational behavior of all their members, as has been shown in the beginning of Chapter 4.

These facts have important implications not only for internal but also for foreign policy. Foreign offices and their agencies are always more probable than any individuals composing them to pursue inconsistent policies and to change aims more or less abruptly. The consequences of this state of affairs can be grave. In a world of states competing for power, the danger arises that countries with often changing foreign policy goals and contradictory courses of action will in time be outmaneuvered by the politicians of more consistent states, and more or less slowly be reduced in power and perhaps be obliterated.

One of the major preconditions of a successful foreign policy is to provide organizational structures furthering the transmission of adequate knowledge and the preservation of meaningful goals in spite of the problems described above. To create and to preserve such an organizational structure and tradition is a difficult task and can probably never be fully accomplished. It should perhaps not even be fully accomplished since this would prevent the inflow of important new ideas and a change of goals warranted by new insights and experiences. Still such changes should only be taken in full knowledge of the old aims and the wisdom and information accumulated by former politicians. For only then some guarantee exists that even well-educated innovators will not overlook relevant knowledge and make fateful mistakes in engineering the policy changes.

What are the factors furthering the consistency of foreign policy methods and of goals over time? There can be no doubt that the recruitment and training of new politicians and civil servants entering the field of foreign policy are of the utmost importance. Before people are allowed to make foreign policy decisions they should be well-acquainted with the bases of relative power, with the instruments of foreign policy, the different possible international systems and their workings and with the present situation including the relative strengths and weaknesses of the relevant states and of their politicians including the aims and methods which they follow. To be able to absorb the necessary information, only individuals with adequate intellectual capabilities, strength of will and education should be allowed to enter the foreign service and its preparatory institutions. Further, a strong loyalty towards the state and its goals seems to be an important precondition for a successful integration into the existing foreign policy system.

When people have been found worthy and capable to enter the foreign service and when they have become acquainted with the main goals and all the relevant information, it is important that they gain practical experience by taking different positions in the administration of the foreign office, in consulates, embassies and missions in and to foreign countries before they are allowed to move up to become political leaders shaping foreign policy.

Next we have to ask ourselves which political systems and structures are most favorable to further institutions capable of pursuing a stable and consistent foreign policy. First of all, popular democracy is certainly not very well-suited to develop the necessary competence and consistency. Here the leading politicians are elected and their foreign policy experience is usually of very minor importance for their election or reelection. It follows that their education and experience are mostly inadequate for their foreign policy tasks. It is, therefore, not surprising that, for instance, many American Presidents proved to be very inexperienced in foreign policy in recent decades, and sometimes had to learn costly lessons in their first years in office. This inexperience and lack of knowledge would not have been so dangerous, if these political leaders would have relied on well-informed and experienced foreign ministers. But this was not always the case, and thus serious blunders were committed, as we have seen in the first chapter.

Another weakness of democratic systems is the frequent change in leading foreign policy positions. Presidents, prime ministers, chancellors and their foreign ministers have mostly to leave office when their parties or they themselves have been defeated in elections or in parliament, or if the party coalition supporting them has broken down. The newcomers are often not only inexperienced, but follow different goals and ideas, since they are members of the former opposition party (parties). Even quite a number of secondary positions are filled with new people, since the old office-holders are thought to be politically unreliable or since the newcomers have to be rewarded for their support during the election campaign. Here, again, information about and experience in foreign affairs as well as loyalty to long-term goals are usually not required of the candidates for these secondary positions.

Whereas democracy is not a very fertile ground for a stable and successful foreign policy, things seem to be quite different for states ruled by oligarchic elites or aristocracies. Aristocracies share a common educational and cultural background, which makes the transfer of knowledge of and loyalty to long-term policy goals of the state which they and their ancestors have directed for generations much less difficult. If the more talented members have a chance to serve for years in political bodies discussing and partly controlling foreign policy and to go abroad as military commanders or as emissaries of the state, these people have the chance to acquire the necessary knowledge and experience in foreign affairs before they move up to the levers of power. All of this seems to have been true in some of the states which have been most successful in long-term foreign policy like the Roman Republic, Venice and Britain during the eighteenth and nineteenth centuries. If it happens that, additional to the common background and the favorable organizational structure, there is always at least one talented and experienced member of this aristocracy who is able to control foreign policy in a given period, then the chances of success are substantial indeed, since this removes the possibility of inconsistent actions following from the very nature of collective decision-making.

Sometimes even absolute monarchies and dictatorships may be a better guarantee for a stable and successful foreign policy than democracies. This is true if they enjoy a sequence of talented kings or dictators able to transmit their goals and knowledge to their successors. Even if the successors are not brilliant they may be wise enough to find talented and experienced ministers following the goals inherited from their predecessors. The stability is enhanced, if great kings, leaders or dictators are able to pass on their goals and methods in 'testaments' which are respected by their successors because of their own foreign policy successes. We have seen that Frederick II of Prussia did exactly this. The same is true for Cardinal Richelieu and King Louis

XIV of France. These testaments had a measure of success. Lenin's writings and speeches have served and probably still serve the same purpose in the Soviet Union.

To conclude, however, one should not overlook the inherent weakness of absolute monarchies and dictatorships. If unqualified kings or dictators succeed to the throne or take over power, foreign policy may become inconsistent and follow different and even vacillating aims. In a dictatorship it is quite probable that people with different policy goals and without adequate training and experience in foreign policy follow each other, since no rule of succession exists, with the consequence that usually leaders come to power with the help of internal fighting and intrigue. Finally, the absolute power of monarchs and dictators may prevent the establishment of durable foreign policy organizations which are able to transmit the necessary knowledge to the future generation and to provide the insight and training which are a precondition of successful and stable foreign policies.

3. The Dilemma between External and Internal Policies

The famous German historian of the nineteenth century, Leopold von Ranke once coined the phrase of the 'primacy of foreign policy'. By this he meant not only that the fate of nations is often determined by foreign policy, but also that domestic policy should be subordinated to the requirements of foreign policy. The former statement refers to observed relationships, whereas the latter amounts to a value judgment. Whether it is accepted or not depends on the goals followed by the respective state.

The statement that the fate of nations and their domestic policies have often been strongly influenced by foreign policy, has certainly been true in many historical cases. But there have been other cases, too, in which the influence of foreign policy on national developments has been very limited indeed, and where foreign policy has been almost totally shaped by domestic policies. A good example are the United States during the time from 1815—1914. During this century the influence of foreign developments on the US and on its domestic policies and politics has been negligible due to the isolated geographical situation and the policy instituted by Washington and Jefferson to keep hands off European involvements. It is true that the US fought a war with Mexico in 1846—47 in which it acquired California, Arizona and New Mexico. Moreover, there were quite a number of fights with the Indians. But these international involvements took place outside of the balance of power system and could thus be solved with very small resources.

Another example is provided by Japan from the beginning of the seventeenth to the middle of the nineteenth century. Here the Tokugawa Shoguns had brutally driven out the Europeans and severed all outside relations with the exception of a very limited trade confined to the port of Nagasaki. It was only after the naval invasion of American Commander Perry in 1854, that they had to open their country again to Westerners and their trade. Even then it lasted until the reforms under Emperor Meiji, that is until Japan started to take over Western science and technology and to move on its path of economic growth, that it began to be involved in international politics again. During the long period before no foreign influence to speak of, and of course no foreign policy influences was present in Japan.

The situation looked quite different to the members of the European Balance of Power, and especially for the countries which were centrally located in Europe, like Austria-Hungary and Prussia (later Germany). They had always to be on the alert against potential aggressors and their dangerous schemes, quite apart from their own foreign policy aims. If only one of the big powers was bent on expansion they had to keep up their armies and their armaments not to loose valuable provinces or even their independence and to prevent the aggressor from gaining supremacy in Europe. Thus the economy had to be strengthened, population growth to be stimulated and private wants and public welfare to be subordinated to the requirements of foreign policy for larger armies and for more and better weapons. Different aims concerning domestic policies between opposing factions and parties often dwindled to insignificance because a great part of additional resources had to be spent mainly on military requirements, on wars and contributions exacted after defeat. All of this was, of course, also true for expansionary states, which had first of all to build up their relative military power. It is obvious that it was a world of this kind which Ranke studied and to which his statement referred. Moreover, if one accepts the goal that a state should first of all try to preserve its territory and its independence, then one can derive at once also the normative statement that internal should be subordinated to external policy.

It should by now be clear under what conditions foreign policy tends to exert a strong influence on domestic policy. This is usually the case when a country is an essential actor in a multipolar, a balance of power or a bipolar system. In such a system a state can only follow independent domestic policies at the risk of loss of population and territory, of its role as an essential actor, and possibly of its very existence. Foreign policy exerts, on the contrary, no influence on domestic policy if a state is isolated from the essential members of the above systems, if it is stronger than possible inessential members and if it has no foreign policy goals of any importance. This was clearly the case in the examples of Japan and the United States mentioned above. As soon as these countries gave up their hands-off policies or (and) became members of the balance of power or bipolar systems they were soon involved in strong international tensions and had to build up and to keep large armed forces. Their domestic policy was now strongly influenced by foreign policies. It is interesting to note that Japan again was able to thrive without a military establishment of any importance until today (1983) after it had been defeated and disarmed by the Americans led by General MacArthur in and after World War II. There can be no doubt that this was again a consequence of its rather isolated position (as compared for instance to West Germany) and of the fact that it was no longer an essential actor of the new bipolar system established after 1945.

A similar role as that played by states isolated geographically from the strong essential actors of the international system has been and is often played by small, weak and (or) neutral countries. In fact, Japan after 1945 has already been an example, since the value of its geographical isolation has been strongly reduced by modern technological developments especially in the field of airplanes, missiles and nuclear weapons. Small, weak and (or) neutral states have in common with isolated nations that they are not essential actors. But because of their relative weakness they can at best hope to build up a defensive force which would make an invasion too expensive to be worthwhile to an aggressor. This has been and is until today the official policy of countries like Sweden and Switzerland. It is obvious that even if such a defensive force is maintained, it does not usually lead to the same expensive drain on economic resources as that experienced by essential actors. Apart from this military strategy small and weak countries have to rely on diplomacy and common interests with some of the essential actors for their security and independence. They can either join an alliance with essential states or decide to become neutral. In the latter case they have to rely apart from their own relatively weak defensive potential on the hope that no essential actor would allow others to occupy them, because this would change the balance of power unfavorably. But the division of Poland in the eighteenth century has shown that this is not a certain possibility. Joining an alliance with essential members, as several European countries have joined NATO, often provides a somewhat more reliable security. However, because of the dominating influence of essential actors, it usually means a reduction of actual independence. The smaller partners of the alliance are asked to act in conformity with the treaty and to carry their share of the common defense burden. Still, this burden is usually relatively smaller than for the essential actor, since the latter knows that the balance of power would break down without his efforts, whereas this is not true for the smaller members of the defensive alliance.[1]

We conclude that the military burden carried by neutrals as well as by inessential members of alliances with essential states is usually lighter than that of the latter. Some of these nations may even risk or be able to have a very small military establishment. Moreover, in both cases the freedom of diplomatic action is rather limited: inessential actors can be either neutrals or allies, but it would be very dangerous for them to change sides often and to develop too much initiative. But if this is true, then the resources necessary for foreign policy should be much smaller relatively, than for essential states. Consequently domestic policies of inessential countries will be less influenced by foreign policies, too.

It has been shown under which international conditions strong, weak and scarcely any influence at all of foreign on internal policy is to be expected. But even if the influence of foreign policy is strong this does not necessarily mean that it is dominant and that domestic policy does not influence the international policy of states. Nor is the international system and the position of a state within this system the only factor determining the degree of dependence of domestic on foreign policy.

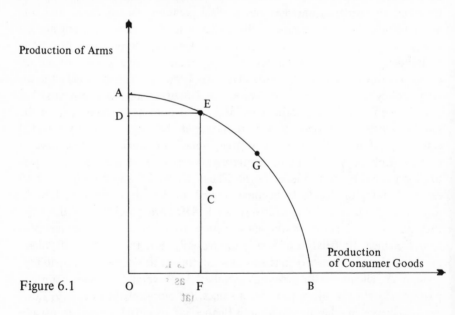

Figure 6.1

The demands of foreign policy and, therefore, the tensions with domestic policy are strongest in states which are essential actors in the given international system. They are present, but weaker, if the respective states are non-essential but not isolated from the big powers of the system. Perhaps the most important conflict between foreign and domestic aims is caused as a consequence of the competing demands on economic resources, which has already been discussed in the section dealing with the arms race. The resulting problem is sketched in Figure 6.1. AB is called the Production Possibility Frontier. It depicts the largest combinations of amounts of consumer goods and of military equipment which can be produced in a country, given the limited resources in the form of labor, capital goods, land, raw materials and available production techniques. The curve slopes down from left to right since a higher production of goods for consumption implies a smaller arms supply. OA is the biggest amount of arms, OB the greatest amount of consumer goods which could be supplied if production would be totally concentrated on this category of goods. It is, however, obvious that OA cannot be realized, since at least a minimal production of consumer goods, say, DE is absolutely necessary to care for the minimal needs of the population. It follows that all possible production plans which allow the survival of the population are given by area FBE. Of these only those on curve BE are efficient production plans. A point like C is inefficient since there are other production plans like G allowing a higher supply of both categories of goods. Of course, this does not exclude that there can be times like big depressions, in which points like C are realized, because many resources are unemployed in such a situation.

Consider a country geographically isolated from the big powers, like the USA in the nineteenth century. Such a state needs scarcely any military establishment. No tension exists between foreign and domestic policies. A point on EB very close to B can be realized. By contrast the situation of a country which is an essential member of the international system is quite different. Because of the expenditures on arms spent by other big powers it may be necessary to select points E or G just to keep up with the others. The question whether E or G is the corresponding point may depend on such factors as the relative economic strength of the country and on its geographical position. If a country is centrally located in the international system it has to spend more on arms to keep up with its competitors. If it is relatively weak economically it has to forego relatively more consumption goods to preserve the balance of power.

Let us assume that E has to be selected just to preserve the relative international power position. In this case a strong dependence of domestic on foreign policy would be present. But this does not mean that E will be selected. The people may just not be prepared to carry the burden implied by E and the government be forced to prefer a point on EB to the right of E. In this case domestic policy has not totally succumbed to foreign policy requirements, but the consequences would be grave. The relative international power of the state would be eroded and the country may slowly lose its position as an essential actor with all the dangers for territorial integrity and independence implied. The leading statesmen may realize this danger and try to move to E. Especially in a democracy, however, they may have a hard time doing so, since voters are not well-informed and well-educated about international problems and about the position of their country. They will thus usually underestimate the international dangers and prefer a higher consumption level with less armaments. Politicians trying to realize E will be defeated in elections by opposition parties promising 'to solve international tensions by peaceful negotiations and a reduction in the level of armaments'.

We conclude that strong tensions can exist between foreign and domestic policies especially in democracies. It is obvious that these tensions may be resolved in different ways. Either the country loses its status as a big power with possibly grave consequences, or some leading statesmen succeed in establishing a dictatorship or oligarchy in the face of what they believe to be vital foreign policy requirements.

Tensions are less pronounced, if the necessary military requirements to keep up the balance of power correspond to point G. Here a viable compromise may be found even in a democracy at or near G (between E and G), if the demand for consumer goods on the part of voters does not exceed or is lower than the amount provided by G. Whether this is the case or not depends on historical developments, especially whether the population has in the past enjoyed higher or lower living standards than that implied by G. If the former has been the case, then the difficulties sketched above arise again, since it is very difficult to reduce a level of consumption to which a population is accustomed. Only in exceptional circumstances like a defensive war are democracies able to reduce the supply of consumer goods below this level.

We have still not quite exhausted all aspects of the problem, namely those connected with economic developments over time. If a position like E has to be selected by an essential country just to preserve its relative power position, then it has to use its total resources to produce arms and consumption goods and to keep up its productive apparatus. Thus no additional resources are available for innovative efforts and for net investments to increase the capital stock.

By contrast a country which could preserve its relative power position by realizing point G in Figure 6.1 could make net investments and innovate in the current period, i.e. increase its capital stock, and thus its production in later periods.

The resulting relationship has been sketched in Figure 6.2. If the country in question could reduce the production of consumer goods by G-G′ to G′, the respective resources would be free for net investments. With this use of resources the country would be able to produce during the current period the combinations of arms and consumer goods given by curve A'B'. Points to the right of G' could only be selected, if this would not endanger the relative power position. The situation is, however, quite different in later periods. For then the production possibility frontier has moved to the right to EF, because of the increase of the capital stock and (or) of successful innovations. Now the leaders of the nation are in a more favorable position than before. They can, e.g., realize H, so that the population gets more consumer goods *and* more arms can be produced than in G. Thus internal demands can be satisfied and the relative power position be strengthened. It is obvious that such net investment and innovation policies can be pursued in each period.

We conclude from the above that if at least one essential competitor exists in the international system which can and does follow a policy of net investment and innovation, then the other members are under strong pressure to follow the same course of action to keep up their relative power. But from what has been said before this means an especially strong burden, if not an impossibility for economically relatively weak and democratic members of the international system.

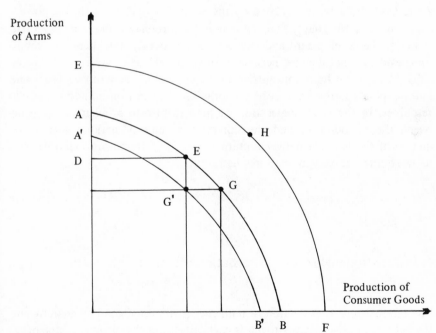

Figure 6.2

Our deliberations allow us to draw several conclusions. First, democracies can only act as big powers and remain essential actors, if their economic resources and productivity are higher than that of other essential actors. Their stability is enhanced, if they are not located in a central position of the international system. Second, the less these conditions are fulfilled, the higher the chance that a country will either lose its status as an essential actor or abolish or never fully develop democracy. Third, non-essential states provide better opportunities for democratic regimes. Finally, democratic regimes have the highest chance to survive in potentially powerful states which are geographically isolated from the big powers of the international system.

Drawing together these conclusions it should perhaps not be surprising to find that the big powers of the balance of power system on the European continent had great problems with the development of democracy before World War II. Even France relapsed twice into dictatorship under Napoleon I and Napoleon III after the Revolution of 1789. Great Britain, on the other hand, had not only the best geographical position of the big powers, but was wealthier than the other countries on a per capita income basis. On the continent, moreover, inessential actors like the Scandinavian states, the Netherlands and Switzerland were the most flourishing democracies. Democratic United States was isolated by the Atlantic Ocean from the big powers of the system. No doubt, that the conditions formulated above are not sufficient for the development and existence of democracy. But there is certainly some evidence that they are necessary conditions for its survival.

Until now we have concentrated on the tensions between external and internal policies brought about by conflicting demands on limited economic resources. In the following section we have to turn to problems created between the surroundings and the domestic systems of nations as a consequence of the tensions between international disorder and national order and between international and national morality.

4. International Disorder, International Law and Morality

The international organization of humanity is still dominated by anarchy and the actions of governments towards each other and the citizens of the other countries strongly influenced by what we have called the law of minimal international morality (Chapter 2). The absence of a world state with international courts, with armed forces and police able to enforce the rules of a worldwide legal system guaranteeing peace and security, has tempted in the past and will tempt again in the future the politicians of one or the other nation to try to extend the power, territory and resources of their state and thus their own power and prestige by employing military forces or threats against countries.

Given this situation, even peace-loving political leaders have to react by building up the military, economic and ideological potential of their states. International distrust, intrigues and maneuvers become everyday affairs. Competition for power and arms races are widespread and wars, infiltration, international reprisals and terrorism are nearly inescapable. International law and agreements will only be followed as long as they are believed to be in the interest of the participating political leaders.

The moral conflicts resulting from this predominantly anarchic state of the international system are obvious. The same people who are obliged by law and morality not to harm other citizens and their property, and even to follow meticulous traffic rules, are allowed as statesmen to blackmail foreign politicians, to threaten whole states and their populations with hunger through blockades and with outright annihilation, and to command their own people to mutilate and to kill thousands or millions of people during wars. Law-abiding citizens, loving fathers and husbands have to kill and to destroy cold-bloodedly if the 'necessities of international politics' reassert themselves.

Statesmen have usually been well aware of this conflict between 'national' morality and 'international' immorality brought about by the anarchic character of the international system. Louis XIV, the Sun King of France, wrote in his memoirs of 1661:[2]

I touch here, my son, on one of the most difficult and controversial points in the behaviour of princes. I am far away from teaching you faithlessness. . . . But it is necessary to make certain differences in this field . . . . The two crowns of France and Spain are in the same situation today as in the past, if one of them increases its power then the other has to lose power correspondingly. This leads to an envy between both countries which is essential to them, if I may say so, and which can be covered up but never extinguished by treaties. . . .
If one shall speak the truth quite frankly, treaties are concluded from the beginning with this mental reservation. All the beautiful provisions about alliances, affirmations of friendship and the promises to grant advantages, do only mean according to the experience of centuries, as understood by the two signatories, that they want to abstain from armed encroachments and from public enmities. Secret violations of the treaties which are not visible to the public are expected by everybody as a consequence of the natural principle I have explained to you.

Similarly, Frederic II of Prussia explained in 1752:[3]

Thus our behaviour has to differ according to situation, time and person. If the time is ripe for an open break a decided and proud comportment is advisable. . . . If there are many enemies, one has to divide them, to single out and to throw oneself on the most irreconcilable, but to negotiate with the others, to lull them into sleep and conclude with them a separate peace treaty even with losses. After first having cast down the main enemy, it is time to return to them and to go for them under the pretext that they did not fulfill their obligations.

The conflict between domestic morality and the behavior towards potential or actual enemies may sometimes pose a scarcely solvable problem to conscientious citizens. The refusal of people belonging to Jehovah's Witnesses to serve in the military establishment even if they risk imprisonment or death, provides on adequate example. Other people may be satisfied to have some superficial rationalization of the different ethical standards used at home and against foreigners. Louis XIV goes on to explain in the quotation mentioned above:[2]

Thus one could say that both sides dispense each other of the obligations to follow the treaties and that, consequently, one can really not violate the agreements. For one has not taken the provisions verbally.

Things have been worse in many historical cases. Human beings are easily prepared to identify themselves with certain groups, organizations, ideas and ideologies. If this happens, they are often ready to convert, to fight, to kill and even to torture outsiders, who do not belong to their group or organization or do not share their beliefs, for the higher aims and goals of the entity with which they identify. The members of the in-group are thus amply justified to treat others differently depending on whether they are members, too, or are hostile, wicked or heretic outsiders. In fighting, maiming and killing such persons or, in destroying their property they may even risk their health and their lives for the higher aim and at least not follow any selfish interests.

The psychic mechanism just referred to has been noted and described by many people. It has been nicely sketched in a book written by Arthur Koestler who concludes:[3]

Yet I think most historians would agree that the part played by impulses of selfish, individual aggression in the holocausts of history was small; first and foremost, the slaughter was meant as an offering to the gods, to king and country, or the future happiness of mankind. . . . The number of victims of robbers, highwaymen, rapers, gangsters and other criminals at any period of history is negligible compared to the massive numbers of those cheerfully slain in the name of the true religion, just policy, or correct ideology. Heretics were tortured and burnt not in anger but in sorrow, for the good of their immortal souls. . . . Wars of religion were fought to decide some fine point in theology or semantics. Wars of succession, dynastic wars, national wars, civil wars, were fought to decide issues equally remote from the personal self-interest of the combatants. The Communist purges, as the word 'purge' indicates, were understood as operations of social hygiene, to prepare mankind for the golden age of the classless society. The gas chambers and crematories worked for the advent of a different version of the millennium. Heinrich Eichmann . . . was not a monster or a sadist, but a conscientious bureaucrat, who considered it his duty to carry out his orders and believed in obedience as the supreme virtue; . . .

Let me repeat: the crimes of violence committed for selfish personal motives are historically insignificant compared to those committed *ad maiorem gloriam Dei*, out of self-sacrificing devotion to a flag, a leader, a religious faith or a political conviction. Man has always been prepared not only to kill but also to die for good, bad or completely futile causes. And what can be a more valid proof of the reality of the self-transcending urge than his readiness to die for an ideal?

It follows that man by his very nature has mostly been able to fill the gap between domestic morality and immorality against 'hostile' foreigners by identifying with the higher causes of an idea, religion or nation. States have thus themselves been focal points for the formation of such loyalties and political leaders have often not hesitated to ask for the unconditional support and sacrifices on the part of the citizens of their states, whatever the nature of their foreign policy goals. The age of nationalism and democracy has at least since the times of the French Revolution asked for the undivided loyalty of all citizens, and it is not by chance that universal conscription of men was introduced in the wake of this very revolution.

Before this age the king, the feudal lord, the city and especially the different Christian churches and sects could often command more loyalty than the state, as witnessed by religious wars and persecutions. The advent of communism, fascism and National Socialism has again signalled the weakening of identification with the nation state, and a substitution of this loyalty by the adherence of many people to these pseudo-religious creeds. We have already discussed how ideological leaders can employ the state as an instrument for their widespread goals, and how they can sometimes be used themselves to try to accomplish the aims of a given government just by making use of the loyalty commanded by these ideologies not only among nationals but also among foreigners.

It is thus not surprising that the most severe conflicts in the hearts of men arise if they are torn by conflicting loyalties towards their nation, towards a nation-transcending belief system, their firms, families or other groups and organizations. For due to the very nature of states and of international relations, governments must take a different attitude towards foreign countries and, therefore, foreigners. To defend the state or to expand its territory by force the citizens have to behave differently with respect to foreigners and their property than with respect to their fellow citizens. But such prescriptions certainly contradict the Christian command to love one's enemy. They contradict, too, the communist command to fight the capitalist class enemy and to join the forces of the proletariat, whether they are compatriots or foreigners. They may contradict, too, the loyalty towards a transnational firm or towards foreign family members. Here the individual has to make his choice, often a bitter choice, since it may be connected with heavy penalties or reprisals, not to speak of the contempt and loss of close family relationships and of friendships of those people who decide to join the other side. In recent decades totalitarian regimes have often asked individuals to forego family relationships and to betray suspicious relatives and friends to the authorities in charge.[5] 'Aryan' husbands were requested to divorce their Jewish wives and communist sons to report their parents' antiparty views. Totalitarian governments no longer drew the dividing lines between foreigners and nationals but between different races or classes and thus aggravated and multiplied the ethical conflicts within the hearts of individuals.

Loyalty towards the state is always in potential conflict with the loyalty to other groups, organizations or belief systems. This conflict may arise with the family, with a language group not coinciding with the boundaries of a state, with corporations and with religious or other organizations. Such divided loyalty becomes a problem for the state and poses an ethical conflict for individuals concerned, whenever the state and the relevant group follow conflicting goals. This is, however, especially true, if the group in question spreads over several nations. By distracting the loyalty of citizens from the ends of a state it may help to erode severely the bases on which the relative power of the country rests. This is quite obvious if strong minorities in a state are by language and culture closely related with the population of neighboring states. This was true for the Sudeten Germans in Czechoslovakia during the 1930s. As a consequence the Czech government could not be sure any longer of the loyalty of a substantial segment of its population. The same was (and probably is) true for a substantial part of the German population in East Germany. Here the communist regime had to revert in 1961 to the desperate means of building the Berlin wall and heavily guarded fences with self-shooting devices and watchtowers all along its border, when two out of eighteen million inhabitants had left for West Germany.

Present-day Lebanon is a country which is slowly being destroyed because the different parts of its population identify more with their religious groups than with the state. An important reason for the outbreak of the civil war in the 1970s seems to have been the presence of Palestinian guerrilla forces. These forces fought against Israel from Lebanese territory and thus invited Israelian counter-attacks harmful to Lebanon. The adherents of Islam obviously sympathized with their Palestinian brethren and were not prepared to set an end to their military activities as demanded by their Christian compatriots. As a consequence the internal power of the Lebanese state was eroded by the stronger loyalties towards religious groups and old tensions flared up into a protracted civil war. Similar problems have exploded during the last decade in Northern Ireland (Ulster).

Conflicts of loyalties can also arise between states and international organizations, like churches, communist parties, multinational corporations and unions. If employees identify more with their multinational corporation than with the state, the latter may well be able to influence deeply the internal politics of weaker states, especially if the influence of the corporation on the respective economy is great and thus the well-being of the population strongly dependent on its economic decisions. In this case it can firmly rely on the help of its employees and many people may support its policies, since they are dependent on the corporation economically. With the development of international unions, and especially of international professional organizations loyalties may arise which are able to pose another threat to the power of certain nation states in case of conflicting goals.

Let us conclude by looking at the problems of international disorder, law and morality from a somewhat different angle. If we analyse nation states we find that they have developed quite a number of organizations, institutions and procedures to deal with internal social, economic and political conflicts which may exist or may develop over time. There are not only systems trying to preserve order and the rule of law including the safety of persons and of property, but also institutions for the redistribution of income and wealth, for help during unemployment, invalidness, old age and poverty, for stabilizing lagging or shrinking sectors of the economy, like agriculture, and for settling internal disputes and conflicts.

This machinery may be more or less adequate or inadequate depending on the country in question. But it does exist and is able to solve at least part of the problems and conflicts within a country without leaving individuals or groups with no other help than to take recourse to violence and other forms of self-help or self-justice. Things are quite different in international relations. It is true that some international organizations like the United Nations, the International Monetary Fund, the International Red Cross, the International Court in The Hague, etc. exist and that there are a great number of multilateral and bilateral treaties between states, which all try to solve some of the existing and developing international problems and conflicts. But these international organizations, institutions and rules are not only less comprehensive than the national ones but depend for their ultimate success on the free cooperation of the nation states concerned. It follows that such important and changing international problems as the access to raw-material resources, international cartels and monopolies, redistribution of income and wealth, different growth of populations, vastly different densities of population, border conflicts, the use of oceans, pollution across borders, complaints against other states because of maltreatment of minorities speaking the same language or adhering to the same religion as the people in the complaining countries, can often not be adequately solved by the existing international machinery. This very fact should by itself explain many cases in which countries feel compelled to seek a solution to the conflicts with the help of threats, boycotts and wars, since they see no other possibility to solve their grievances. It is clear that these sources of international threats and violence are a consequence of an inadequate organizational and institutional machinery and need not be caused at all by expansionary or imperialist aims of the states involved.

Notes

1   For an excellent treatment of this problem compare M. Olson Jr. and Richard Zeckhauser: "An Economic Theory of Alliances." In Bruce M. Russett (ed.): *Economic Theories of International Politics*. Markham, Chicago 1968, pp. 25–44.
2   Louis XIV: "Memoirs." Quoted from Walter Schätzel (ed.): *Der Staat*. Carl Schünemann Verlag Bremen. Without date, 2nd ed., pp. 171–172.
3   Friedrich der Grosse: *Das Politische Testament von 1752*. Philipp Reclam jun., Stuttgart 1974, S. 73.
4   Arthur Koestler: *The Ghost in the Machine*. Pan Books, London 1971, pp. 268–269.
5   Compare Hannah Arendt: *Totalitarianism*. Harcourt, Brace and World, New York 1968.

Chapter 7

The Present World System

1. The Bipolar Post-War System

We have seen how the present bipolar international system supplanted the old European-based balance of power system, which dominated Europe and the world for three to four centuries. The bipolar system comprising the USSR and the USA was firmly established in the wake of World War II, but had been slowly approaching for decades as a consequence of relative changes in the power bases given by the size of population, territory and especially of economic strength. Thus de Tocqueville could already predict in 1835 for the USA and Russia:

Their starting-point is different and their courses are not the same; yet each of them seems marked out by the will of Heaven to sway the destinies of half the globe.

The military equilibrium established and carefully preserved after World War II, and the lethal threat posed by the existence of nuclear weapons, which can be transported by intercontinental missiles into the very heartlands of the enemy, sufficed to preserve peace between the two super-powers and their industrially developed allies and satellites. Forty years of peace in Europe and between the industrialized countries are certainly not a mean accomplishment judged by the records of European history.

Still, the international situation is far from giving reason for complacency. Indeed, in a sense the situation is more dangerous than during any time of former history. It is the first time that the arsenals of weapons accumulated by the big powers are sufficient to exstinguish all human life. And nobody can be sure that one day an atomic war not wanted by any of the nuclear powers may not be triggered by sheer accident, by false alarms, by miscalculations or by human failure. Perhaps still greater is the danger posed by the spread of nuclear weapons and missiles to countries with less stable political systems, less rational leaders and with ideological or religious commitments, which make the use of such weapons much more probable. The supposed advances made by countries like India, Pakistan, South Africa, Iraq and Israel in the development of such weapons must strike every thinking observer with the most pessimistic forebodings. There can be scarcely a doubt that Israel and

South Africa would use nuclear weapons to defend their very existence against dangerously threatening attacks of their Arab or African neighbors. If one day leaders like President Gaddafi of Libya or Ayatollah Khomeini of Iran would get atomic weapons one could certainly not be sure whether they would not be used to defeat or to exterminate Israel or other 'heretic' neighbors. Given, moreover, the political instability of such countries, there exists even the danger that some ideological, political or terrorist group may have a chance to lay its hands on nuclear weapons and to use them for their sinister purposes.

The two big powers are at least partly responsible for the spread of nuclear weapons. Had they acted together they would have been able to forbid and on the whole to prevent the development and use of such weapons. It is true that the two countries promoted the Nonproliferation Treaty, in which many countries obliged themselves to forego nuclear weapons. But they themselves did not live up to the obligation to reduce their own arsenals, nor did they force countries which were opposed to sign this treaty. But it is obvious that with the spread of atomic weapons more and more countries will feel themselves forced to follow suit to be able to defend themselves and not to have to rely on the promises of the big powers to assist them against nuclear threats and attacks.

The dangers brought about by increasing nuclear arsenals and the spread of atomic weapons to more and more countries are not the only factors threatening the present balance of power. We have seen that the very existence of nuclear weapons, which makes a major war between the two big powers impossible as a rationally calculated act of foreign policy, must necessarily further the use of other measures, if some states still want to reach their expansionist aims. Limited wars with 'conventional' weapons, guerilla warfare, terrorism, ideological and economic warfare will be increasingly used and have in fact be observed more and more often since World War II especially in and among less developed countries.

From the historical facts one can conclude that the United States are not striving for world domination. They did disarm after World War II quite in contrast to the Soviet Union. They tried to placate Soviet leaders with territorial and other concessions in Europe, gave up domination of the Philippines, and above all they did not use their monopoly of atomic bombs in the last phases of the war and in the years immediately following it to move towards world empire. It follows from the internal workings of democracy, too, that a sudden reversal of foreign policy against a war-time ally and the use of force against the Soviet Union for the sake of world domination would have been impossible.

Since then the United States of America have been on the defensive, whereas the facts seem to show that Soviet policy still aims at a communist universal empire, quite in accordance with Lenin's statement:

Only after we have thrown down, perfectly defeated and expropriated the bourgeoisie in the whole world and not only in one country, shall wars become impossible. And it would be quite wrong and unrevolutionary from a scientific point of view, if we evade or hush up just the most important: the suppression of the resistance of the bourgeoisie, which is the most difficult and requires most fighting during the transition to Socialism. 'Social' preachers and opportunists . . . are different from revolutionary Social Democrats by the fact . . . that they do not intend the bitter class fight and class wars to realize this glorious future.[1]

A look at Soviet expansion since World War II gives an impression which is in conformity with these ideas. The Soviet Union annexed Eastern Carelia, Petsamo, the Baltic States, the northern part of East Prussia, Eastern Poland, the Carpatho-Ukraine, the Bukovina and Bessarabia, and established its Eastern European satellite empire (see Map 14). It also supported communist aggression in Greece and Malaya, against South Korea, helped communist or leftist take-overs in Vietnam, Cambodia, Cuba, Ethiopia, Mozambique and Angola and it invaded Afghanistan in 1979. To help takeovers it supported communist or leftist forces by sending military advisors and weapons, and in some cases even had its satellite Cuba directly intervene with troops (e.g. in Angola and Ethiopia). This is certainly an impressive record and does not cover other less successful subversive actions. Considered together with the heavy rearmament, the communist program and ideology it is hard to believe that the Soviet Union has really embarked on a policy of peaceful coexistence in the western sense of the word. It seems, quite on the contrary, to follow from Soviet sources that the idea of peaceful coexistence has been looked upon by the Soviet leadership as a means of lulling western attention, to weaken its determination to keep up the balance of power and to undermine its will of resistance by ideologically undermining its position. The rearmament program pursued in the 1970s during the period of 'peaceful coexistence' and the communist expansion followed towards and in underdeveloped countries encourage such an interpretation.

There is thus some danger today of a successful Soviet drive towards universal domination, towards a Universal Communist Empire. It seems, however, that this danger is rather limited in spite of the successful communist or Soviet expansion in different regions of the globe. First of all, the Soviet Empire seems to be rather weak internally. The crude planning system appears to be the less able to bring about a tendency towards economic efficiency, the more developed the economy. With a great number of different consumer and investment goods, it is less and less possible to solve the more and more complicated information problem with the help of bureaucratic planning devices, not to speak of the lack of motivation inherent in the system. The shortages of many consumer goods, the rationing of supplies, the dismal state of agriculture, the low productivity and the low quality of goods after sixty years of communist rule point into the same direction. Black markets and corruption are rampant and people are totally disenchanted with the system. Politically, especially after the events in Poland in 1980–1982 and in other satellite states before, one must doubt, whether many adherents of their regimes are left in the communist countries, who still believe in communist ideology. Moreover, Soviet domination seems to rest on rather shaky ground in Eastern Europe. It is highly doubtful, whether Poland, Hungary, Czechoslovakia and East Germany would still be communist without the presence of Russian troops, as witnessed by Soviet military intervention in the latter three states in 1953, 1956 or 1968, respectively, and the pressure exerted on Poland in 1980–82.

Finally, the Soviet Union has lost its influence not only on Yugoslavia but, more important, on Communist China. The common communist background with the Soviet Union does not prevent the Chinese to be so afraid of this country as to motivate them to move closer to the capitalist USA. A similar estrangement may easily happen with other communist or leftist countries like Ethiopia, Cuba, Angola and Mozambique, which are geographically separated from the Soviet Union, if their leaders do not feel any longer a need for Soviet support, or if they hope to secure western economic aid or want to reassert their independence. The facts just mentioned do, however, not preclude further regional Soviet advances. Even Western Europe may be in danger if the present movement for one-sided disarmament and the mood against the USA should prevail.

Considering the weaknesses and drawbacks of the Soviet system it seems to be rather improbable that the Soviet Union will be able to gain world domination in the future, even if it has several foreign policy advantages over democracies like the USA. But if this is true, what are then the more probable courses of future development? It is this question to which we turn in the following section.

2. Possible Future Developments of the Present International System

We have come to the conclusion that the development of one of the two leading powers, the USSR and the USA, into a universal empire or into a power dominating the globe does not seem to be very probable. What then, apart from the possible doomsday-scenarios of atomic holocaust, are the more probable future developments of the international political system?

Table 7.1: Population and Area of the Fourteen Most Populous Countries of the World (million persons)[1]

Country	1950/51	1965/66	1981/82	Area (1000 km²) 1982
Federal Republic of Germany	49.1 (0.32)	59.7 (0.30)	61.6 (0.27)	248.7 (0.027)
France	42.2 (0.27)	49.5 (0.25)	54.2 (0.24)	547.0 (0.058)
Great Britain	50.2 (0.33)	54.7 (0.28)	55.8 (0.25)	244.0 (0.026)
Italy	46.6 (0.30)	53.1 (0.27)	56.3 (0.25)	301.2 (0.032)
Soviet Union	193.0² (1.26)	230.6 (1.17)	268.8 (1.19)	22402.2 (2.393)
Mexico	25.6 (0.17)	44.1 (0.22)	71.2 (0.31)	1972.5 (0.211)
United States	153.5 (1.00)	196.8 (1.00)	226.5 (1.00)	9363.1 (1.000)
Brazil	53.4 (0.35)	84.7 (0.43)	127.7 (0.56)	8512.0 (0.909)
Nigeria	24.0 (0.16)	57.5 (0.29)	79.7 (0.35)	923.8 (0.099)
China (People's Republic)	455.9 (2.97)	700.0 (3.56)	1008.2 (4.45)	9561.0 (1.021)
India	356.9 (2.33)	498.7 (2.53)	713.8 (3.15)	3287.6 (0.351)
Indonesia	60.4 (0.39)	104.5 (0.53)	150.5 (0.66)	1904.3 (0.203)
Japan	83.2 (0.54)	98.9 (0.50)	118.7 (0.52)	372.3 (0.040)
Pakistan	75.7 (0.50)	105.0 (0.53)	87.1³ (0.83)	803.9³ (0.086)
European Community	–	182.7 (0.93)	268.4 (1.18)	1529.0 (0.163)

SOURCE: *Statistische Jahrbücher der Bundesrepublik Deutschland.*

[1]   The figures in brackets give the relative size of population and area compared to that of the United States.
[2]   1944
[3]   After the loss of East Pakistan, now Bangla Desh.

In trying to answer this question it seems advisable to look first at the basic factors underlying the relative power of states, the size of territory and population and the degree of economic development. For we have convinced ourselves (see Chapter 3) that these factors have been surprisingly good indicators of the changes in the relative power of states during the past. Indeed, de Tocqueville's prediction of 1835 concerning the USA and Russia ". . . each of them seems marked out by the will of Heaven to sway the destinies of half the globe" rested mainly on his correct appreciation of the development of these underlying factors. We will thus present and draw some conclusions from the respective facts and then try to complete the picture by considering some additional factors which may exert their influence on the future international system.

Let us first turn to population and territory. Table 7.1 presents the development of the populations (from 1950/51 to 1981/82) and the areas of the fourteen most populous states of the world. The relative sizes of populations and areas compared to the USA are given in brackets, the USA having been the strongest power in the world in 1950. Thus the population of France in 1965/66 was 0.25 or 25 per cent of that of the USA (1.00 or 100 per cent) and its territory 5.8 per cent of the area of the USA.

Looking at the figures one realizes at once the rather limited importance of the European members of the former balance of power system. The territories of West Germany, France, Great Britain and Italy are tiny indeed compared not only to the areas of the USSR and the USA, but also to those of Brazil and China. They are even small in comparison to the territories of Mexico, India and Indonesia. The European countries mentioned are in a somewhat better position concerning their populations. Still, in spite of the fact that the absolute number of inhabitants has increased from 1950 to 1982, the relative size of the population has decreased. In the case of Great Britain, for instance, the figures fell from 33 per cent to 25 per cent and in the case of Italy from 30 per cent to 25 per cent of the population of the United States. This happened during a period, in which the relative population of China rose from 297 to 445 per cent, of Brazil from 35 to 56 per cent, of India from 233 to 315 per cent, of Indonesia from 39 to 66 per cent and of Nigeria from 16 to 35 per cent of that of the USA, reflecting the far higher birth rates of these less developed countries. Judging from the present birth rates, some European countries like West Germany will even experience an absolute decrease of their population during the next decades.

Comparing these developments with those from 1790 to 1937 (contained in Table 3.3 of Chapter 3) we find that the deterioration of the population strength of the European countries relative to the USA is just a continuation of earlier developments. Note further that the relative population strength of Japan remained about the same during the past-World War II period.

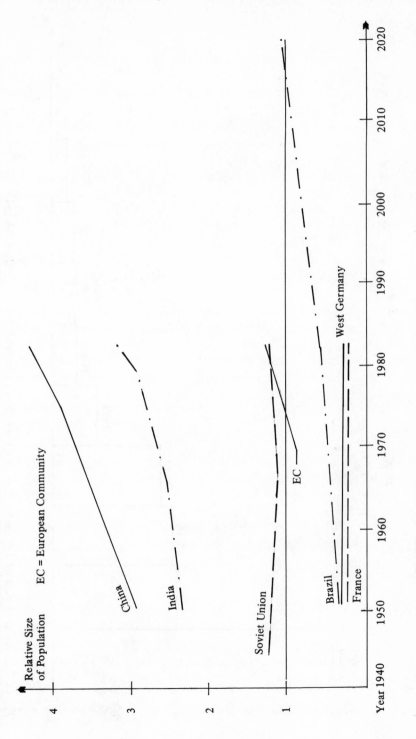

Figure 7.1: Development of Size of Population in Several Countries Compared to that of the USA (=1)

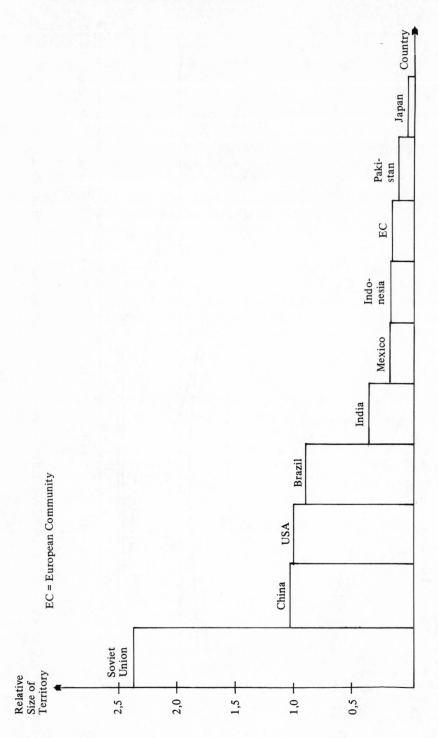

Figure 7.2: Relative Size of Territory of Several Countries Compared to that of the USA (=1)

Next, judging from territory and population alone, one would expect the following states to develop into big powers on a par with the USSR and the USA: Brazil, China, India and, perhaps, Mexico and Indonesia. The latter countries have however, only a territory of about 20–21 per cent the size of the USA. The population of Mexico is still only 31 per cent compared to the USA and smaller than that of Nigeria (35 per cent). But it will grow rapidly in the decades to come and Nigeria's territory is only 10 per cent of that of the USA. Japan does qualify from the size of its population as a future big power, but has a very small territory, relatively speaking (4 per cent of the USA).

None of the medium-sized Western European states qualifies as a future big power. Size of population and territory are in each case smaller than those of the possible candidates mentioned above. From these criteria alone, the only chance left to these countries is to combine their strengths and to form a European political community, a federal state. This would give them a population bigger than that of the United States and approaching that of the Soviet Union and a territory which is at least 16,3 per cent of that of the USA, that is if this system would only comprise the present member states of the European Community. Other states like Portugal, Spain and Norway might then decide later to join this European Union, thus increasing its territory and population. Especially the latter would be welcome because of the slow or stagnating growth rates of Western European populations. Whether the Western European countries will be able to form a political union in the next two decades remains to be seen. Looking at the developments during the last decade one may be rather sceptical about the prospects. Still, without a unification there is a great danger that Europe will remain a pawn and a possible victim on the chessboard of international politics. We shall return to this problem in the concluding section of this chapter.

In moving on we have to ask ourselves, whether the conclusions drawn are reliable, since they are only based on the size of territories and populations and on the growth rates of the latter. Isn't it true that economic and technological factors have become more and more important determinants of relative international power and that, consequently, population and territory have become less and less decisive? Did not the very high growth rates of the population in underdeveloped countries turn even into an impediment for economic development and thus into a weakness of these countries?

There is a lot of truth in these arguments. European powers like Great Britain, France and Russia have not developed into world powers because they started with great territories and populations. Rather, their technological and economic development gave them the superior strength to acquire large colonial empires and to support incredible population increases as a consequence of their industrialization. Even in the case of the white North American settlers it was the superiority of the European civilization which made them the masters of a continent and allowed the manifold multiplication of their number (compare Tables 3.2–3.6, Chapter 3). Spain, on the other hand, which could not follow the economic and technological development of the other European powers during the last one and a half centuries, did not experience a comparable population growth and lost its status as a big power and its colonial empire much earlier.

Table 7.2: Average Annual Growth Rates (in per cent) of Real Gross National Product and of Gross Domestic Product of Some of the Most Populous Countries

Country	1951/57[1]	1956/64[1]	1963/71[2]	1970/81[2]
West Germany	7.41 (2.58)	6.31 (1.88)	4.84 (1.32)	2.56 (0.90)
France	4.66 (1.62)	5.25 (1.57)	5.67 (1.54)	3.31 (1.16)
Italy	5.27 (1.84)	5.66 (1.69)	4.66 (1.27)	2.83 (0.99)
Great Britain	2.60 (0.91)	3.33 (0.99)	2.68 (0.73)	1.50 (0.52)
Mexico		6.14 (1.83)	7.04 (1.92)	6.60[4] (2.31)
United States	2.87 (1.00)	3.35 (1.00)	3.67 (1.00)	2.86 (1.00)
India		4.13 (1.23)	3.48[3] (0.95)	2.91[4] (1.02)
Japan	9.47[6] (3.30)	10.54 (3.15)	10.58 (2.88)	4.67 (1.63)
Brazil			5.76[3] (1.57)	7.47 (2.61)
Indonesia			5.20 (1.42)	7.45 (2.60)
Soviet Union[5]			7.64 (2.08)	4.73 (1.65)

SOURCE: *Statistische Jahrbücher der Bundesrepublik Deutschland.*

[1]   Gross National Product
[2]   Gross Domestic Product
[3]   1963–1969
[4]   1970–1980
[5]   Net Product. Not corrected for inflation
[6]   1950–1956. Inflation corrected with cost of living index. Not quite comparable with other figures.

Still, size of territory and population are not unimportant. First, we know that Russia would not have successfully withstood the invasions of Napoleon and Hitler had it only been the size of France. Second, even a highly developed small country with a small population loses its relative power when states with a bigger territory successfully embark on industrialization and economic growth and thus experience a corresponding increase of their populations. For by doing so they become stronger economically and in the size of their populations than the formerly superior small industrialized country. The importance of the Netherlands and of Sweden in the seventeenth and early eighteenth centuries is well-known. Especially the Netherlands were at that time more developed economically than even Great Britain. But with the economic development of states with greater territories they soon lost their status as important or — in the case of Sweden — even as essential powers.

We conclude that a country with a relatively small territorial base can only hope to gain and (or) to maintain a role as an essential actor in the international political system, if it continues to move ahead of other powers economically and technologically. Only in this case size of territory and of population shall be of minor importance. With these conclusions in mind, let us cast a glance at recent economic developments and their future prospects.

In Table 7.2 average annual growth rates of gross national products or gross domestic products have been put together for several important countries for the past World War II period. These figures contrast strongly with those for the growth of the respective populations, at least for Western European states. From 1951 to 1971 Italy, France and West Germany show markedly higher economic growth rates than the USA, not to speak of the even bigger rate of Japan. This period thus witnessed an incredible economic performance of these countries which nearly allowed them, with the exception of Japan, to catch up with the United States on a per capita income basis. Only Great Britain could not match this performance and is now badly lagging as far as per capita income is concerned. For 1970/81, however, the growth rates of gross domestic products diminished in all these countries compared to the earlier periods. The same is true for the Soviet Union, which showed a rather high growth rate form 1963—71. In spite of this deterioration, higher growth rates than that of the USA are still enjoyed by France, the Soviet Union, and above all, by Japan. It is possible, however, that the figures for the Soviet Union are misleading and too high compared with other countries, since they are calculated by using different methods and have not been corrected for inflation (the same is true for the corresponding figures of Table 7.3).

Table 7.3: Development of Gross National and Gross Domestic Product of the Twelve Most Populous Countries (Excluding China and Nigeria)[1]

(Billion dollars at 1978 constant prices and at 1978 $ exchange rates)

Country	1950[2]	1956[2]	1963[2]	1963[3]	1970[3]	1981[3]	1978 Exchange Rate per $
West Germany	86.12 (0.111)	156.35 (0.157)	261.49 (0.205)	256.60 (0.202)	505.14 (0.398)	677.75 (0.307)	0.4975
France	111.73 (0.144)	160.84 (0.161)	240.96 (0.189)	221.16 (0.174)	350.12 (0.276)	498.66 (0.227)	0.22388
Great Britain	152.56 (0.197)	174.57 (0.175)	213.84 (0.167)	210.33 (0.166)	262.70 (0.207)	301.79 (0.137)	1.9154
Italy	53.23 (0.069)	78.59 (0.079)	121.28 (0.095)	125.08 (0.099)	230.32 (0.181)	286.93 (0.130)	0.001194
Soviet Union				240.62[4] (0.190)	413.25[4] (0.326)	681.10[4] (0.309)	1.42549[5][6]
Mexico					59.22 (0.047)	108.32[7] (0.049)	0.04353
United States	774.78 (1.000)	997.94 (1.000)	1277.93 (1.000)	1269.55 (1.000)	1648.76 (1.000)	2205.30 (1.000)	1
Brazil		29.46 (0.030)	34.79 (0.027)	43.27 (0.034)	83.95 (0.066)	207.09 (0.094)	0.05468
India					80.40 (0.049)	98.52[7] (0.045)	0.11144[6]
Indonesia					16.91 (0.013)	39.48 (0.018)	0.00144[6]
Japan	103.73 (0.134)	177.79 (0.178)	342.01 (0.268)	358.17 (0.282)	743.35 (0.586)	1107.94 (0.502)	0.004776
Pakistan					12.60 (0.008)	22.29 (0.010)	0.09129[6]

Looking at the figures for developing countries, we observe higher growth rates for Mexico, Brazil and Indonesia. For the latter two these growth rates have even increased from 1963/71 to 1970/81, quite in contrast to all other states. Finally, the Indian performance does not look very good, especially if one takes into account the great poverty in this country. In the period from 1963 to 1971 its growth rate was lower than that of the USA and in 1956–71 lower than the growth rates in all other countries with the exception of Great Britain and, for 1956–64, of the USA.

The consequences of the different growth rates for gross national and gross domestic products are shown in Table 7.3 (in billion dollars). The figures give an interesting picture, but the reader should be warned that they are not very reliable, especially if one compares absolute levels between different countries. The main reasons are somewhat different methods in calculating total products and, above all, the exchange rates used to convert the domestic currency figures into dollars. Dollar exchange rates have fluctuated widely, some have been influenced by exchange controls and the rate for the Soviet Union is not even a market rate. Thus the selection of a specific exchange rate had to be necessarily somewhat arbitrary.

Still, the figures tell an important story, especially if we look at those in brackets which present the relative magnitudes of gross national or gross domestic products compared to those of the United States. They show that West Germany moved up from 11.1 to 30.7 per cent, France from 14.4 to 22.2 per cent and Italy from 6.9 to 13.0 per cent of the gross national or domestic product of the United States, whereas Great Britain saw a fall from 19.7 to 13.7 per cent. We conclude that the relative economic strength of Western Europe, with the exception of Britain, has about been doubled in the post-war period. This outstanding performance was, however, easily surpassed by Japan, which moved up from 13.4 to 50.2 per cent. The Soviet Union did quite well from 1963 to 1981. Here the figures are 19 and 30.9 per cent of the gross domestic product of the USA. The absolute level is, however, rather low for a country of its size and population. The level is still lower than that of Japan and comparable to that of West Germany. But as

---

[1]   The figures in brackets give the relative size of Gross National or Domestic Product
      compared to that of the United States.
[2]   Gross National Product.
[3]   Gross Domestic Product.
[4]   Net Product, not corrected for inflation.
[5]   Official Russian DM exchange rate multiplied by DM/$ rate.
[6]   End of December 1978: DM exchange rate multiplied by DM/$ rate.
[7]   1980

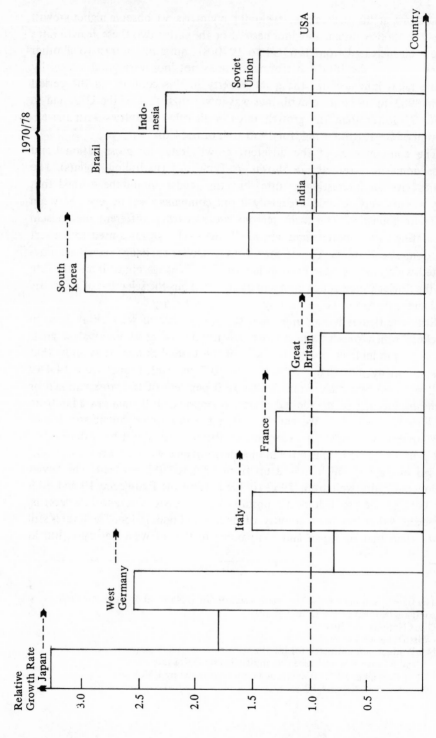

Figure 7.3: Annual Growth Rates of Real Gross National or Domestic Product of Some Countries Relative to the USA (=1), 1951/57 and 1970/78

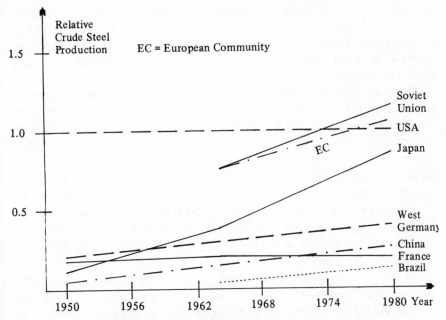

Figure 7.4: Development of Production of Crude Steel in Several Countries Relative to that of the USA (=1)

mentioned before, one should not put too much trust into the absolute figures in such comparisons.

Turning to underdeveloped countries, we see that Brazil moved up from 3 to 9.4 per cent of the United States from 1956–1981. Mexico nearly kept its 4.7 per cent and India experienced a fall from 4.9 to 4.5 per cent during the period 1970–80/81, whereas Indonesia moved ahead a bit. The relative level of this country, however, 1.8 per cent, as well as that of Pakistan, 1.0 per cent, is still abysmally low compared to the United States.

Taking everything together one gets the impression that only the Western European Countries and Japan would be capable of becoming essential international actors in the near future, because they have sufficiently developed economic strength. China, for which no comparable figures are available, may be a third candidate. There can be no doubt that even when including territory and population into our considerations a United Western Europe could easily become a world power already today, reaching or even surpassing the United States of America in population and economic capacity. Japan, on the other hand, has the disadvantage of a small territory and a smaller population (52 per cent) than the United States, whereas it will soon reach an incredible economic strength, if it can only maintain its higher economic growth rate. This leads to the question, whether a country with a small territory and not too big a population, but with a very highly developed economy and sophisticated technology can become an important international actor in the future. This is a question to which we will have to return at the end of this section.

The past, even the immediate past, is not the future. Cannot countries like Mexico, Brazil, India and Indonesia grow into big powers later, if not in the next two decades? Quite possible for Brazil, doubtful for Mexico and Indonesia and much more doubtful for India, if we speculate from recent developments. Let us take the gross domestic products of 1978 and their average annual growth rates from 1970–1978, thus excluding the consequences of the following recession. Then it is easy to calculate how long it would take several countries to catch up with the United States. It follows from this simple calculation that Japan would reach the gross domestic product of the United States in 2018, that Brazil would do so in 2022, the Soviet Union in 2066, Indonesia in 2083, Mexico in 2167 and France in 2211. Brazil would surpass the Soviet Union already in 29 years, that is in 2007. On the other hand, West Germany, Britain, Italy and India would fall back further and further behind the USA and the other countries since the average annual growth rates of their gross domestic products have been smaller than that of the United States in 1970–1978.

Somewhat different conclusions hold for the development of the populations of these countries. Applying the average annual growth rates experienced from 1965/66–1978/79 and starting from the size of the populations in 1978/79 one gets the following results: Indonesia will reach the population of the USA in 2004, Brazil will do so in 2014, Mexico in 2023 and Japan in 2175. Moreover, Brazil will have the same population as the USSR in 2029. The population of the Western European countries by contrast will lag more and more behind those of the USA and the other countries.

Now, there can be no doubt, that these figures are, as pure trend extrapolations, absolutely fictitious. First, we know from historical experience, that population growth rates increase in the initial phase of the industrialization process, but decrease later with rising per capita incomes. This has happened in Europe and the USA and is now taking place in Japan and the Soviet Union. Population growth rates of the countries mentioned can thus be expected to decline from their present levels. Still, the growth rates in the USSR and the USA may decline further, too, so that the relative population position of the other states would· increase in spite of falling growth rates.

Similarly, we know again from experience that economic growth rates of countries leading in the development of science, technology and the economy, like formerly Britain and now the USA, have become lower after some time than those of the countries which are lagging in their development but have already entered the path of industrial development. Part of this difference follows from the fact that the lagging states can make use of the experience and knowledge of the more advanced countries. Part of it is a consequence of the fact that the political and economic structure and organization, the resistance of interest groups and bureaucracies against changes and the growth of the state petrify and fossilize a system the more the longer it exists and develops without serious disruptions. Note in this connection that West Germany, Japan, France and Italy suffered either total defeat or at least occupation during World War II. Thus their rigid structures were shaken or weakened, so that they could experience rather high economic growth rates for at least two decades, quite in contrast to Great Britain and the USA. Similarly, Russia underwent the Bolshevik Revolution, the Civil War and foreign intervention from 1917, and suffered heavy destructions and losses of life during the German invasion in World War II. The growth rate of its total product has also been higher than that of the USA and Great Britain, and this in spite of its rather inefficient planning system (compare Table 3.4, Chapter 3, and Table 7.1).[2]

From these deliberations it follows that the growth rates of gross domestic products shall decline with the passage of time and with an approach to the per capita income in the USA in Japan, Brazil, the Soviet Union, Indonesia, Mexico and France, as they have already done in West Germany and Italy during the last decade. Thus the level of economic development of the USA on a per capita basis will probably be reached later than suggested by the figures given above. Some countries may perhaps even never be able to catch up with the USA.

Collecting all arguments developed, it seems probable that only Japan and Brazil and perhaps Western Europe have a good chance to become essential members of the international political system during the next two to four decades. The situation of Western Europe, which could as a United Europe become a world power already today, will somewhat weaken relatively to the USA and the USSR if economic growth rates do not move up again. Brazil has the additional advantage of a relatively isolated geographical position on the South American Continent with rather weak neighbors, so that it may be able to pursue its economic development for a long time without the burden of heavy military expenditures. Nearly the same is true for Japan, especially given the military umbrella provided by the USA and given the tensions between the USSR and Communist China. Japan's small territorial base keeps its position, however, somewhat precarious. Finally, Communist China, which has not been very successful economically, but

Table 7.4: Production of Selected Goods in the Twelve Most Populous Countries (Excluding Indonesia and Nigeria)[10]
SOURCE: Statistische Jahrbücher der Bundesrepublik Deutschland and the Stateman's Yearbook.

	Electricity (bill. kwh)			Cement (mill. t.)[1]			Crude Steel (mill. t)[1]		
	1950	1964	1981	1950	1964	1981	1950	1964	1981
West Germany	45.6 (0.117)	165 (0.152)	369 (0.156)	11.0 (0.284)	34.1 (0.546)	31.5 (0.485)	14.1 (0.160)	37.3 (0.324)	41.6 (0.371)
France	33.1 (0.085)	94 (0.087)	264 (0.111)	7.4 (0.191)	22.3 (0.357)	28.2 (0.435)	8.7 (0.099)	19.8 (0.172)	21.2 (0.189)
Great Britain	56.5[2] (0.145)	172 (0.159)	260 (0.110)	9.9 (0.256)	17.0 (0.272)	12.7 (0.196)	16.6 (0.189)	26.7 (0.232)	15.3 (0.136)
Italy	24.7 (0.064)	74 (0.068)	173 (0.073)	5.0 (0.129)	20.7 (0.332)	41.6 (0.641)	2.4 (0.027)	9.8 (0.085)	24.8 (0.221)
Soviet Union		459 (0.423)	1325 (0.560)	16.0[4] (0.413)	72.4 (1.160)	127.0 (1.957)		85.6 (0.742)	148.5 (1.325)
China People's Republic	11[5] (0.028)	55[6] (0.051)		12.3[4] (0.318)	20.0[7] (0.321)		2.0[4] (0.023)	11.0 (0.095)	35.6 (0.318)
India	5.1 (0.013)	29 (0.027)	41.2[3]	2.7 (0.070)	10.6 (0.170)	20.8 (0.320)	1.5 (0.017)	6.0 (0.052)	10.8 (0.096)
Pakistan	0.2 (0.001)					2.66[11] (0.041)			
Japan	44.9 (0.116)	176 (0.162)	523 (0.221)	4.5 (0.116)	32.7 (0.524)	84.8 (1.307)	4.8 (0.055)	39.8 (0.345)	101.7 (0.906)
Mexico	4.4 (0.011)	16 (0.015)	74 (0.031)	1.5 (0.039)	4.3 (0.069)	17.8 (0.274)	0.3 (0.003)	2.3 (0.020)	7.6 (0.068)
United States	388.7 (1.000)	1684 (1.000)	2365 (1.000)	38.7 (1.000)	62.4 (1.000)	64.9 (1.000)	87.9 (1.000)	115.3 (1.000)	112.1 (1.000)
Brazil		29 (0.027)	142 (0.060)	1.4 (0.036)	5.2 (0.083)	26.1 (0.402)	0.8 (0.009)	3.1 (0.027)	13.2 (0.118)
European		355[8]	1215[9]		80.3	149.0		87.9	126.1

for which we have scarcely any reliable figures, may with economic reforms now taking place turn into another essential actor. As a defensive power, it has perhaps already reached this status, for it seems impossible to occupy this huge country, with a substantial part of its approximately one billion inhabitants engaged in guerilla warfare against an invading army.

We thus see the picture of a new balance of power system as a probable development during the next two to four decades. The essential actors could be, besides the USSR and the USA, Japan, Brazil, China and possibly a United Western Europe. This would be a big change from the present bipolar system and we will have to discuss this prospect more fully later on. Further, we notice that Mexico and Indonesia may be able to join this system in the second half of the twenty-first century, but that India can only succeed in doing so if she is capable of strongly improving her economic performance and embarking on a path of sustained development.

Let us conclude our considerations concerning the development of the economic base of relative international power by looking at Tables 7.4 and 7.5, which present the development of the production of several selected goods in some countries. The respective figures confirm and complete the impression gained from the development of gross national or domestic products. For all goods considered the same strong growth performance of the Western European countries (with the exception of Great Britain) and of Japan emerges. The production of all these goods (excluding electricity) by the European Community surpasses that of the USA in 1981. Japan is ahead of the United States in the production of cement, motor cars and television sets in 1981 and approaches it for crude steel. The Soviet Union produced more cement and crude steel than the USA in 1980, but is strongly lagging in passenger cars and synthetic materials and television sets. Communist China and India moved on in the production of electricity, cement and steel relative to the USA, but even China has reached only 32 per cent of

---

1   Metric tons
2   Without Northern Ireland; only public production.
3   1970
4   1953
5   1954
6   1960, official figure
7   1959, official figure
8   Without Luxemburg
9   Without Ireland and Luxemburg
10 The figures in brackets give the relative amounts of production compared to the production of the United States.
11 1970/71

Table 7.5: Production of Selected Goods in Some Populous Countries[1]

Country	Passenger Cars (1000)			Synthetic Materials (mill. t)[2]		Television Sets (mill.)	
	1950	1964	1981	1964	1981	1964	1981
West Germany	216.1 (0.032)	2650 (0.342)	3590 (0.574)	1.75 (0.380)	6.61 (0.506)	2.30 (0.240)	4.61 (0.445)
France	257.3 (0.039)	1351 (0.174)	2612 (0.418)	0.61 (0.133)	2.42 (0.185)	1.33 (0.139)	1.96 (0.185)
Great Britain	522.5 (0.078)	1868 (0.241)	955 (0.153)	0.88 (0.191)	2.05 (0.157)	2.18 (0.228)	2.36[3] (0.228)
Italy	115.0 (0.017)	1029 (0.133)	1254 (0.200)	0.76 (0.165)	2.15 (0.164)	0.81 (0.085)	1.54 (0.149)
Soviet Union	77.4[4] (0.012)	185 (0.024)	1324 (0.212)	0.72 (0.157)	3.40 (0.260)	2.93 (0.306)	8.19 (0.791)
United States	6665.9 (1.000)	7752 (1.000)	6253 (1.000)	4.60 (1.000)	13.07 (1.000)	9.57 (1.000)	10.36 (1.000)
India[5]	4.9[4] (0.0007)	34 (0.004)	46 (0.007)				
Japan	1.6 (0.0002)	580 (0.075)	6974 (1.115)	1.35 (0.293)	5.89 (0.451)	5.27 (0.551)	14.58 (1.407)
European Community		6272[6] (0.809)	8489 (1.358)	3.42[7] (0.743)	17.33[8] (1.326)	4.86[8] (0.508)	11.29[9] (1.083)

SOURCE: *Statistische Jahrbücher der Bundesrepublik Deutschland.*

[1] Figures in brackets give the relative size of production compared to that in the United States.
[2] Metric tons
[3] 1980
[4] 1953
[5] With cars assembled from imported parts
[6] 1965
[7] Without Luxemburg
[8] Without Ireland, Greece and Luxemburg
[9] Without Netherlands, Denmark, Ireland, Greece and Luxemburg

US production of crude steel in 1981. Mexico and especially Brazil have advanced strongly and certainly more rapidly than India. But they, too, started from a rather low base and thus even Brazil has not yet reached the production level of Italy in 1981. Still, at recent growth rates (1964—1980) the Brazilian production would reach that of the USA for electricity in 2021, for cement in 1991 and for crude steel in 2002, figures which correspond to our earlier calculation. The low production levels for China for cement and electricity reflect the relative weakness of the Chinese economic performance. This may at least partly be caused by the disorganizations of the 'Big Leap' and the 'Cultural Revolution'. It is quite possible that the resulting weaknesses may be overcome by the present reforms.

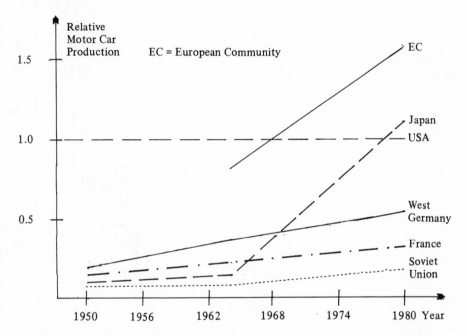

Figure 7.5: Production of Motor Cars (Private) in Several Countries Relative to that in the USA (=1)

On the whole, the figures presented for individual products do confirm the conclusions drawn above. Economic developments seem to provide a base for Japan, Western Europe and Brazil to become essential powers of the international system during the next two to four decades. Communist China will probably remain weaker economically than these countries, at least in certain sectors, but it has the advantage of a big territory and of a huge population. It is, therefore, probable that the present bipolar world system will develop into a new international balance of power system, containing two to four additional actors besides the USA and the USSR.

The new balance of power system, which is the most probable international system to emerge, would, however, probably function somewhat differently from earlier balance of power systems. True, the same kind of

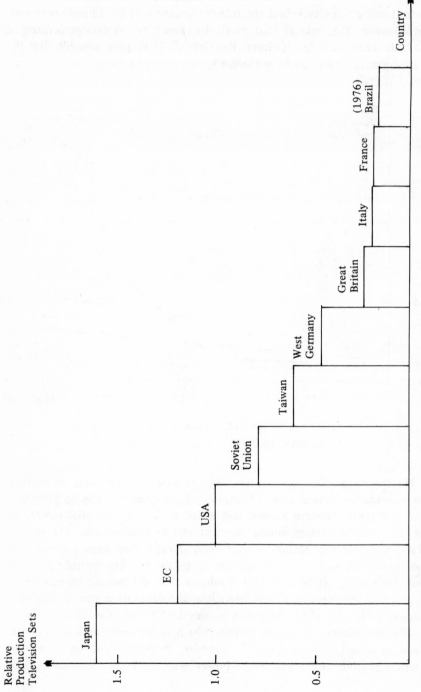

Figure 7.6: Production of Television Sets in Several Countries Relative to that in the USA (=1) (1980)

international diplomacy forging and changing alliances with the intention of furthering expansionary foreign policy goals and, even more important, of containing the strongest member among the big powers, will probably play its part again as in earlier periods. But recall, the military situation has changed radically with the advent of missile-borne thermonuclear weapons. All essential actors will be able to produce these weapons and to direct them against the major cities and vital centers of any other great power. This fact makes a full-fledged and open war between essential countries impossible, at least as far as rational calculations are concerned. True, a limited war, not touching the core territory of the enemy, using only traditional and 'strategic atomic' weapons with limited objectives is more probable. But even here the big powers may hesitate to embark directly into such a war with the forces of another essential actor as opponents, since the risk of an escalation into a major nuclear war is too high and the greater the more successful the actor's own forces.

We conclude that because of this stalemate wars against non-essential states, possibly not with an actor's own troops but with those of a satellite, guerilla wars, ideological and economic warfare, terrorism and revolution will more and more prominently be employed by members of the new balance of power system. No doubt that such a world would be dangerous with risk of atomic war caused by miscalculations or human failures. The possibility of a guerilla war, revolution, war with or between third states or of economic pressures turning into a major war would continue to exist.

Such a situation can develop especially because of the extreme dependence on outside supplies of energy and raw materials on the part of some of the prospective members of the new balance of power system, especially Japan and Western Europe. Suppose, for instance, that guerilla warfare, revolutions or civil unrest supported by Soviet arms and advisors would develop in Saudi-Arabia and the Gulf States and cut off near-Eastern oil supplies. In such a case Japanese and Western European industrial activity would be substantially reduced, perhaps even by more than 40 per cent of their capacity. This would not only deal a serious blow to employment and the provision of goods to the population, but also erode the international power and domestic political stability of these states. Even today the USA would probably decide to intervene in the Near East to help its allies under such circumstances. But the reaction would be almost inescapable if Western Europe and Japan had already developed into essential international actors. On the other hand, the dependence on oil will probably be much lower in twenty to forty years from now. But there can be no doubt that the dependence of these countries on rawmaterials supplied, for instance, by South Africa with its domestic racial problems will be at least as big as today, so that similar critical situations may develop.

Before concluding this section let us push our speculations about the future one step further. If Japan with its small territorial base, its high dependence on imported energy and raw materials and a population of less than half the size of that of the Soviet Union can become a world power, could then not some smaller countries, which are industrially developed, be capable of building up a system of nuclear weapons combined with intercontinental missiles, and thus be able to defend themselves against any aggression by the big powers through the threat to use these weapons? But if this is true, would then the international system not slowly be transformed from a balance of power into a multipolar system? What would be the consequence of such a development?

In trying to answer these questions we have to keep two factors in mind. First, even countries like India, which is rather weak economically, South Africa, Israel and possibly Pakistan have already or are presently developing atomic weapons, Second, to develop, to produce and to employ such weapons a certain scientific, technological and economic sophistication is necessary. It follows from this that some smaller countries like South Korea and Taiwan, which have been developing rapidly recently, should already have or at least be able to gain in the future the necessary know-how and economic resources to develop thermonuclear weapons and intercontinental missiles. The sophistication reached by these states is highlighted by the fact that Taiwan produced 6.92 million television sets and 9.66 million radios, Korea 5.13 million radios and 7.7 million television sets in 1981, which is quite an achievement if you compare these figures to the 8.19 million television sets and the 8.7 million radios produced by the Soviet Union. The figures for West Germany are 'only' 4.61 and 2.85 million, respectively. Korea, moreover, produced 247 thousand household sewing machines, West Germany 304 thousand. The population of Taiwan has reached 18.46 and that of South Korea 39.33 million inhabitants (1982). Average annual growth of South Korean gross domestic product amounted to 9.98 per cent from 1970–1979, a figure which is higher than any growth rates for the same period of the countries represented in Table 7.2. No doubt, this has been an impressive economic performance.

Judging from these facts, countries like Taiwan and South Korea should be able to develop nuclear weapons and perhaps intercontinental missiles in the next two decades. Other countries may follow, especially if the production costs of such weapons should decrease further which is quite possible with technological developments. The only question would then be whether these countries would have a chance to acquire the necessary raw materials. From the experiences of the last two decades one would expect no insurmountable obstacles.

Let us sum up. If the above analysis is correct — and it can always be wrong since it is impossible to know all future developments — the balance of power system to be expected would in time be transformed into a multipolar system. The latter would contain, in addition to five or six big powers, a number of smaller countries able to defend their independence and integrity even against essential actors with atomic weapons arsenals. Unfortunately, this would probably enhance the danger of nuclear war brought about by irresponsible politicians, by miscalculations, accidents or as a consequence of an erosion of the status quo by terror, guerilla war, revolution and economic or ideological warfare. Indeed, the future world which is the most probable one does not look very safe, even if the existence of nuclear weapons lowers substantially the risk of outright major wars.

3. What Kind of World do we Want?

Man belongs to the few cases in the animal kingdom able to kill members of their own species. It is the biological heritage of human beings which provides the last cause of intrahuman violence, man-slaughter, murder, torture and war. To quote Arthur Koestler:[3]

... when one contemplates the streak of insanity running through human history, it appears highly probable that *homo sapiens* is a biological freak, the result of some remarkable mistake in the evolutionary process. The ancient doctrine of original sin, variants of which occur independently in the mythologies of diverse cultures, could be a reflection of man's awareness of his own inadequacy, ...

What are the reasons of this human predicament? Here no agreement seems to exist among scientists until now. Koestler, who heavily leans on MacLean's experimental work and theoretical conclusions,[4] goes on to explain:[5]

The cause which contemporary research seems to indicate is not increase in size [of the brain], but *insufficient coordination* between archicortex and neocortex — between the phylogenetically old areas of our brain, and the new, specifically human areas which were superimposed on it with such unseemly haste. This lack of coordination causes, to use a phrase coined by P. MacLean, a kind of 'dichotomy in the function of the phylogenetically old and new cortex that might account for differences between emotional and intellectual behaviour'.[6]

Konrad Lorenz, the well-known zoologist, has a different, but not necessarily contradictory theory:[7]

The inhibitions controlling aggression in various social animals, preventing it from injuring or killing fellow members of the species, are most important and consequently most highly differentiated in those animals which are capable of killing living creatures of about their own size. A raven can peck out the eye of another with one thrust of its beak, a wolf can rip the jugular vein of another with a single bite. There would be no more ravens and no more wolves if reliable inhibitions did not prevent such actions. Neither a dove nor a hare nor even a chimpanzee is able to kill its own kind with a single peck or bite. Since there rarely is, in nature, the possibility of such an animal seriously injuring one of its own kind, there is no selection pressure at work to breed inhibitions against killing. One can only deplore the fact that man has definitely not got a carnivorous mentality! All his trouble arises from his being a basically harmless, omnivorous creature, lacking in natural weapons with which to kill big prey, and therefore, also devoid of the built-in safety devices which prevent 'professional' carnivores from abusing their killing power to destroy fellow-members of their own species. No selection pressure arose in the prehistory of mankind to breed inhibitory mechanisms . . . until all of a sudden, the invention of artificial weapons upset the equilibrium of killing potential and social inhibitions. When it did, man's position was very nearly that of a dove which, by some unnatural trick of nature, has suddenly acquired the beak of a raven.

Whatever the merits of these theories, it seems clear that man's biological inheritance leaves him the inner freedom and sometimes the motivation and provides him with the intellectual capabilities to construct the means to mutilate and to kill fellow members of his species. But it is hard if not impossible to influence or even to change inherited traits. Koestler's hope that some hormone or tranquilizer may be synthesized and applied which could act as a stabilizer between the old and the new brain must strike the observer as a rather utopian proposal. Given these facts quite different measures changing social institutions have to be used to overcome the problems stated in or implied by our earlier analysis. Man is a very pliable being. The same is true for his organizations and institutions. There are not only murderers and fanatics, there are also saints and martyrs. Aggressive social organizations and states exist side by side with small, peaceful countries which have not engaged in wars for centuries. The number of people killed has been lower in universal empires or in countries isolated from the international system of essential states than in regions of competing essential actors. True, it might be better if we could change the essential nature of man, given by his inherited genes. But the situation might be improved, too, if international and domestic organizations and institutions could be introduced capable of reducing the level of intrahuman aggression, violence and mass-murder.

The problem itself, the question how to reduce intrahuman violence, torture, murder and mutilation of fellow-humans by changing organizations and institutions can be separated into two subproblems. First, how should an adequate order and its institutions look like? Second, how can such an order be introduced starting from the present situation? In this section we will take up the first, in the next section the second of these subproblems.

We begin by observing that the division of the world into more or less independent or sovereign states has proved to be a dismal failure. The nation

Table 7.6: Estimate of War Casualties in Europe, by Centuries, 1000–1925 (in 1000)

Country	11th	12th	13th	14th	15th	16th	17th	18th	19th	20th (to 1925)
France	1	4	11	59	61	107	658	1055	1769	3682
Austria-Hungary		8	11	7	100	257	1560	1505	226	3000
Great Britain	1	7	17	64	86	91	160	310	141	3095
Russia	5	12	29	37	38	118	119	752	777	6371
Germany								360	459	6060
Spain						160	559	94	166	44
Netherlands						64	290	170	34	
Italy							17	41	54	1783
Poland and Lithuania	7	31	68	167	285	66	91	348	219	
Total						863	3454	4635	3845	24035
Per 1000 population	2	5	8	10	15	37	33	15	54	

SOURCE: Pitirim Sorokin: *Social and Cultural Dynamics.* vol. III. Tables 6–19

state has been able to further internal tranquility, rule of law and order in many countries. In doing so it has helped to bring about an incredible increase in economic well-being in industrialized countries during the last decades by providing the stability which is a precondition for a well-functioning economy. In addition, it has been instrumental in most developed countries in constructing an extensive social security net preventing the poor, sick and old people from becoming victims of misery and depravation. A minimal level of general education and a chance to enter higher levels of the educational system has been provided to the whole population at least in the more affluent states. By contrast, in countries where these successes have not been reached this is at least partly a consequence of the absence of well-established and stable national governments, which have the monopoly of power and are relatively free from corruption.

The internal accomplishments of the nation state are in strange contrast to its failure as an organizing principle of the international system. We have already discussed several examples of international disorder. Let us add a few additional facts. States restrict people to the use of their often rapidly depreciating national monies, limit the free movement of goods and services by import duties, import quotas and tax and health regulations, control and often prohibit free travel and movement of people and of their properties, punish those who violate more or less haphazard and arbitrary regulations and sometimes even prohibit the free circulation of foreign newspapers and books or forbid their subjects to listen to foreign radio or television.

Worse still, citizens are forced to participate in wars and to kill and to maim other people for higher national or ideological interests. Sorokin estimates that from 1900 to 1925 about 24 million people have been killed in Europe alone (see Table 7.6).[6] During the second World War the number of deaths amounted to about 16 million who died in military actions or through their consequences. The number of civilians killed is estimated to have been 20–30 million, of which 1.5 million died by bombardments from the air.[9]

We have already stated that the number of violent struggles leading to deaths is much lower in organizationally integrated territories than in comparable territories comprising several independent states.[10] Moreover, the formation of larger states has led to the removal of many internal barriers to trade and the movement of people, to more unified legal, economic and monetary systems and to mechanisms providing for income and wealth redistribution in larger regional systems. No longer was it necessary within these newly formed nations to settle disputes arising between subunits by force as it was during feudal times. Instead this task was taken over by the courts supported by the police. Internal violence between citizens and groups of citizens was outlawed in greater territories than before and thus the level of violence substantially reduced. The rule of law and order instituted in many modern states has certainly been a major accomplishment.

However, as shown by the absolutely and relatively increasing number of war deaths (Table 7.6) and by the danger of nuclear holocaust, the consolidation of nation states, their marriage with ideological creeds and the development of modern weapons have in spite of their internal accomplishments sadly increased the sum total of the dangers for humanity. The disfunctional division of mankind into independent states is one of the most important social causes of our present predicament. It is, therefore, high time to replace it with a better form of international organization. In the face of a threatening suicide of humanity the outmoded organization of the world into independent countries can no longer be tolerated. A world state has to take the place of outdated sovereign nations.

But what kind of world state do we want? Certainly not a centralized state levelling all regional, cultural, religious and traditional differences of humanity. We all enjoy diversity and want to live and to develop according to our own traditions, predilections and creative potentials. A first precondition of a world state would then be a strongly federalized system. This is, however, not the only precondition. Another one would be the absence of dictatorship, of totalitarian rule and of religious or pseudoreligious belief systems with a claim supported by world government that everybody had to become a member of this creed. Individual liberty and free development as well as the respect for different traditions, cultures and ways of life would not be safeguarded under dictatorship, totalitarianism or a world state dominated by an obligatory belief system.

A rigid federal system building on the fortuitous composition of states at the moment of federation would not be satisfactory. It would not only be burdened with the consequences of former misdevelopments often brought about by force and, therefore, possibly causing future dissention and violence, but would also inhibit future changes wanted by the inhabitants of certain regions, communities and cities. Because of this the following rules should be proposed. Each state or nation is divided into different provinces. The adult and sane inhabitants of each province have the right to declare by simple majority in a referendum its independence within the World Federation. The authorities of the province would be obliged to organize a referendum, whenever a corresponding initiative signed by, say, 100,000 inhabitants were presented to them. Similarly, each region neighboring another state has the right to join this country by using the same procedure, if the majority of the population of this state is willing to accept them. Moreover, each community bordering another province or state is entitled to secede and to join this other province or state. Such procedures would allow the formation of new states and a change of frontiers of old provinces and states according to the needs felt by the majority of the population. A kind of competition between states and provinces would arise forcing them to correspond more closely with their organization, the surroundings provided and the goods and services offered to the preferences of their citizens, who would otherwise prefer to secede from their present territorial organization.

What other necessary ingredients should be contained in the constitution of the World State? First, it is obvious from our former discussions that the Universal Federal Government should have, apart from local police a monopoly of armed forces. All other forces would be abolished, all other arms including all nuclear weapons be destroyed. No barriers to international trade of goods, services and capital should be allowed, and there should be a common and stable federal money – preferably a commodity standard providing the price stability of the old gold standard. Federal courts would be instituted to settle disputes between individual states and to judge any alleged violation of the federal constitution and of federal laws. The decisions of federal courts would, if necessary, be enforced by the federal police and, in case of emergency, by the federal armed forces.

The use of violence between states, between citizens or groups of citizens and foreign states should be absolutely prohibited by the federal constitution, be suppressed by federal armed forces and judged by federal courts. Moreover, the same should be true for any propaganda trying to spread hatred against foreign nations, against religious and other groups and against linguistic and other minorities. Legal prescriptions of this kind would, of course, imply some censorship, thus contradicting the principle of free speech and religion postulated below. But note that this minimal censorship is necessary to preserve the freedom and safety of the members of foreign nations, of religious groups and of minorities. It is as necessary for the existence of a free, just and safe society as limitations on the freedom of everybody to use weapons. Minority groups would be allowed to establish an independent school system. To finance its activities, the Federal Government should be able to rely on its own taxes, the tax revenue, however, should be limited by the constitution.[11]

To remove possible sources of tension and unbearable inequalities the Federal Government should have some limited additional means at its disposal, which could correspond to the part of the present armament and military expenditures in the world not needed to keep up the much smaller federal military establishment. Thus the resources currently wasted because of the dilemma of the armament race could be transferred to development aid and to other uses reducing international problems.

An important part of the federal constitution would refer to human rights. Here the well-known principles should be stated, namely the rules forbidding arrest and imprisonment without a warrant from a judge and without due process of law, the rules allowing freedom of speech, of religion, of assembly and of the free formation of organizations and associations not directed against the constitution. Moreover, the constitution should contain an article requiring just compensation in case of nationalization of property and a limitation of the tax burden which can be put on individuals and their associations. Very important, each individual should have the right to emigrate if he is accepted by any other country. Everybody would, of course, have the right to turn to the federal courts in case he felt these rights to be violated by a state or other individuals and groups of individuals.

We turn now to the necessary limitations of federal power, which are in a world state the only guarantee against a misuse of these powers by an eventual dictatorship or oligarchy usurping the Federal Government by a coup d'état or even by regular elections. Legally, the constitution should postulate for this purpose that each state has the right to leave the World Federation if such an event happened. Moreover, the constitution itself should declare any dictatorship or oligarchy to be unconstitutional. The basic ingredients of the constitution should be declared to be unchangeable even by substantial majorities of the Federal Parliament.

An additional safeguard would be the Federal Parliament itself. The House of Representatives would be elected directly by districts all over the world containing about the same number of voters. The Senate would represent the different states, each Senator one state, or if some states are too small, like Grenada or the Kingdom of Tonga in the Pacific, a group of smaller countries. The Senators would be elected directly, too, by the population of their states.

A third safeguard would be the limitation of the federal tax revenue by the constitution which has already been mentioned. A similar restriction would apply to the tasks which could be taken up by the Federal Government. All tasks not mentioned in the world constitution could only be assigned to the Federal Government if three fourths of the House of Representatives and of the Senate voted in favor of a reassignment.

Finally, the armed forces as well as the police force of the Federation and the police forces of the individual states should be strictly limited as to their sizes and weapons. The federal forces should be able to suppress violence between two or more states, but not be big enough to subjugate all states resisting a possible world dictatorship or oligarchy. Only in case of an emergency would three-fourth majorities of both houses of parliament be entitled to increase the size and the weapons arsenal of the federal armed forces.

Finally, an independent commission elected by both the House of Representatives and the Senate should have the right and the duty to control the size of armed forces and police, the quality and quantity of their weapons and the production of weapons all over the world.

The above sketch of some important ingredients of the constitution and organization of a possible world state is certainly incomplete. But it seems at least to contain some proposals adequate for the preservation of a peaceful, free and just, but culturally differentiated and federalized world system. Still, there can be no once and for all guarantee against an erosion of such an order and of the corresponding constitution. A turn towards world dictatorship or oligarchy cannot be precluded with certainty, even if the organization sketched above should once have been established. Nor is a breakdown into a system of competing states impossible. In spite of this, there is a good chance that such an organization once created, would function better and hold greater promises for human survival and well-being than the present disorganized system of sovereign states. It is more difficult to imagine with our present knowledge how a world federation like that described could be introduced given the present status quo. This is the problem to which we have to address ourselves in the concluding section.

4. Can We Move Towards an Improbable Future?

We have sketched a possible, but a utopian future, that is a future with a negligible probability of being realized. The most probable future, a system between a balance of power and a multipolar system, with an increasing incidence of civil unrest, terrorism, guerilla warfare and minor wars incited by major powers provides a rather gloomy picture. A far less probable development leading towards a universal empire gives the Soviet Union a bigger chance than the USA to acquire a predominant position, and is thus likely to be connected with authoritarian suppression and dictatorship rather than with the rule of law, with freedom and human rights. Finally, there remains the small, but slowly increasing probability of a nuclear holocaust eradicating or at least decimating and barbarizing humanity. For there should be no doubt: the occurrence of a 'zero' when playing roulette is an improbable event, but if you play it long enough it is virtually certain to happen. The same is true for the game with thermonuclear weapons, even if the probability of atomic war has a much lower probability than the one-thirty-seventh probability that a 'zero' occurs in one round of roulette.

Humanity is thus threatened with extinction or a scarcely reversible relapse into barbarism. Perhaps this may be considered by some a fitting end for a species, concerning which Konrad Lorenz states:[12]

Obviously instinctive behaviour mechanisms failed to cope with the new circumstances which culture unavoidably produced at its very dawn. There is evidence that the first inventors of pebble tools, the African Australopithecines, promptly used their new weapons to kill not only game, but fellow members of their species as well. Peking man, the Prometheus who learned to preserve fire, used it to roast his brothers: beside the first traces of the regular use of fire lie the mutilated and roasted bones of Sinanthropus Pekinensis himself.

Again, perhaps a fitting end for a species, which lamented already in one of its earliest written documents (about 2000 B.C.) the destruction of the old Mesopotamian city of Ur by foreign invaders:[13]

City, whose name has been widely-known, you are destroyed to me,
Oh city, whose ramparts rose highly, your domain has perished,
My town, your lambs are separated from you like lambs from their mother sheep, . . .
For Ur, which has been destroyed to her [the Goddess] bitter wailings are raised. . . .

Before the invention of nuclear weapons one could, in spite of human suffering, misery and death, at least comfort oneself with the thought that the survival of humanity was not at stake; that the low probability for a future world state would be sufficient to bring it about in the long run one day; that the world state once established would prove rather stable, since no barbarians would be left this time outside of its borders; that thus an end would be set to the worst sufferings brought about by international disorganization and war; and that, last but not least, there would be a chance then for the development of a free world society preventing or suppressing organized violence, but guaranteeing human rights, self- and codetermination, individual liberty, justice and democracy.

This hope has faded with the fruits of human inventiveness, with thermonuclear weapons. Time is running out. The probability of a future atomic holocaust appears to be greater than that of the occurrence of a universal state. But what can be done to change the course of history, to make the more probable future events less and the least probable utopia more probable? At first sight this problem seems to be unsolvable and, what is more, it may even remain unsolvable. The very fact that we had to assign much higher probabilities to other future outcomes is caused by the strong forces working towards their realization. But we should not despair too easily. All our surroundings including the international organization are manmade human artifacts. It follows that the very forces working towards the more probable outcomes of human history are dependent on human action. Human action is dependent not only on man's given surroundings but also on the degree and quality of his information and on his goals. Thus if everybody who knows about the dangers imminent in the international situation starts today to inform others and to influence their goals, the probability of a world federation and of international peace may be increased sufficiently to prevent in time the horrors of human nuclear self-destruction.

In the following let us try to be somewhat more concrete in spite of the depressing lack of knowledge concerning possible paths to utopia, in spite of this most dangerous dilemma of international politics: We know how a better international organization of humanity should look, but we scarcely know anything about how to get there. We can see the summit of the promised land at a far distance in brilliant sunshine but the path to it is hidden by fog and darkness.

A first important step towards the utopian world state has already been considered: Keep up the military balance at as low a level as possible against threatening powers but try with all decisiveness and stubbornness to reduce the level of nuclear and conventional arms in disarmament talks and agreements. Try even to gain an agreement of the USA with the Soviet Union to prevent, if necessary, by force the further spread of nuclear weapons. Put pressure on governments with the help of all available political means, which may, however, be very restricted or even be non-existent in authoritarian states, to enter and to promote such talks. Do, however, not entertain the illusion that one-sided disarmament of a few, say, European states would secure world peace. On the contrary, it would remove all leverage to bring other countries to a reduction of their arsenals and would invite aggressors to wage the very war which should be prevented.

The latter remark leads us to the role of Western Europe. We have convinced ourselves that Western Europe would already today be able to become a world power, if it were willing to unite into a European Federal State. By doing so it would be able for the first time since World War II to behave as an essential actor and not to remain a mere pawn on the chessboard of international politics. It could enter international disarmament talks itself and put pressure on other participants by threatening to build up a nuclear arsenal of its own if they were not prepared to reduce their armaments.

These are not the only advantages of Western European unification. The formation of an European Federal State with a thriving economy, a constitution guaranteeing human rights, rule of law, freedom, democracy, strong federalism and protection of minority rights in each of the composing states would be an attraction to Eastern Europe and help to dissolve the petrified Soviet system, which is today the most dangerous stumbling block on the way towards a peaceful and free world federation. Even if the path towards a federal world state should prove impossible, Western Europe would then be able to throw its own weight on the side of peace and to reassert, if necessary, its independence and identity against the goals and vagaries of the present superpowers, especially the dangers posed by the Soviet Union. Moreover, Western Europe could try to move towards a federation with other industrialized, free and democratic societies like the USA, Japan, Canada, Australia and New Zealand, that is towards a worldwide federal state, with a constitution similar to that proposed above and open to all countries willing to accept its constitution. A possible erosion of the Soviet bloc furthered by an attractive Western Europe would then bring the world state wanted within reach of possible realization. It follows from these considerations that all Europeans interested in peace should work with all political means available for an attractive European Federal State open to their Central and Eastern European brothers, and for the formation of a broader federation of all free and democratic nations.

A further step towards a world state can be done by strengthening existing and by creating new international organizations, private associations, trade unions and corporations. It is true that the United Nations and its organizations have been a sad failure, if their accomplishments are compared with the hopes engendered in many at the time of foundation. But given the absence of a monopoly of power of the UN and the veto rights of the USSR, the USA, China, France and Britain in the Security Council, exaggerated hopes had no valid foundation from the very beginning. Still, some useful accomplishments have been reached by preventing or limiting wars. The suborganizations have been able to tackle some international problems or at least to draw widespread attention towards them. In recent years, however, the organization has been more and more often misused for the aims of non-democratic governments, for instance in trying to limit the freedom of the press, of radio and television, and the free flow of information. Countries like Israel and South Africa have been banned from several UN organizations, a procedure certainly not helpful in removing the dangers of confrontation in the respective regions. Perhaps industrialized democratic governments could do more to suppress or limit such tendencies by using the leverage available to them as the most important financial contributors of the UN and its suborganizations.

Other international organizations like the International Monetary Fund and the World Bank (both in Washington) have been somewhat more successful. The IMF played an important role in organizing a rather stable international monetary system at least until 1973, when most of its more important members went from a system of fixed to flexible exchange rates. The World

Bank, too, has been important in channelling funds first to European countries during the period of reconstruction after World War II, and then to underdeveloped countries. Both organizations are entitled to set conditions for their aid in the case of balance of payments difficulties and for development projects, respectively, and are thus able to exert some pressure on governments to introduce sound fiscal and monetary policies. Another international institution which has been valuable in promoting free trade and in removing trade barriers has been the General Agreement on Tariffs and Trade, GATT (Geneva).

All three organizations should be further developed and be used to promote a freer movement of goods, services and capital and the security of foreign property all over the world. The IMF could possibly be revitalized if the more important member countries moved towards commodity monies based on an identical commodity bundle. This would mean that everybody had the right to exchange (convert) at any time money into the commodity bundle at a fixed price (parity) at the respective central bank and vice versa. Such rules would not only remove the inflationary pressure inherent in the present currency systems but lead to exchange rate stability between the participating countries, thus strongly promoting the international flow of goods and capital, which could be further strengthened by promoting GATT. The greater international interdependence resulting from extended trade and capital movements would increase the risk of using wars and international violence, since the interruption of economic relations between the countries concerned would be more costly.

These beneficial tendencies could be made more forceful if the World Bank and the IMF would make it a policy not to extend credits to countries, which are not prepared to liberalize international trade, which are engaged in war or spend more than a certain portion of their gross domestic products on armaments. Again, since Western countries supply the biggest shares of the funds available to the two institutions, they should have a good chance to initiate a corresponding policy, if they could only agree on common principles.

The countries of the Eastern Bloc are not members of the institutions mentioned above, but Poland, Roumania and Hungary seem to be prepared to join them in the near future. A membership of such Eastern Bloc countries should certainly be encouraged, if they are willing to accept the necessary conditions, as a means to promote their integration into the system of international economic interdependency lowering the risks of war and of international violence.

As important or more important for the promotion of a future world state than official international organizations may be private organizations like international trade unions, professional associations, multinational corporations and institutions like the Euro-money market. The Euro-money market is now a worldwide international money and credit market which cannot be controlled by any individual nation state and which has grown into huge dimensions during the last two decades. This market has extended more credits, has done more to finance balance of payments and budget deficits of many countries as well as development projects, not to speak of normal private investments, than all official international organizations and institutions together. Even Eastern Bloc countries have long been participants in this market, at least as debtors, and the huge transfers (the so-called recycling of the earnings surpluses on crude oil) which became necessary as a consequence of the two big increases of oil prices in the 1970s were only possible with the help of the Euro-credit market. It is understandable from a national point of view, that some governments and central banks showed uneasiness about the uncontrollable features of this highly developed international market, but on the whole it seems to have been a very advantageous institution. From our point of view everything should be done to strengthen the Euro-money market. It is an innovative international adventure which has outrun the outdated nation state and has done a lot for the integration of world capital markets and, therefore, for international interdependence.

Similar observations can be made in favor of multinational corporations. It has become fashionable to blame these organizations for all kinds of exploitations of underdeveloped countries and for cartelistic and monopolistic practices, certainly not always without justification.[14] One should not overlook the fact that multinational corporations are by their very nature against international wars and violence disrupting their international business, and that they are cores of innovation and of the spread of knowledge in the international system. An increase in their number should, therefore, be favored as another means of reducing the probability of international violence.

An important recent tendency has been the move towards worldwide trade unions and professional associations. Closely-knit international associations of physicians, of air traffic controllers and pilots, of maritime unions, of engineers, etc., could be of great importance in reducing international violence and promoting a world state. A boycott by such associations of all flights and all traffic to countries giving refuge to terrorists or engaged in war with other countries would be not only a powerful measure to bring about a change of behavior of states, but also a means of preventing similar actions in the future. Still, the countries with dictatorial or oligarchic regimes usually do not allow free unions and associations so that the possibility of worldwide organization finds its limit at the borders of the respective countries. Here, again, communist states prove to be a stumbling block on the path towards a peaceful world system.

We have concluded our discussion of some of the measures and of organizational and institutional developments, which could be promoted to make a future more peaceful international organization and possibly the emergence of a world state more likely. Human inventiveness and innovation may, however, be able to invent and to explore quite different measures and instruments in the future, which may be much better suited to move towards the end of a peaceful organization of the globe. It is, therefore, of the utmost importance to further all research and innovation which may be moving into that direction, and not to stifle them like other initiatives in an ever-increasing net of state expenditures and taxes, of official regulations and of a rigid bureaucracy.

Man presently faces a number of awesome problems. Pollution of the environment, exhaustion of resources and of fossil energy, the possibility of thermonuclear war and the overcrowding, famine and misery threatening as a consequence of the population explosion. With the growth rate of world population observed from 1950–1980 each square meter would be inhabited in 545 years by one person. Already in 2030, the earth would be crowded by 11.38 instead of 4.42 billion people in 1980, and in 2080 the number of human beings would have surged to 29.35 billion. Still, none of these dangers is as threatening as the possibility of nuclear holocaust. Over-population would be regulated by malnutrition, starvation and death from famine and violence caused by overcrowding. It would thus lead to a life brutal, nasty and short, but not to an extinction of the human race. The exhaustion of raw materials and of other scarce resources would be either overcome by the same dismal processes or by human inventiveness and innovation leading to savings, recycling and substitution by more plentiful substitutes. Similar conclusions hold for energy. The final limit on energy is given by the incredible amounts supplied each year by the sun and by the amounts which would be available if the fusion of nuclear particles would become controllable and safe. Energy would thus be available in sufficient amounts for millions of years, if human inventiveness would succeed in mastering the transformation of energy stemming from the sun and the techniques of fusion processes. In fact, we are rather optimistic that the problems of resources and energy can be solved if their prices are allowed to move up with scarcity, such that the necessary innovative efforts become more and more profitable and as long as they are not hindered by official regulations. We are optimistic, too, that environmental problems can be controlled as witnessed by recent success in industrialized countries. All these problems do not pose questions which are not solvable. Perhaps even the increase of the population can be stopped by the spread of information about birth control and by the lowering of birth rates traditionally following industrial development, before the situation becomes utterly miserable. But here one cannot be too optimistic. Again, a threat to the survival of humanity as a whole as opposed to that of human beings is only posed by thermonuclear holocaust. Our main efforts should, therefore, be directed towards the solution of this problem, and especially towards the reorganization of the international system. The steps proposed above for that purpose may prove to be inadequate. Still, we should endeavour to take them and to find additional and possibly better means. The aim is too important to give up hope even if the chances of success are low. Even when working against probability let us recall Ovid's statement:[15]

> Ut desint vires, tamen est laudanda voluntas.

> Even where strength is missing, intentions are praiseworthy still.

Notes

[1] Wladimir I. Lenin: "Das Militärprogramm der proletarischen Revolution." Published Sept./October 1917. See Lenin: *Ssotschinjenija* [Works], 3rd Ed., vol. 19, Moscow 1935, p. 325.

[2] A statement and discussion of these assumed relationships can be found in Mancur Olson: *The Rise and Decline of Nations. Growth, Stagflation, and Social Rigidities.* Yale University Press, New Haven (Conn.) 1982. Dennis C. Mueller (ed.): *The Political Economy of Growth*, Yale University Press, New Haven and London 1983.

[3] Arthur Koestler: *The Ghost in the Machine.* Pan Books, London 1970, p. 304.

[4] P.F. Mac Lean: "Contrasting Functions of Limbic and Neocortical Systems of the Brain and their Relevance to Psycho-physiological Aspects of Medicine." *American Journal of Medicine,* vol. 25, no. 4, October 1958.

[5] Arthur Koestler: Op. cit., p. 312.

[6] P.F. Mac Lean: op. cit., p. 613.

[7] Konrad Lorenz: *On Aggression,* London 1966, pp. 206–208. It should, however, be noted that the view that animals rarely kill members of their own species has recently been disputed. Probably most intra-species killing is not an expression of aggression, but a fight over resource distribution.

[8] Pitirim Sorokim: *Social and Cultural Dynamics,* vol. 3, Tables 6–19.

[9] Der Grosse Brockhaus [Encyclopedia], vol. 12, Wiesbaden 1957, pp. 447–448.

[10] Lewis F. Richardson: *Statistics of Deadly Quarrels,* Pittsburgh and Chicago 1960, chs. XI and XII.

[11] A modern discussion of federalism from the point of view of an economist can be found in Wallace E. Oates: *Fiscal Federalism,* New York 1972. For an interesting proposal concerning world organization after World War II see Henry Simons: Trade and the Peace. In: Seymour Harris (ed.): *Post-war Economic Problems.* McGraw-Hill, New York 1943. Reprinted in: Gordon Tullock (ed.): *Simons' Syllabus.* Center

for Study of Public Choice, George Mason University, Fairfax (Va.), 1983. The author postulates free trade and goes on to explain: "Free trade and free exchange require and permit that rather minimal government which is compatible with democracy. . . . Likewise, . . . they offer the possibilty of enduring peace with that loose and flexible international organization which requires no large sacrifice of sovereignty and autonomy on the part of participating national states, and no large exercise of force by dominant powers." (p. 55, Tullock's edition)

"It is useful . . . to recognize that free trade is a nearly meaningless conception where collectivism (or totalitarianism) is present. . . . The larger the area governed by a legislature, the weaker are the defenses of democracy (or of dictatorship) against special-interest groups and political logrolling. We must either limit drastically the positive functions and activities of large governments or accept both internal disintegration of democracy into syndicalism and increasing nationalist barriers to world trade and peace." (p. 58)

"The good future of the world . . . is the good future of small nations. Its menace is great federalisms like Germany and the United States, in which government from above grows steadily at the expense of government by states or provinces and by smaller units wherein the processes of democracy have their origin historically and their only strong foundations. It is the great nations which really constrain trade; it is the great nations which give rise to global war. . . . On this view the function of a world state is not so much that of governing the world as that of preventing great nations from governing it. The ideal world state would thus be mainly a repository of powers denied to nations (and to monopolies), held not for exercise from above but merely to prevent their exercise and to assure that systematic dispersion of power which is the only guarantee of liberty at home and the only hope of enduring peace for the world". (p. 64)

[12]   Konrad Lorenz: Op. cit., p. 205.

[13]   A. Falkenstein and W.v. Soden (eds. and translators): *Sumerische und Akkadische Hymnen und Gebete.* Artemis, Zürich and Stuttgart 1953, p. 195.

[14]   For a critical discussion see Frank L. Long: Restrictive Business Practices, Transnational Corporations and Development. A Study. Dissertation, Universität Basel, (Switzerland) 1979.

[15]   Ovid: *Letters from Pontus* 3, 4, 79.